Bill Drath

BRITISH DRUMS
ON THE
SOUTHERN FRONTIER

BRITISH DRUMS
ON THE
SOUTHERN FRONTIER

The Military Colonization of Georgia, 1733–1749

by

LARRY E. IVERS

The University of North Carolina Press
Chapel Hill

Library of Congress Cataloging in Publication Data

Ivers, Larry E
  British drums on the southern frontier.

  Bibliography: p.
  1. Georgia—History—Colonial period.   2. South Carolina—History—
Colonial period.   3. Anglo-Spanish War, 1739–1748.   I. Title.
F289.I93   975.8'02   73-4837
ISBN 0-8078-1211-0

Contents

Preface   xi

I *Southeastern North America, 1565–1732* / 3

II *"Cover and Protect That Settlement," 1733–1735* / 11

III *Mackay among the Creek, 1734–1736* / 31

IV *Occupation of the Spaniards' Doorstep, January–June 1736* / 50

V *The Coveted Indian Trade, June–November 1736* / 65

VI *Preparations for War, 1737–1739* / 72

VII *Beginning of the War of Jenkins's Ear, 1739–1740* / 90

VIII *The British Invasion of Florida, May–June 1740* / 105

IX *The Battle of Fort Mosa, June 1740* / 113

X *Defeat and Withdrawal, June–July 1740* / 125

XI *On the Defensive, 1740–1742* / 133

XII *The Spanish Invasion of Georgia, May–July 1742* / 151

XIII *Oglethorpe's Revenge, July–September 1742* / 162

XIV *Raid and Counterraid, 1742–1743* / 174

XV *In the King's Pay, 1743–1747* / 184

XVI *The End of an Era, 1747–1749* / 204

Notes / 217

Bibliography / 255

Index / 265

Illustrations

South Carolina Provincial Soldiers in Georgia, 1733–1737 / 15

Fort Argyle, 1734 / 22

The Scout Boat *Carolina,* ca. 1728–1743 / 54

A Small Piragua / 57

Fort Frederica, 1736 / 59

The 42nd Regiment of Foot, 1737–1749 / 81

Georgia Provincial Soldiers, 1739–1747
(Highland Ranger, Seaman, and Creek Indian Warrior) / 190

Georgia Provincial Soldiers, 1739–1747
(Marine, Ranger, and Highlander) / 191

Maps

South Carolina, 1717–1732 / 8

Southeastern North America on the Eve of the Colonization
of Georgia, January 1733 / 12

Savannah's Defenses, 1733–1736 / 24

Palachacola, 1704–1747 / 26

The Creek Nations, 1733–1749 / 43

Georgia's Southern Frontier, 1736–1739 / 56

The Upper Savannah River, 1737–1749 / 76

Florida, 1740 / 93

Saint Augustine, 1740 / 110

Georgia, 1740–1742 / 135

Saint Simons Island, 1742 / 158

Florida, 1743 / 179

Georgia, 1743–1747 / 187

Southeastern North America, 1747–1749 / 210

Preface

This is a military study of the southern colonial frontier during the colonization of Georgia and the War of Jenkins's Ear–King George's War. It was the era in which the implimentation of British military policy in that part of North America was, to a great degree, the responsibility of James Edward Oglethorpe. Of necessity, Oglethorpe's character and his political, diplomatic, and military activities on the southern frontier have been subjected to considerable scrutiny. Few pages here are devoted to the formulation of British imperial policy and decision-making; other studies have dealt more than adequately with activities at that level. Rather, the emphasis here is placed upon southern frontier politics, Indian diplomacy, and military campaigns from the British colonial viewpoint. A large part of this study is concerned with the British, Georgia, and South Carolina soldiers' personalities, assigned tasks, efficiency, and life on campaign and in garrison.

I have long been fascinated with Georgia's and South Carolina's colonial military histories. During several years as an army infantry officer my assignments fortunately placed me near several libraries, particularly the British Public Record Office and the Georgia and South Carolina Departments of Archives and History, where I was able to conduct detailed documentary research. My principal research was confined to British sources; however, I have consulted Spanish sources for the purposes of clarifying and checking the accuracy of British accounts, especially those concerning combat actions. One of my most valuable periods of research was a year of duty in Vietnam's Mekong Delta where I lived in a primitive earthen walled fort with Vietnamese provincial soldiers. Now I feel a kinship with the early British, Georgia, and South Carolina soldiers by knowing firsthand the boredom of frontier garrison life, the discomfort of patrolling under a hot sun in an open paddled boat, the exhaustion of marching in enemy country with a stomach full of ambush fear, the excitement of a brief clash and victory, the loss of morale during a retreat, and the dismay of viewing the remains of a friendly fort destroyed. The filth, smells, rats, mosquitoes, and sickness of the little forts are imbedded in my senses. The crudity and cruelties of the illiterate soldiers continue to rankle my sense of civilization.

Thanks for the preparation of this study go to my wife, Kristin, for typing, proofreading, and general motivation. I am grateful to Charles Lee of the South Carolina Department of Archives and History who encouraged my interest in southern colonial history and provided constructive criticism. Audrey Feaster, Judith Putnam, and Mark Magnussen provided valuable assistance by proofreading the initial drafts. Pat Bryant and Marion Hemperley of the Georgia Surveyor General Department also proofread the initial drafts and provided extensive skillful assistance in locating obscure sites and trails. The pen and ink illustrations of soldiers and of Fort Argyle are by Bill Drath of Atlanta, Georgia. Others who made this study possible are Mary Bryan (deceased) and Carroll Hart of the Georgia Department of Archives and History; John Bonner, Jr., of the University of Georgia Libraries; Lilla Hawes of the Georgia Historical Society; Mrs. Granville Prior of the South Carolina Historical Society; and Doris Wiles of the Saint Augustine Historical Society. Thanks go to the Marquess of Cholmondeley, the Georgia Historical Society, the South Carolina Historical Society, and the Florida State University for permission to cite and reprint certain materials.

In order to avoid confusion concerning dates, the days of the month are cited according to the period Julian calendar (whose new year began on 25 March, instead of 1 January, and was eleven days behind in its calculation) and the years are cited according to the modern Gregorian calendar.

Materials were consulted in the following libraries: Army Infantry School Library, Atlanta Public Library, British Public Record Office, Cambridge University Libraries (England), Emory University Libraries, Georgia Department of Archives and History, Georgia Historical Society Library, John Carter Brown Library,

Margaret Davis Cate Library, Newberry Library, South Carolina Department of Archives and History, South Carolina Historical Society Library, University of Chicago Libraries, University of Georgia Libraries, University of Iowa Libraries, University of Nebraska Libraries, and the University of South Carolina Libraries.

LARRY E. IVERS

BRITISH DRUMS
ON THE
SOUTHERN FRONTIER

I

Southeastern North America
1565–1732

Spaniards were born and buried in southeastern North America for a hundred years before the arrival of the first English colonists in the Carolinas. Saint Augustine, Florida, the first permanent Spanish settlement, was established in 1565 to protect the treasure galleons en route from Central and South America to Spain, to Christianize the Indians, and to prevent rival European nations, especially France and England, from colonizing the region. As in all of their other North American settlements, the Spaniards induced the Indians to become Catholics and Spanish subjects through the efforts of missionaries operating from a chain of fortified missions garrisoned with royal soliders. Three mission provinces were established in southeastern North America. West of Saint Augustine was the province of Timucua where the missions were located along the major east-west path. Further to the west was the province of Apalachee, the most prosperous economically and politically. The province of Guale (pronounced Walie) included the Atlantic coast and coastal islands of present Georgia. Revolts by the mission Indians, attacks by fierce inland Indians, and raids by English pirates drove the Guale missions ever southward until, by the end of the seventeenth century, the northernmost mission was located on Amelia Island in present Florida.[1]

By the middle of the seventeenth century England was developing into an imperial power with colonies in North America at Virginia, Maryland, and New England. King Charles II, coming to the throne in 1660, looked at the vacant land between Virginia and Spanish Florida with covetous eyes. An expedition formed by the Carolina Proprietors, eight of Charles's friends, established Charles Town near the mouth of Ashley River in South Carolina during 1670. Ten years later the small settlement was moved to its present location (Charleston) where it became the leading city of the southern English colonies.[2]

Spain and England were old enemies who shared a common dislike stemming from religious differences and imperial clashes. By the early eighteenth century the balance of power had shifted to England's favor. Spain, after serving as a major power in Europe for two hundred years, was in decline. Beginning with the destruction of the Spanish Armada in 1588, the English had begun to despise and underestimate the Spaniards. Warfare between the two countries soon extended to the American colonies where old feuds were sharpened by the Carolina proprietors' charter that attempted to award them land encompassing not only North and South Carolina but also Saint Augustine and the Spanish mission provinces. The first serious clash occured when the Spaniards destroyed the two-year-old Scottish settlement of Stuart's Town on Port Royal Island, South Carolina, in 1686. The South Carolinians did not immediately retaliate, but in 1702, after the outbreak of Queen Anne's War (1701–13), they conducted an unsuccessful attack on Saint Augustine. Between 1704 and 1710 South Carolinians and their Indian allies raided and completely laid waste the Spanish mission provinces of Timucua and Apalachee. In 1706 the Spaniards, with the aid of French ships, retaliated by invading South Carolina; however, the militia and a small flotilla of provincial boats forced the Spaniards to retreat, following some skirmishes outside Charles Town's earthen walls.[3] Queen Anne's War left Spanish Florida in a dismal condition. Most of its Indian allies had deserted or had been killed, the garrisoned missions lay in ruins, and the few settlers were forced to live in Saint Augustine under the protection of a small garrison and the walls of Fort San Marcos.

North Carolina, under a separate government since 1689, suffered a near disastrous war with the Tuscarora Indians during the period 1711–13. The Tuscaroras were defeated largely because two expeditions composed of South Carolinians and their Indian allies marched to North Carolina's assistance and conducted spirited offensive operations.[4]

The South Carolinians had developed into a confident people, extremely warlike as a result of a decade of continuous and usually successful skirmishes with Spaniards and Indians. The introduction of rice culture gave the colony a cash crop that prompted the organization of large plantations at the expense of small farms and increased the black slave traffic from Africa until by 1715 the white population was only about 6,250 while black slaves numbered about 10,500. However, land was readily available on the frontier where cattle and corn could be raised without the necessity for large gangs of slaves, thereby assuring the existence of a small number of yeomen farmers for frontier defense.[5]

Despite the South Carolinians' confidence, growth, and prosperity, they were destined to suffer greatly for their increasingly poor relations with the Indians. The balance of power in southeastern North America was controlled by a small number of powerful Indian nations, most of which were loose federations of several towns whose populations usually spoke dialects related to the Muskhogean, Iroquoian, or Siouan languages. The principal nations and their geographical locations (in reference to modern states) were as follows: the Creek in Alabama and Georgia; the Choctaw in Alabama and Mississippi; the Chickasaw in Alabama, Mississippi, and Tennessee; the Catawba in South Carolina; the Yemassee in Georgia and later in South Carolina; the Tuscarora in North Carolina; and the Cherokee in South Carolina, North Carolina, Georgia, and Tennessee. Smaller nations roamed the area either as independent groups or as subsidiaries of the larger nations.[6] South Carolina traders and their caravans of Indian bearers or pack horses traversed the southeastern forest paths from Charles Town inland for hundreds of miles to practically every town, exchanging their trade goods for the Indians' deer skins and captive slaves. Indians became so dependent upon English woolens, cutlery, and guns that some nations moved closer to Charles Town, the source of the coveted trade goods. Guarding each of the principal entrances into the colony was a friendly Indian sentry-town, protecting the settlers from attacks by enemy Indians. However, by the first decade of the eighteenth century, South Carolina was taking her Indian allies for granted. The colonial government refused to control the conduct of the traders who extended unnlimited credit to the Indian hunters until the debts became impossible to pay, sometimes collected the debts by selling Indian wives and children into slavery, cheated on the weighing of skins with false weights and measures, and conducted themselves like barons in the Indian towns where they were licensed to trade.[7]

By 1715 the Indians would bear no more. A conspiracy of gigantic proportions was formed and in April the Yemassee, whose settlements were then located in South Carolina between the Combahee and Savannah Rivers, began a war by killing the traders in their towns and several scores of settlers living between Port Royal and the Edisto River. Most of the nations and independent towns were members of the conspiracy, but the English discovery of their intentions had caused a premature initiation of the war, resulting in subsequent uncoordinated attacks. In June the Catawba and other northern Indians attacked the Santee settlements north of Charles Town. During July the Creek and Apalachee penetrated South Carolina defenses, destroying the plantations southwest of Charles Town between the Edisto and Stono Rivers. Most of the women and children of the colony were forced to take shelter in Charles Town, but the militia, reinforced with armed slaves and settlement Indians, responded superbly and followed each of the three invasions by defeating the Indians and forcing them to withdraw. A decade of war had well prepared the South Carolinians to defend their colony. The Yemassee retreated to Florida under the protection of the Spaniards, and the former sentry-town Indians along the frontier fled to the interior to live with the larger Indian nations. During the winter of 1715 a South Carolina army, bolstered with Virginia and North Carolina soldiers, marched into the Cherokee nations and compelled their allegiance.[8]

By 1718 the major fighting was over, but the Yemassee and Apalachicola continued to conduct small-scale raids and ambushes against the settlements between the Savannah and Edisto Rivers. South Carolina developed a system of defense against the raids which became the standard for the southern frontier. Small garrisons of soldiers manned the cannons of the following fortifications: Fort Moore, guarding the principal western crossing over the upper Savannah River; Congaree Fort, covering the main northern path on Congaree Creek; and Fort Johnson, protecting the entrance to Charles Town Harbor. Scout boats patrolled the southern entrance into the colony via the Inland Passage (present Intracoastal Waterway) from stations at Beaufort Fort, located in the town of Beaufort, and Water Passage Fort on present Pinckney Island. Protecting the settlements were three companies of rangers who patrolled the forest paths on horseback. The Northern Rangers were probably stationed at John Hearn's plantation on the Santee River, the Western Rangers were at James Rawlings's Edisto Bluff plantation on the big bend of the Edisto River, and the Southern Rangers were stationed initially at John Woodward's plantation near the head of the Ashepoo River and later at Palachacola Fort on the lower Savannah River. Only about a hundred men manned the entire system. Although changes were made in locations of some forts and in the number of soldiers employed, this basic system of defense remained in use throughout most of the colonial period and served as the model for the defense of Georgia.[9]

The French, who had established the small colony of Louisiana in 1698, were by 1720 considered more dangerous than the Spaniards. Earlier, during Queen Anne's War, South Carolinians had organized and led armies of Creek and Chickasaw Indians against Louisiana, but they were unable to destroy either the French settlements or their Choctaw Indian allies. As part of their expansionist aims, the French had long desired to extend their influence among the southern Indian nations, and during the Yemassee War they took advantage of South Carolina's precarious situation, making deep diplomatic inroads with the Creek. In 1717 Fort Toulouse was constructed and garrisoned among the Upper Creek near the conflux of the Coosa and Tallapoosa Rivers in present Alabama. South Carolina, fearing that the French were preparing to isolate the British colonies against the Atlantic coast by a fence of garrisoned forts, sought help from England. In 1720 Colonel John Barnwell, an experienced South Carolina soldier, convinced the British government to supply a company of regular British soldiers to assist South Carolina in a program to build a screen of forts to counter French expansion. But the screen did not then progress beyond the erection of one fortification. From

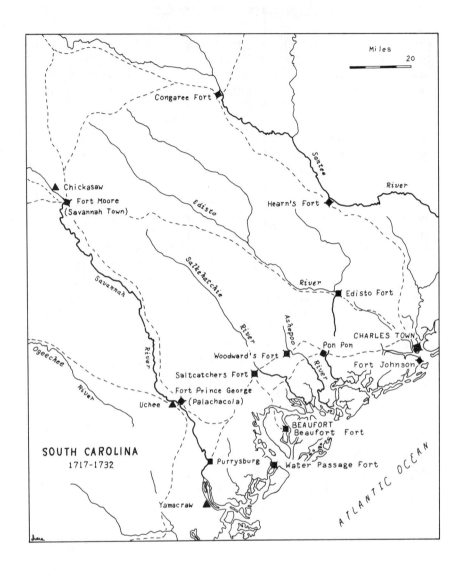

Miles
20

Congaree Fort

Chickasaw
Fort Moore
(Savannah Town)

Santee

River

Hearn's Fort

Edisto

Salkehatchie

River

River

Savannah

Ashepoo

Edisto Fort

CHARLES TOWN

River

Ogeechee

River

Woodward's Fort

Pon Pon

Fort Johnson

Saltcatchers Fort

Fort Prince George
(Palachacola)

Uchee

BEAUFORT
Beaufort Fort

SOUTH CAROLINA
1717-1732

Purrysburg

Water Passage Fort

Yamacraw

ATLANTIC OCEAN

1722 to 1727 the Independent Company of Foot, composed of invalids and old men, garrisoned Fort King George located at the mouth of the Altamaha River near present Darien, Georgia. The ill-conceived fortification was designed to prevent the French from controlling the Altamaha River region and to guard the southern frontier from attacks by Spaniards and Yemassee Indians.[10] However, the French were not then capable of such expansion efforts, and the fort did not prevent the movement of Yemassee war parties from their sanctuary in Spanish Florida to South Carolina.

Between 1726 and 1728 Yemassee attacks became so severe that South Carolina was forced to a near-war footing. The frontier militia was often on alert, two crews of scouts watched the Inland Passage, and mounted rangers patrolled between the Savannah and Edisto Rivers. In 1727 the British Independent Company of Foot was withdrawn to Beaufort Fort to help protect the Port Royal settlers, leaving only a two-man lookout at Fort King George. One of the Yemassee Indians' most successful attacks was the ambush of a scout boat on Daufuskie Island; the crew was killed and the commander was carried to Saint Augustine as a prisoner. Finally, a large South Carolina raiding party under Colonel John Palmer, an experienced scout and militia officer, penetrated Florida's defenses in March 1728, burning and pillaging the Yemassee towns nestled near Saint Augustine.[11]

Border warfare slackened following the raid into Florida, but the frontier settlements still lay open to future raids. Schemes for planting fortified settlements along the edge of the frontier as a buffer zone against the Spanish and French had been considered even before Colonel Barnwell's proposal of 1720. The colonization schemes were finally placed into effect in 1730 when the British Board of Trade, acting upon newly appointed South Carolina Governor Robert Johnson's proposals, ordered settlements laid out. Eleven "townships" were to be established and settled by Protestants from Britain and Europe. Nine of the townships were eventually laid out within the present bounds of South Carolina. East and north of Charles Town were Kingston on the Waccamaw River, Queensboro on the Peedee River, Williamsburg on the Black River, and Fredericksburg on the Wateree River. From the northwest to the southwest lay Amelia on the Santee River, Saxe Gotha on the Congaree River, Orangeburg on the North Fork of the Edisto River, New Windsor on the upper Savannah River, and Purrysburg on the lower Savannah River. Two townships were supposed to have been located near the Altamaha River in old Guale, the virtually uninhabited Atlantic coastal area that was hotly claimed by both England and Spain, but their establishment was delayed until the task was undertaken by the new colony of Georgia during the period 1733–36.[12]

The colonization of Georgia was timely for the British defense of the southern frontier. Although the South Carolinians were finally recovering from the Yemassee War under the excellent guidance of Governor Johnson, they were probably unwilling, at that moment, to extend the frontier south and west of the Savannah River where conflict with the Spaniards was certain. The extremely hard fighting of the Yemassee War, the long discouraging guerrilla war that followed, financial difficulties, political quarrels, and the danger of slave revolts had cooled their aggressive spirit. Nevertheless, the South Carolinians could and would gladly assist a colonizing effort from England. They unselfishly placed their tiny army at Georgia's disposal, assisted with materials and supplies, and they provided frontier experts such as Colonel William Bull to advise and assist in building a fortified community on the southern frontier.[13]

The Georgia project was the fusing of two requirements into one solution. The first requirement was philanthropic. James Oglethorpe, Dr. Thomas Bray, Sir John Percival, and many other Englishmen considered colonization one of the best methods of solving the problem of Britain's debtors, unemployed, and poor. This coincided perfectly with the second requirement, military colonization of the Altamaha-Savannah Rivers region as ordered by the Board of Trade. Slavery was prohibited in Georgia; villages of white protestant yeomen, planting crops and training as soldiers, were to act as a buffer against the Spaniards in Florida and the French in Louisiana.[14]

II

"Cover and Protect That Settlement"

1733–1735

About the latter part of January 1733 a messenger from Charles Town rode his horse into Saltcatchers Fort at the head of Combahee River on the South Carolina frontier and delivered a message to Captain James McPherson, the commander. Inside were marching orders from the governor. "You . . . are hereby order'd immediately with fifteen men to repair to the new Settlement of Georgia, there to Obey orders and directions as you Shall receive from Mr. Oglethorpe, in order to Cover and protect that Settlement from any insults; of this fail not."[1]

At that moment 113 people, newly arrived from England, were temporarily camped in Fort Frederick at Port Royal, South Carolina, awaiting transportation to the southern bank of the Savannah River where they planned to establish a new British colony called Georgia. South Carolinians correctly viewed the new settlement as a godsend; it would absorb the bloody raids of the Florida Spaniards and their Yemassee Indian allies which had previously been directed toward South Carolina. A grateful South Carolina General Assembly had provided the new colonists with boat transportation, breeding cattle and hogs, provisions, and military protection by the provincial scout boat and Captain McPherson's Company of Southern Rangers.[2]

The governor's orders severely disrupted the frontier rangers' monotonous daily routine. They selected riding and pack horses and strapped provisions and ammunition to pack saddles. Captain McPherson chose six of the company's twenty

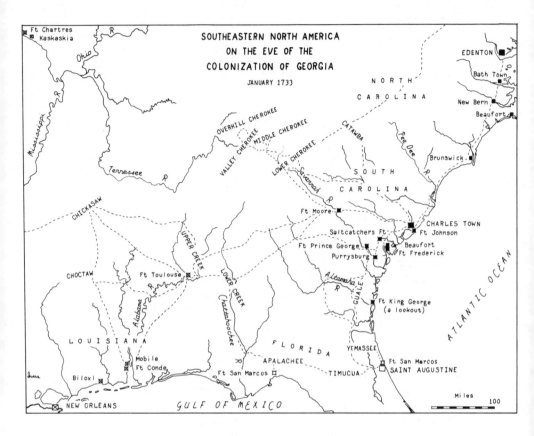

SOUTHEASTERN NORTH AMERICA
ON THE EVE OF THE
COLONIZATION OF GEORGIA
JANUARY 1733

privates to remain in garrison at Saltcatchers Fort. Within a few days they were reinforced by the temporary assignment of a lieutenant and four rangers from Fort Prince George on the Savannah River.[3]

McPherson owned a five-hundred-acre cowpen (cattle ranch) near the fort upon which he had built his home. His wife, thirty-three-year-old Rachel Miles McPherson, born and raised on the frontier, assumed full responsibility for maintaining the cattle and preparing for the approaching corn planting season.[4] Unknown to either of them, five years would pass before he returned permanently from the expedition to Georgia.

The company probably began its movement to Georgia at

dawn one day during the first week of February 1733. The governor had made preparations for the rangers to ride to the Savannah River, cross on riverboats called piraguas, ride down the western bank, and then rendezvous with the Georgians. The path was a new one, a ride of over forty miles which followed the ridges and crossed a number of creek swamps, perhaps a two-day journey for the rangers and their pack horses. They probably spent a night at Purrysburg, a new frontier "township" of Swiss immigrants on the east bank of the Savannah River. The next morning they pulled and shoved their horses onto the piraguas which had been assembled to transport them down river to the Georgia settlement. They probably landed near the Yamacraw Indian town located in the present city of Savannah. The Yamacraw were a mixed Yemessee-Creek band of about one hundred people who had moved there three years before. John Musgrove and his wife Mary, who were part white and part Creek Indian, had the trade monopoly of this band and were living among them.[5]

The Georgia colonists had already landed at Yamacraw Bluff on Thursday, 1 February, about half a mile southeast of the Indian town and were laying out a settlement called Savannah. James Oglethorpe, the Georgia trustee who acted as the colony's leader, was proceeding under the advice of Colonel William Bull, a prominent South Carolina frontiersman. When the rangers rode into the Georgians' camp they found them hard at work hacking a town out of the wilderness. A third of the men were clearing trees from the town site, another third were working on a blockhouse, and the remainder were clearing land for the planting season just a month away. Cold rains fell in torrents that February, making working conditions miserable.[6]

The Georgians must have thought the rangers exhibited a poor appearance when compared to the smartly dressed British dragoons they had seen in England. Their small Spanish horses were quite ugly after three days on muddy trails, saddles and other leather gear were unpolished, and Captain McPherson, with a personal servant in attendance, was probably the only one who made a decent appearance. Most of the rangers' faces were scarred from smallpox and partially covered with three days' growth of whiskers. Because of the cold weather some wore wool caps or caps of fox fur, some with the foxtails still attached. Others wore hats in various degrees of dilapidation. The upper garments probably included a checked shirt and sometimes a waistcoat, worn beneath a coat or pea jacket. Buckskin knee breeches and heavy knee-length stockings, which were often covered with canvas spatterdashes or leather Indian leggins, clothed the legs. Shoes protected their feet. Each man carried a flintlock carbine and two large pistols; the latter were attached to the front of the saddle in holsters. The firearms were each loaded with a bullet that was covered with three or more large turkey or swan shot, an excellent short-range brush load. The rangers made their own cartridges by rolling powder, ball, and shot into paper cylinders that were carried in a leather or leather-covered wooden box hanging from a sling over the shoulder or from a belt at the waist. There was no mention of their carrying swords, although Captain McPherson may have worn one. Most men probably carried hatchets that were utilized as both tools and weapons.[7]

Their appearance as a company of British provincial soldiers might have severely disturbed the king, but anyone who thought their crudeness was an indication of their incompetence would have been badly mistaken. Since their activation in October 1726 the Southern Rangers had patrolled the thickets and swamps of the Edisto, Ashepoo, and Combahee Rivers on the alert for Yemassee war parties who raided the frontier from their sanctuary in Spanish Florida. The company initially included Captain William Peters, an experienced Indian fighter from Saint Bartholomews Parish; Sergeant William McPherson, James's brother; and fourteen privates. A mico, or chief, named Harry and ten of his Kiawah Indians, Muskhogee of the Cusabo group, were attached to the company for at least a year. By December 1726 the company was stationed in the Pon Pon settlement on the western bank of the Edisto River near present Jacksonboro, perhaps on Captain Peters's nearby plantation. There are few surviving accounts of the company's early patrols, but the rangers occasionally scouted as far as the Salkehatchie River to check on reports of war parties camped there. On one occasion a detachment of the company was in hot pursuit of a raiding party when Sergeant William McPherson's horse was shot from under him. In June 1727 James McPher-

South Carolina Provincial Soldiers in Georgia, 1733–1737
Scout, Ranger, and the Scout Boat Carolina

(*Drawing by Bill Drath*)

son became sergeant in his brother's stead, and about November of that year the government commissioned him captain when William Peters resigned. During the year 1727 Yemassee war parties struck at will in their former settlement, the "Indian Land," which lay between the Savannah and Combahee Rivers. During the following year, or shortly thereafter, the company, which totaled twenty-two men, transferred to the Indian Land. On the western bank of the Salkehatchie River, then called the Saltcatchers (which is actually the upper portion of Combahee River), the rangers constructed Saltcatchers Fort, also called Rangers Fort, near the present town of Yemassee. They were responsible for patrolling the area between their fort and Fort Prince George near the Savannah River, thirty miles to the west. By January 1733 the members of the company had served as frontier rangers for an average of four years each, and during patrols they had ridden over much of the South Carolina frontier. They knew the Indians' method of war and adopted it as their own. Lawrence Cooke, William Finley, William Fitchet, William Small, and others made the ranger service a career and continued to serve in Georgia as rangers for several years.[8]

Oglethorpe stationed the company up river about five miles northwest of Savannah at a place called the Horse Quarter from where they patrolled the area close around Savannah during the remainder of the winter and spring of 1733.[9]

With the beginning of summer Oglethorpe began the organization of a defensive screen on the exposed south and west sides of the town. On June 12 he ordered Captain McPherson and his rangers to accompany him on a reconnaissance of the area around Savannah to find the best locations for ranger stations and villages.[10]

Oglethorpe and McPherson had undoubtedly already inventoried each other and liked what they found. Oglethorpe was to have many disagreements and make many enemies among South Carolina officials and McPherson was later disliked by several Georgia officials, but both men continued to think highly of each other.

James Oglethorpe was a thirty-seven-year-old wealthy English bachelor with extensive leadership training and a complicated personality. He was not a handsome man. He possessed a long face having a large Roman nose, slightly protruding eyes, a high forehead, and a prominent double chin. Nevertheless, the gaze he delivers from a surviving portrait exudes self-confidence. By the age of twenty-six he had served as a British infantry lieutenant, attended Oxford University, experienced combat in eastern Europe as the aid-de-camp to Prince Eugene of Savoy, inherited the family's English estates, sat as a member of Parliament, and killed a man in a drunken brawl. He possessed a fantastic amount of energy and had the self-confidence to use it; however, he was quick of temper and often bold to the point of recklessness. He purposely suffered the same privations as those with whom he was in company, despite their social class, and he espoused the cause of oppressed debtors, seamen, and soldiers. Nevertheless, critics were accurate in insisting that he was vain and belligerent. For reasons of philanthropy and nationalism, he had been involved in the plans for the colonization of Georgia from the beginning and was a member of the Board of Georgia Trustees, the colony's governing body, who considered him their representative in Georgia. He lived to the advanced age of eighty-nine, a remarkable achievement for those times.[11]

James McPherson was a forty-five-year-old native of South Carolina who was known for his friendly disposition. After a lifetime on the frontier he naturally lacked Oglethorpe's social polish, but he was an experienced frontier soldier, having served in the militia during the Yemassee War and in the Southern Rangers for the past six years. He continued to command South Carolina ranger troops during periods of frontier crises until the age of sixty-two. It is a credit to McPherson's leadership ability that his rangers averaged several years each under his command, unlike most frontier soldiers who did not stay with a company or garrison for more than six months or a year. He lived to the advanced age of eighty-three.[12]

Using Yamacraw men as pathfinders, they probably worked their way northward on the incomplete paths following the Savannah River. Not far north of Savannah, Oglethorpe ordered a change of direction to the west. After about ten miles of hard going they came upon the well-marked warpath that began near Saint Augustine in Florida and ended at the Palachacola crossing on the Savannah River. Oglethorpe decided this path had to be blocked against the Yemassee Indians who had long used it to penetrate the South Carolina frontier. When the expedition arrived at the ford where the path crossed the Ogeechee River, Oglethorpe ordered McPherson to build and garrison a fort for Savannah's defense.[13]

Oglethorpe agreed to pay Captain McPherson and his men £200 for building the fortification; eighteenth-century soldiers did not construct forts without receiving extra wages. Both men would have discussed the type of fort needed, where to erect it, and the required construction techniques. Oglethorpe was completely familiar with European fortification practices, and McPherson had constructed Saltcatchers Fort and had probably helped with a number of others. The favorite type of fortification on the South Carolina frontier at that time was the small palisade fort that differed little from small field forts in Europe. The shape varied according to the topography, but it was usually square with diamond-shaped bastions protruding from the corners. The outworks usually consisted of earthen walls, a moat, and a wooden palisade planted in the moat, with huts, a stable, and other buildings grouped inside. This was the type of fort built on the Ogeechee River. Oglethorpe named it Fort Argyle in honor of his good friend, the second Duke of Argyle. The initial site was on the east bank of the Ogeechee above present Morgan Bridge, about eight and three-quarters miles north of its junction with Canoochee Creek.[14] After tracing the outline of the proposed fort, Oglethorpe evidently returned to Savannah.

If McPherson followed customary practice, he divided his men into work crews. One party continued clearing the site and began building crude shelters as protection from rains, another group was composed of loggers who fell the trees needed for construction, and those men designated as sawyers dug a saw pit and began sawing planks. After a squared timber was extended over the excavation, the sawyer, on top of the pit, and his assistant, in the pit, sawed planks with a two-man saw set into a frame, a process that required a considerable amount of work and time.[15] The youngest rangers probably drew the unpopular assignment of sawyers' assistants, sweating in hot pits with sawdust falling in their faces.

The limbs and tops of the trees that were cut from the fort site were dumped into the adjacent Ogeechee River, which is narrow at that site and has many turns because of the extreme lowness of the land. About the first part of August, after most of the trees had been cut, the trimmings created a tight jam in the river just below the fort, rendering the site untenable. Boats could not bypass the jam, and there was no other practical way to transport heavy supplies to the fort because the numerous streams and swamps rendered movement by wagon or cart nearly impossible. Work was halted and McPherson informed Oglethorpe, who then paid £50 for the labor on the ill-sited fort and ordered him to move downstream and begin again. The company, unquestionably complaining and cursing, picked up their tools and belongings and crossed the river. The partially completed fort, afterwards called First Fort, or Old Fort, was left standing.[16]

McPherson and his men moved about five miles down the west bank of the Ogeechee to a point three and two-tenths miles above the mouth of Canoochee Creek where the channel widens and a ten-foot bluff crowds against the river. Here they began work on a new Fort Argyle.[17] Tactically it should have been located on the east bank where the river would have served as an obstacle to war parties approaching from Florida; however, swamps crowded the river banks elsewhere, leaving precious little high ground for a fort site.

Even though the South Carolinians were inured to the extreme heat of July and August, they probably did not work much during the afternoon when the heat was most stiffling. More likely, the working day began at dawn and continued until near noon when they probably relaxed in the shade drinking beer, smoking clay pipes, and sleeping during the hottest part of the day, resuming work in the cool of the evening. Swarms of flying insects harassed the sweating rangers all day and at sundown the mosquitoes began their attacks. The only relief was gained from a smoky fire or a pipe. The South Carolina rangers accepted those inconveniences as an inevitable part of their lives.[18]

McPherson probably defined the outline of the walls and bastions with stakes. The design was a square, 110 feet to the side. Outside of this line the rangers dug a moat four or five feet deep and about fifteen feet wide. The dirt shovelled from the moat was piled upon the inside and used to build the earthen wall or curtain. One method of building the wall was to dampen each layer of newly piled earth and walk back and forth to pack it. In order to achieve at least a forty-five degree slope on the outside and seventy-five degrees or more on the inside, a facing material was normally utilized to retain the loose sandy soil. Perhaps a layer of swamp mud, six inches to a foot thick, was packed on both the outside and inside of the sandy wall, or a facing of logs, planks, or fresh sod could also have been used. The wall was shaped upwards to a height of about four and one-half to five feet so that a man could stand erect and fire over the top. The top was about six feet wide and flat, sloping slightly forward.[19]

A bastion protruded perhaps thirty to forty feet beyond each corner of the wall. According to fortification practice they were diamond shaped, but if exact measurements were not followed and if McPherson did not insist, they might have been carelessly finished in a rather oval form. Defenders of such fortifications normally fought from the bastions, where flanking fire could rake the walls to either side and prevent attackers from climbing inside. Four small cannons had been carried to the fort and two were probably mounted in each of the bastions facing the land side.[20]

The final portion of the outworks constructed was a fence of logs called a palisade which served as an additional obstacle to attackers. Logs about eleven feet long and a foot thick were trimmed and set into a narrow ditch about three feet deep along the center of the moat. Each log was individually set about three inches apart. A row of small, split logs was nailed horizontally to the back of the palisade, about two feet from the top, to support angle braces that were fixed diagonally against the back of the palisade at spaced intervals. The completed palisade was eight feet high, a little lower than the earthen wall, to allow the rangers to fire over it. Since an attack from the river was unlikely, that side of the fort was probably protected by only half-bastions and a palisade, without the addition of a moat and an earthen wall.[21]

Twelve buildings were constructed, some of which were probably frame houses. The process of building structures of whole logs was seldom used in Georgia or South Carolina except for the construction of fortified houses. Instead, a house was normally built by erecting a stout frame and siding it with clapboards. Square beams were slowly hewn out with a broadax and used by those designated as carpenters to construct the house frame. Unfortunately, no stones lay in the tidewater lowlands of Georgia and bricks were not yet available; therefore, large beams were laid on the ground in the shape of a rectangle to form the foundation. After the side frames were pinned together on the ground, the entire company raised them into place on the foundation beams. The whole frame was held together by the use of mortise-and-tenon joints and wooden pins called treenails. Clapboards, tapered boards about four feet long that were split from small logs with a hatchet-like tool called a froe, were nailed horizontally to the house frame. Finally, rafters were added and covered with shingles, also split from small logs with a froe. A frame building was probably used as a storehouse with a cellar underneath for a powder magazine.[22]

Most of the barracks were probably crude huts constructed of frames of poles lashed together with clapboards covering the sides and shingles or bark covering the roofs. Since there were no bricks available for fireplaces or chimneys that year, fires were built on the earthen floors and the smoke escaped through holes in the roofs. A similar hut, only much larger, was built as a stable designed to hold thirty horses.[23]

It is doubtful that a latrine, or "necessary house," was constructed, since their use in early South Carolina and Georgia forts appears to have been practically unknown. It was very likely that frontier soldiers and their families used the woods surrounding the fort as a latrine, and during periods of alarm, when it was thought unsafe to leave the fort, individual "cathole" toilets were probably dug in the moat or behind the barracks huts.[24]

At about the beginning of September six families were sent from Savannah to Fort Argyle to farm the adjacent lands.[25] With their help the fort was probably finished about Christmas 1733.

Oglethorpe had raised two companies of volunteer Indian militia from among the Yamacraw, one of which, commanded by a principal warrior named Skee, was to hunt and patrol along the fork of the Altamaha River. Oglethorpe ordered that they were to be given free provisions when visiting Fort Argyle or the other settlements, but the Indians usually imposed upon their hosts by remaining a week or longer in a place where the food was free. If the warriors' habits were similar to Skee's they could also have stayed drunk for a similar period.[26]

The Indians would have found liquor available at Fort Argyle despite the fact that, because of Oglethorpe, Georgia was officially "dry." Oglethorpe apparently was not an ardent prohibitionist, he was just an incompetent diagnostician. The Georgians were unaccustomed to the southern climate and many of them died that first year as the result of dysentery and typhoid, but Oglethorpe thought the cause was an excessive intake of rum. He convinced the Georgia trustees in London to pass a law making rum drinking unlawful and staved in

Fort Argyle, 1734
(*Conjectural*)

(*Drawing by Bill Drath*)

all the rum barrels he could find. He had little success in his personal prohibition, however, because drinking rum punch was the popular escape from the hardships of daily living for the poor settlers on the southern American frontier. McPherson was very tactful in procuring liquor for his South Carolina rangers; as late as the spring of 1735 he was having rum, disguised as cider, delivered from Charles Town. Oglethorpe had no prejudice against wine or beer; all ages, sexes, and classes normally drank those beverages instead of water. Beer was always cheap and usually available in Georgia, and a homemade substitute could be created by boiling molasses, sassafras roots, Indian corn, and the tops of fir trees in water.[27]

Early in 1734 South Carolina reinforced the Company of Southern Rangers by adding five men to the detachment at Fort Argyle. William Elbert, a South Carolinian, received a

Georgia trustees' commission as lieutenant of the company, and Captain McPherson accepted a Georgia commission in addition to the one from South Carolina. Lieutenant Elbert and half of the twenty rangers transferred to First Fort where they built a few huts from the unused lumber lying there. In June of that year Elbert married seventeen-year-old Sarah Greenfield, one of the original Georgia settlers, but it is not known whether she shared his primitive living conditions at First Fort. He and his detachment patrolled northeast along the Yemassee war path to Palachacola on the Savannah River.[28]

Palachacola had long been a strategic point on South Carolina's southwestern frontier. The name was derived from Palachacola Town, a settlement of friendly Apalachicola Indians which had served as a South Carolina sentry-town, guarding the principal crossing site on the lower Savannah River. However, when the Yemassee War began in 1715 those Indians joined the conspiracy against South Carolina and were soon forced to vacate Palachacola Town and flee to their ancient home in present southwestern Georgia. Without a guard on the lower Savannah crossing site, war parties could cross the river and penetrate the settlements at will. The Company of Southern Rangers (1716–18) built a fort across the river from the abandoned town and patrolled along the east bank of the Savannah River during the first six months of 1718 in an attempt to secure that portion of the frontier. From March 1719 to September 1721 the location served as a factory, or Indian trading center, and it may have included a fort with a small garrison.[29]

For a while Palachacola lay unguarded, but in early 1723 the settlers living north of Beaufort began clamoring for government rangers to protect their plantations from the raids of Yemassee war parties operating from Spanish Florida. In February the South Carolina government ordered a captain, a lieutenant, a sergeant, and nineteen horsemen to be recruited to build and garrison a "small Pallisade Fort" at Palachacola. They were to range east above Beaufort and north to Fort Moore, keeping the Indians west of the Savannah River. William Bellinger, a local landowner, was appointed captain and Edmond Maxwell, a former ranger, was commissioned lieutenant. The men were probably enlisted during March. In April

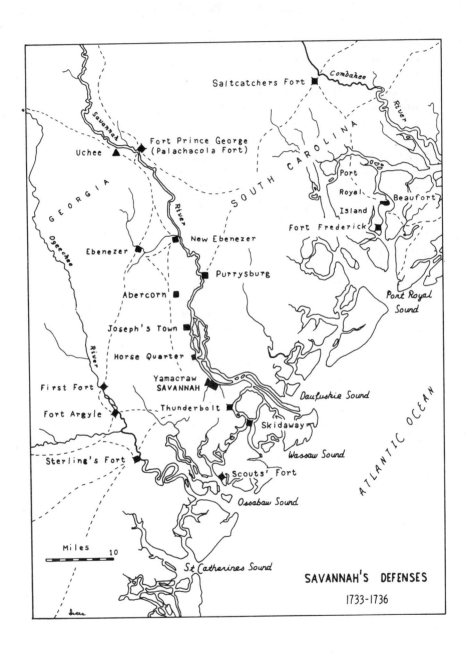

SAVANNAH'S DEFENSES

1733-1736

or May they began building the fort on the east side of the Savannah River in the northwest corner of present Jasper County, South Carolina. In late August, Captain Bellinger dejectedly reported that the fort was not yet completed because most of the men were sick and he was doing most of the carpentry himself; snakes from the nearby swamps were also a problem. In June 1724 Captain Bellinger and Lieutenant Maxwell became thoroughly discouraged and resigned. Rowland Evans, a former garrison commander during the Yemassee War, was appointed captain and Philemon Parmenter was selected as his lieutenant. The garrison's strength was reduced from twenty-two to seventeen.[30]

The fortification's official name was Fort Prince George, but the rangers were usually known as the Palachacola Garrison. The fort may have undergone at least two major rebuildings by the time Georgia was settled; timber and earthen fortifications on the southern frontier required rebuilding every four or five years. Wooden structures and palisades decayed quickly and torrential rains eroded the earthen walls into the moat.[31]

Life in Fort Prince George was lonely at best, but frontiersmen were accustomed to loneliness and did not expect to be entertained. The rangers probably drank too much rum and kept company with Indian girls from the Uchee, or Yuchi, town across the river. Most of those men who spent more than a few months in the garrison probably "went native." Young soldiers stationed among a foreign people quickly adopt many of the habits and customs of that people no matter how primitive, when provided the impetus of pretty mistresses. There were usually Indians from one nation or another loafing around the fort because of the requirement that all Indians entering South Carolina via the Palachacola entrance had to stop there and wait for permission from the govenment in Charles Town before continuing on. Garrisons were supposedly not permitted to engage in trade with the Indians, but a considerable amount of bartering probably took place. The government encouraged the garrison to farm and raise corn, their staple food, and paid them a good price for each bushel. A contractor provided other provisions such as salt, flour, and meat. The men had little if any religious guidance; the nearest minister was located at Beaufort. Nor was there a doctor in

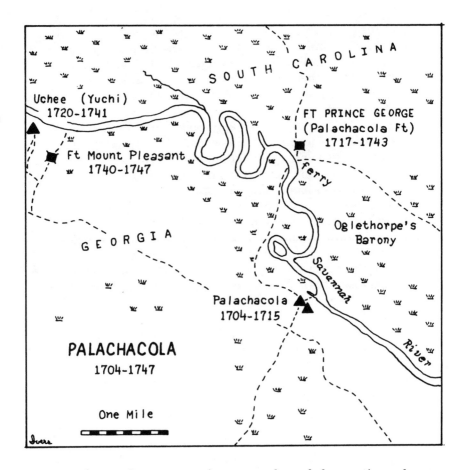

attendance. On one occasion a member of the garrison almost died before he could be transported to a doctor in the settlements.[32]

During part of the year 1725 the government stationed Lieutenant Parmenter and seven of the rangers near present Jacksonboro on the western side of the Edisto River. Each "scout" was ordered to "find his own horse and accoutrements, and provisions . . . and be armed with a gun, a pistol, and cutlass, a hatchet, powder-horn, with at least a quarter of a pound of powder, and cartouch box, with twelve charges . . . and a large mastiff or mungrel bred dog, to go constantly along with them in their scouting. . . ."[33]

The Palachacola Garrison was instructed to patrol the one hundred miles of frontier between Port Royal and Fort Moore once every two weeks, but it appears very unlikely that they actually covered the terrain that often, if ever. During the period of brutal Indian raids, 1726–28, the garrison's patrols did not discourage all the Yemassee war parties from crossing the Savannah River and penetrating the settlements. The garrison shared surveillance of the Indian Land with McPherson's Southern Rangers after the latter were stationed at Saltcatchers.[34]

During a Creek Indian scare in August 1732, six months before the settlement of Georgia, the Palachacola Garrison went on full alert. Colonel Alexander Glover, the Creek Indian agent, rode to Fort Prince George and assumed command of that section of the frontier. Even though Captain Evans, the commander of the fort, had been too sick to perform duty for some time, he had still been retained in command; however, when war with the Creeks seemed likely Evans was discharged and Lieutenant Parmenter was promoted to captain. Aneas Mackintosh, a Scottish gentlemen and heir to the chieftainship of Clan Mackintosh in Scotland, was commissioned lieutenant. At the end of the first week in September the fear of a major Indian war dissolved when the government discovered that the Creeks had no intention of going to war.[35]

In early February 1733 one of the Southern Rangers from Saltcatchers rode into Fort Prince George with the governor's message concerning the measures to be taken to protect the Georgia settlers. According to the governor's order, Captain Parmenter sent Lieutenant Mackintosh and four men to strengthen the remaining ranger garrison at Saltcatchers Fort, leaving both garrisons with ten men each.[36]

South Carolina officials informed Oglethorpe, in early 1734, that Fort Prince George might not be necessary much longer because the rangers at Fort Argyle and First Fort adequately protected that portion of the frontier. Oglethorpe, impressed with Fort Prince George's location, told them that if they ever decided to abandon the fort he would garrison it. The fort was a ready-made station for rangers patrolling the area north of Savannah, and it was also a good location from which to control traffic on the Savannah River. By March 1734 the South

Carolina government realized that the organization of frontier defense would have to be permanently altered because of the settlement of Georgia. The rangers at Saltcatchers were needed in Georgia and were ordered to join McPherson there. Lieutenant Mackintosh and his men demolished Saltcatchers Fort, probably setting fire to the huts and palisade to prevent its being used by hostile Indians.[37]

South Carolina disbanded Captain Parmenter's Palachacola Garrison, but Oglethorpe placed four of his men in Fort Prince George to maintain the buildings and cannons. The Georgia trustees assumed responsibility for the men's wages and South Carolina agreed to provide them with corn for provisions. However, a change of plans became necessary before the moves could be completed. The South Carolina settlers on the frontier near Port Royal were outraged by the removal of all the soldiers from their portion of the frontier, and to pacify them the government in Charles Town ordered Mackintosh and his ten rangers to station themselves at Fort Prince George instead of Fort Argyle.[38]

Under the new establishment Mackintosh was promoted to captain and his men became known as the Palachacola Rangers. They patrolled the eastern bank of the Savannah River as part of Captain McPherson's Company of Southern Rangers until April 1735 when the South Carolina Assembly absolutely refused to provide any more money for their pay. The fact that they knew Oglethorpe would undertake the maintenance of the fort probably helped prompt their decision. Georgia immediately assumed responsibility for the fort and Mackintosh's men, who were thereafter considered a separate party of rangers and independent of McPherson's company.[39]

Fortunately for the British, neither Spain nor France chose to attack Georgia's meager defenses during this initial settlement period. The South Carolina rangers, the scout boat (which will be discussed in Chapter IV), and the Yamacraw Indian militia patrolled the avenues of approach in order to give early warning of an advancing invasion force; they did not possess the numbers or firepower to repel such incursions. If an invasion had occurred Georgia's survival would have depended upon the performance of its small militia, which mustered only 397 men and boys by early 1735. The citizen soldiers were unconventionally organized into tythings that were each composed of approximately ten men commanded by a tythingman, a militia noncommissioned officer who was also a law-enforcement official. Constables, who were also law-enforcement and court officials, functioned as militia officers, each commanding four tythings. Although most of the militiamen lived in Savannah, a significant portion of them and their families farmed small land grants near tiny fortified villages that were designed to provide a defensive screen to protect Savannah from minor raids. The more important villages were Thunderbolt and Skidaway to the southeast of Savannah, Sterling's Fort and Fort Argyle to the southwest, and Abercorn and Ebenezer to the northwest. Only a few of the fortified villages were ever very important to Savannah's defense; the soil was poor for farming and sickness rapidly thinned their populations. The Georgia militiamen were too few to withstand an invasion, but they had the promise of assistance from the South Carolina militia, which numbered about three thousand men who were conventionally organized into companies and regiments. In order to carry out this cooperative strategy the British government commissioned the governor of South Carolina as the commander in chief of the Georgia militia, and until at least 1738 Colonel William Bull, Oglethorpe's South Carolina adviser, was prepared to assume active command during emergencies.[40]

Thus, during the period 1733–35 the British system of defense on the Anglo-Spanish border began with the two Yamacraw Indian companies who sometimes watched the crossing sites of the Altamaha River. Behind them Captain McPherson's South Carolina rangers patrolled the west bank of the Ogeechee River, Lieutenant Elbert's detachment rode between the Ogeechee and the Savannah Rivers, and Captain Mackintosh's garrison ranged up and down the east bank of the Savannah. The South Carolina scout boat completed this early warning scheme by scouting the invasion route along the Inland Passage. The tiny fortified villages with their militia garrisons formed a second defensive screen behind the Indians and South Carolinians. In the event an invasion force penetrated these initial defenses, the Savannah militia tythings were prepared to make a stand in the dense woods and swamps around the town. Hopefully, they would delay the invaders for a few weeks until the widely dispersed South Carolina militia could muster and march to their assistance. Unfortunately, the South Carolinians suffered a serious disadvantage; their numerous black slaves were becoming more and more restless and would likely seize an invasion as an opportunity to revolt.[41]

III

Mackay among the Creek
1734–1736

Two hundred and fifty miles west of Savannah, Georgia, were the settlements of the Creek Indians, consisting of several towns loosely joined into two nations. The Lower Creek occupied both banks of the Chattahoochee River while the Upper Creek were divided into three factions—the Coosa (or Abihka), Talapoosa, and Alabama—each living near rivers of those names. The Creek were a farmer-hunter people and first-class warriors. An assured food supply from their corn fields gave them the leisure to engage in war, a very serious game that they played with religious fervor. Their headmen were skillful diplomats; for decades they played Spanish, French, and British against one another, and they sometimes succeeded in achieving a degree of neutrality unobtainable by most modern nations. The Creek men were superb hunters who harvested great quantities of deerskin to trade for English wool, guns, and cutlery. A large share of South Carolina's economy was based upon that trade, but, equally as important, South Carolina was able to maintain a degree of influence with the Creek only because English trade goods were of greater quantity, lower price, and better quality than similar goods from France and Spain.[1]

The Lower Creek were often troublesome to the British, but in the spring of 1734 they were addressing a loyalty of sorts to Georgia because James Oglethorpe had met with some of their headmen during the previous year and had established a treaty of friendship with the help of Tomochichi, the Yamacraw mico (chief), and a large amount of presents. The trustees'

Indian policy was initially wise and fruitful. They lavished presents on the Indians, redressed the Indians' grievances wherever possible, and acquired land through treaty rather than appropriation. Oglethorpe was the perfect man to carry out the trustees' policy. He ate the Indians' food, slept in their houses, sincerely recognized their value as Georgia's allies, and seldom voiced impatience with their alien-appearing customs.[2]

Most of the Upper Creek towns were generally friendly to the British and often helped assure the lower nation's friendship, but previously, in 1717 following the Yemassee War, the Alabama faction had allowed the Louisiana French to build and garrison a fort among their towns. Fort Toulouse, sitting on the eastern bank of the Coosa River two and a half miles above its junction with the Tallapoosa River, gave the French an ideal staging point for diplomatic and military operations among the other two factions of the Upper Creek. The presence of French soldiers was embarrassing for the British and was dangerous to the future of the South Carolina Indian trade. If the trade was ever disrupted the British would lose their only substantial influence among the Creek who, if allied with the French and Choctaw, could destroy Georgia and possibly even South Carolina.[3]

Ships arriving in Charles Town from England in late February 1734 brought rumors that war with France was near. Recent French diplomatic maneuvering among the Creek now appeared frightfully purposeful. In addition, deserting French soldiers reported that Louisiana was preparing to renew its war with Britain's staunch friends, the Chickasaw. The South Carolina Assembly sent a message to Oglethorpe in Georgia requesting "to concert with him about the proper measures to be taken."[4]

Oglethorpe arrived in Charles Town on 2 March and soon afterward met with the assembly's committee on Indian affairs. South Carolina had long considered building and garrisoning a fort among the Upper Creek to serve as a refuge for the traders in the event of an Indian war and to counter the presence of the French fort. The committee did not believe that the Upper Creek would agree to the presence of South Carolina soldiers, but if Oglethorpe's recent success with the Lower Creek was an indication, then perhaps a Georgia garrison would be acceptable to them. Oglethorpe agreed to raise a company for that purpose, but he stated that the trustees' appropriation from the crown was insufficient to meet that expense. The committee approached the assembly on 9 March and recommended that South Carolina equip and pay the company. The commons house absolutely refused, but a short time later they relented after receiving a personal request from Colonel William Bull, Oglethorpe's adviser and a respected member of the governor's council. They agreed to pay for the company's subsistence during its first two years if Oglethorpe would raise the men and direct their activities.[5]

On 13 March Oglethorpe wrote a captain's commission for Patrick Mackay, his choice to command the company destined for duty in the Creek nations. Oglethorpe had known Mackay since at least the previous September when he had recommended him to the trustees as a fit person to receive a five-hundred-acre grant of Georgia land. Evidence suggests that, by giving him the commission, Oglethorpe was providing a fellow gentleman with a second chance. Patrick Mackay was from the Highland county of Sutherland in Scotland. He was the eldest son and heir of Hugh Mackay, a well-to-do and influential man. Patrick had engaged in large-scale business speculation and, as a result of bad luck and some possible fraudulent dealings by others, had lost most of the family fortune and gone into debt. He was forced to sell Siderra, the family estate, and, in 1733, after publishing a pamphlet explaining the reasons for his indebtedness, Patrick and three brothers—Hugh, James, and Charles—took passage to the colony of Georgia, arriving there about September. Patrick brought his wife and infant daughter. He, his brothers, and some other Scotsmen who paid their own way were given grants of land upriver from Savannah at a place called Josephs Town, or Captain's Bluff. Oglethorpe returned briefly to Savannah on 11 March to assist a group of German-speaking settlers who had just arrived from Salzburg, and he probably gave Mackay his commission at that time. Mackay appears to have accompanied Oglethorpe when he returned to Charles Town on 23 March.[6]

On 27 April 1734 Oglethorpe addressed official written instructions to "Mr. Patrick Mackay Agent to the Creeks." He ordered Mackay to recruit his company as soon as possible and march them to the Creek nations where he was to meet with the traders to collect intelligence concerning Spanish and French activities among the Indians. After visiting each of the major towns he was to conduct a conference with all their headmen in order to attain permission to build and garrison a fort in the Upper Creek nation. His power as agent authorized him to hear and redress the Indians' grievances, and having the authority of a constable he could reprimand lawbreaking traders and banish them from the nations if necessary. Instructions covered the conduct of guard duty and the daily tasks of the officers and noncommissioned officers. If the Spaniards or the French threatened military action Mackay was authorized to assume that war had been declared and mobilize the traders and Indians under his command for a compaign to be conducted at his discretion.[7]

Oglethorpe had no authority to appoint Mackay as agent nor to give him disciplinary powers over the traders; the trustees did not pass an Indian trading law assuming authority to regulate the trade in Georgia until the following year. Nevertheless, Oglethorpe was reputed to have remarked to several traders in Charles Town "that "they [the traders] very well knew that the Indian Trade did belong to Georgia, and that it solely did belong to them, but Carolina had begg'd that they might have Liberty to grant License for that Year."[8] Oglethorpe obviously had every intention of assuming control of the trade with those Indians inside the boundaries of Georgia. He wanted Georgia to share the economic benefits of the trade, but, equally important, he realized that the traders' conduct had to be tightly controlled in order to maintain a lasting peace and alliance with the Indians. Previously, in 1715, the traders' lawless conduct had caused a war with the Yemassee nation which had nearly destroyed South Carolina.[9]

There is an indication that Governor Robert Johnson of South Carolina acquiesced to Oglethorpe's plans. He apparently agreed that Georgia should either assume responsibility for regulating the Creek trade or, at the very least, take part in unified control with South Carolina. Perhaps he hoped that Oglethorpe could regulate the traders' conduct even though his own government could not. Both Oglethorpe and Governor

Johnson were careful not to declare their intentions too loudly, since the merchants who participated in the Indian trade were a major political power in South Carolina and would be incensed if they suspected that the trade was about to be lost to Georgia. Having been opposed to the colonization of Georgia from the beginning, they would induce the assembly to withdraw their monetary support for Mackay's company and to halt other funds that had been appropriated for Georgia's assistance.[10]

Oglethorpe left Charles Town on 7 May, bound temporarily for England, and Mackay soon afterward returned to Savannah and began raising and equipping his "Independent Company." Its fully authorized strength was twenty-seven men: a captain, lieutenant, ensign, surgeon, sergeant, corporal, interpreter, messenger, three packhorsemen, and sixteen soldiers, whose term of enlistment was one year. They were equipped for ranging and were called rangers. Few of the mens' names are known, but at least one South Carolinian, William Small, had been a professional ranger under Captain James McPherson since 1727. Oglethorpe had chosen Robert Parker, Jr., as lieutenant and Mackay presented him with his commission during the latter part of May. Parker had arrived in Georgia during the previous December, and during the following April, about a month before he received his commission, Oglethorpe had sent him and three other men to be caretakers of Fort Prince George at Palachacola. He, like his father, was vain and egotistical and later caused the Georgia magistrates considerable trouble. Lieutenant Parker joined the company at Josephs Town where the newly recruited rangers were engaged in clearing land, hewing and sawing logs, and other labors on Captain Mackay's plantation. Hugh Mackay, Jr., Patrick's nephew, was commissioned ensign. The names of the sergeant and corporal are also uncertain but Nicholas Fisher was probably one or the other.[11]

Captain Mackay began outfitting his company. He bought twenty-two muskets from the trustees' store in Savannah, enough to arm everyone but the interpreter, the messenger, and the three packhorsemen who, as civilians, provided their own arms. Two cheap Indian-trading muskets were procured, presumably for two Indian guides. Belt buckles, probably of brass, were purchased for the men to use in making their own belts; each belt would support a cartridge box, a powder flask, and an iron-handled cutlass. The company needed horses for use as mounts and as pack animals to carry their equipment and supplies, but there were no horses for sale in Georgia. In addition, the trustees' store did not stock the great quantity of presents needed for the Indians. About 1 June, Mackay set out on horseback to purchase those items in Charles Town.[12]

Most of the Charles Town merchants soon became alienated by their government's decision to place Georgia soldiers among the Creek. They had undoubtedly heard reports of Oglethorpe's conversations with some of the traders in which he implied that Georgia would assume control of the Creek trade by 1735. They may also have studied Oglethorpe's instructions to Mackay and been shocked to find Mackay addressed as "Agent" with complete disciplinary authority over their traders. During his stay in Charles Town from June through the first half of August 1734 Mackay informed the traders, who were then in Charles Town to purchase their licenses, of his mission among the Creek and suggested that they stop selling rum to the Indians. South Carolina's commissioner of Indian affairs, Tobias Fitch, resented Mackay's intrusion into his domain and began openly advising the traders to disregard the Georgian's counsel. In response, Mackay requested Governor Johnson to personally inform the traders that he was South Carolina's appointed agent for the Creek Indians. Johnson did direct Fitch to order the Creek traders to assist and obey Mackey, but he deftly sidestepped the inflammable request to appoint Mackay as his agent.[13]

Evidently, word of Mackay's earlier defunct business ventures in Scotland had spread to Charles Town, because some people began calling him Mr. Oglethorpe's "poor friend." Mackay realized he would receive little respect from the merchants and traders until he had the authority to issue trading licenses, a power that would allow him to determine who could trade and to assign traders to specific towns. In despair he wrote the trustees that his title as agent was no good unless they also appointed someone (obviously thinking of himself) as commissioner to issue licenses.[14]

Without the merchants' cooperation Mackay found it difficult to hire men and buy the necessary equipment and the large number of horses he needed. Finally, he did succeed in engaging three packhorsemen and a personal servant, and he purchased a herd of pack horses from the executor of a deceased Cherokee trader. He borrowed a forge and purchased axes, saws, nails, other tools to build the proposed fort in the Upper Creek nation, and presents for the Indians including Union Jack flags, one for each of the major Creek towns. He dispatched the equipment to Georgia by water in a piragua that he had previously hired at Savannah.[15]

On 15 August 1734, after a summer of frustrating dealings in a hostile Charles Town, Captain Mackay set out overland for Georgia with the herd of horses. During the first night on the road from Charles Town to Palachacola the servant contracted the ague (malarial fever) and was left in the settlement of Pon Pon (modern Jacksonboro). Mackay did not see him again. On the third day the packhorsemen became so ill that Mackay was forced to camp near the Ashepoo River for two days while they partially recovered. After hiring a man from a nearby plantation Mackay continued the trip on 20 August. That day two of the packhorsemen had relapses and were left alongside the road to recover. Mackay and his two remaining men had considerable difficulty in driving the herd, which probably consisted of about fifty horses of the tough breed raised by the Cherokee. During the week it took to travel from the head of Ashepoo River to Palachacola on the Savannah River, several horses escaped and drifted into the swamps. Finally, on 26 August, Captain Mackay rode into Fort Prince George at Palachacola with his horses. Captain Aneas Mackintosh, the garrison commander, lent Mackay two of his rangers to help corral the herd and tend it until the packhorsemen were well enough to rejoin Mackay. The piragua arrived soon afterward and its cargo of presents and equipment was secured in the fort.[16]

When Captain Mackay arrived in Josephs Town he found his Independent Company in a state of convalescence. All the rangers had contracted a fever and were still too ill for duty. Doctor Hirsh and Lieutenant Parker had gone to Savannah where they were recovering. On 16 September, while Mackay was in Savannah visiting his surgeon and lieutenant, he contracted the same fever and lay in bed during the ensuing two weeks, sometimes delirious. About the first of October his fever broke and he left for Beaufort, South Carolina, to rest and regain his strength in the ocean breezes, but as soon as he arrived he had a relapse and lay near death for twenty days. His fever finally broke again and he returned to Savannah on 31 October.[17]

The outlook for Mackay was discouraging. Seven months had passed since Oglethorpe had ordered him to journey to the Creek nations. Most of his rangers had recovered from their recent sickness, but their morale was low. They told Mackay that they had no intentions of remaining in the company after March when their terms of service would expire. Mackay's chief packhorseman, an Indian trader named John Gray, informed him that the horses were sick and some of them would not survive a journey to the Creek nations. Robert Parker, Jr., resigned his commission as lieutenant because he was too ill to perform his duties, and Mackay could not have felt too strong himself after five weeks of intermittent fever.[18]

Captain Mackay wanted James Burnside, a settler at Fort Argyle, as his new lieutenant, but Thomas Causton, the trustees' representative and storekeeper, gave the vacant commission to Adrain Loyer, his former assistant in the trustees' store. Mackay thought Loyer lacked a "Warlick disposition."[19]

In early November, after months of frustrating delays, Captain Mackay began final preparations to journey to Coweta, the principal town of the Lower Creek. Thomas Wiggins, the trader whom Oglethorpe had engaged to assist and accompany Mackay, advised him to take only a part of the company because there were not enough fit horses to mount all the men and pack their baggage. Captain Mackay agreed and left Lieutenant Loyer and eight rangers in Savannah while he and the remainder took boat passage on 10 November to the Uchee Indian town three miles west of Fort Prince George. He planned to return the horses for Loyer and his rangers as soon as the Upper Creek authorized him to build a fort. The packhorsemen had previously swum the horses (four of which had drowned) and boated the presents, supplies, and equipment across the river to the Uchee town. After arriving, the company stayed under the cover of the Indians' huts and traders' houses for about two weeks while early winter rains delayed their departure. While there, Mackay renewed the trading licenses of the two traders in residence, an act for which he had no authority.[20]

During the last week of November 1734 Captain Mackay and his half of the Independent Company began their overland march to Coweta on the Chattahoochee River. The company probably included Thomas Wiggins who served as guide, Ensign Hugh Mackay, Jr., John Barton the interpreter, Doctor Hirsh, William Clark the messenger, John Gray and one or two more packhorsemen, a noncommissioned officer, and about seven private rangers. Mackay had left two of the rangers at Josephs Town to work on his plantation. Perhaps two or more Yamacraw Indians attended the company as hunters, guides, and scouts.[21]

When traveling the southern forest paths the members of a ranger party awoke and began riding early in the morning. Indian scouts ranged to the front and flanks to hunt deer and turkey for the party's food supply. They stopped before noon each day for two or three hours in order to rest and skin the wild animals that the Indians had killed for the evening meal. Afterwards, the rangers rode until just before sunset when they stopped and made camp near a stream. The horses were not tied but were allowed to wander in the vicinity of the camp with a leather hobble tied between their forelegs to keep them from straying too far. Bells were tied around their necks to inform the rangers of their locations during the next morning's dim predawn light. After guards were posted around the camp, meat and other food was divided among the groups, or messes, of four or five men each who prepared supper over their separate fires. After eating, the men lay down to sleep with their weapons close by, using saddles for pillows.[22]

The exact trace of the path they followed is unknown, but it probably ran from the Uchee town west-northwest to a point just below present Milledgeville, then southwest to present Columbus. The path would have been narrow with tree branches closing in on the riders from all sides, and a man who did not watch the path could have been knocked from his saddle. Almost every creek bed was a swamp where the rangers were forced to dismount and wade through the deep stinking mud. Captain Mackay reached certain conclusions about ranger equipment during that journey. The muskets he had bought were designed as infantry weapons, too long and cumbersome for horsemen negotiating narrow paths. The cheap saddles he had purchased were falling apart. He soon wrote to Oglethorpe, asking him to supply short carbines and a "hunter" type of saddle.[23]

The first major river crossing was the Ogeechee. Crossing large rivers was a time-consuming project for a party with baggage. Horsemen crossed by one of two methods. The first and most dangerous method was to ride the swimming horses across, a maneuver that could and often did result in men being swept off and drowned. The second and most comfortable method was to search the bank until an Indian dugout canoe or raft could be found and then paddle across while the horses were made to swim alongside. The packhorsemen floated the baggage across rivers in a skin boat, a small portable craft made by stretching a leather cover over a wooden frame. It was collapsible and was carried in one of the horse's packs.[24]

About a week after beginning their journey they crossed the Oconee River approximately four miles southeast of present Milledgeville. There the path joined with the Lower Trading Path, which ran from Fort Moore, South Carolina, on the Savannah River to Coweta on the Chattahoochee River. This was the path that joined Charles Town to the Lower Creek nation. A day or two later they passed by the ancient mounds at modern Ocmulgee National Monument in Macon and crossed the Ocmulgee River. About 10 December, ten to twelve days after leaving the Uchee town, the company arrived at the Flint River. Mackay wrote and dispatched instructions to all of the principal traders among the Lower Creek to meet him within fifteen miles of Coweta and accompany him to that town. About two days later approximately fifteen "Gentlemen Traders" met Captain Mackay on the trail and saluted him in frontier fashion by firing their muskets into the air. The next day the combined parties received a friendly welcome from Chigelley, the principal mico of the Lower Creek, as they rode into Coweta on the west bank of the Chattahoochee River, two and one-half miles southeast of Mill Creek, which runs through modern Phoenix City, Alabama. That was Mackay's headquarters for the next three and one-half months.[25]

He spent the remainder of the winter visiting the Lower Creek towns, most of which were similar in appearance. Each of the richest warriors' residences usually consisted of four buildings: a winter lodge and kitchen, a summer hut, a storage hut, and a hut for skins and other trade goods. All faced an open court. The town square consisted of an artificial mound, with a winter hothouse and a summer-cabin court on top, and a large rectangular yard where the game of chungke was played. Surrounding the town were the cornfields that were worked in common by the inhabitants.[26]

Each of the towns probably gave him a customary reception, varying in intensity. Since it was winter the welcoming ceremony likely took place in the hothouse, a circular building about fifty feet in diameter which served as the winter temple and men's club. Inside of this smoky stinking hut the head warriors served a black ceremonial drink made of the leaves of the Yaupon holly tree. Afterward they may have moved outside to watch a game of chungke. A small wheel-shaped chungke stone was bowled down the field followed by two warriors who threw light poles toward the spot where they expected it to stop. The closest pole determined the winner. Food was later served, and that night the Indians probably danced for Mackay's entertainment.[27]

The Independent Company had some success in establishing rapport with the Indians through Doctor Hirsh, who worked among the Indians of the various towns curing many of their minor ailments. The young doctor also served as the company's surgeon and veterinarian, treating both the rangers and their horses.[28]

Mackay unfortunately established a degree of influence over Licko, the mico of a small town called Uchesses, which was probably one of the Uchee, or Yuchi, settlements. Mackay, on his own initiative, had decided to take positive action against the Spaniards because they were supposedly building fortifications in Apalachee, south of the Creek nations. Licko already hated the Spaniards—they had reportedly killed his brother—and only a little persuasion by Mackay through John Barton, the interpreter, was needed to set him on the warpath with twenty-five of his men. Believing that the Spaniards would retaliate if they suffered from Licko's raid, Mackay wrote Thomas Causton at Savannah to suggest that he alert the settlements and send some Yamacraw to scout the crossing sites of the Altamaha River. Licko struck a Spanish outpost named Fort Pupo on the west bank of the Saint Johns River during the first week of May 1735, killing the fort's master gunner. A month later, true to Mackay's prediction, a party of Yemassee Indians from Florida surprised a Yamacraw scouting party camped on the Altamaha River, killing seven men.[29]

During his initial days with the Lower Creek, Captain Mackay was undoubtedly fascinated by their customs. Unlike most Europeans of that period, the Creek bathed daily. Scratching one another until blood was drawn was an obsession; children were scratched when naughty to let out the evil spirits and men scratched each other to pledge friendship. They were often noisy with their whoops, each designed for a special occasion. Their clothing was a mixture of traditional Creek and period English. The common winter dress was a trade shirt, a cloth apron or breechcloth, moccasins, and a blanket. The Creek conducted war by employing small raids and ambushes to gain a few scalps instead of organizing extensive campaigns, like European nations, to destroy entire armies and towns. After killing a few men, women, or children and stealing a few horses they returned home to celebrate and brag. There was very little group discipline; a warrior could accompany or not accompany a war party, and even after joining he could quit and return home at any time with no question asked. If a war party was overwhelmed they seldom stood and fought but instead turned and ran, sometimes for days, to escape death with no loss of face. However, like Europeans, elevated social status served as the reward for courageous actions in battle.[30]

Mackay's fascination with the Creek customs quickly soured. Unlike Oglethorpe, he had no particular respect or tolerance for Indians. He pictured them as being sullen and gloomy, but that was certainly an inaccurate description of their character. He thought their answers to his political questions were ambiguous, but the Creek survived by being ambiguous; Spanish and French captains asked them the same questions. He thought they were too arrogant, but arrogance was their pre-

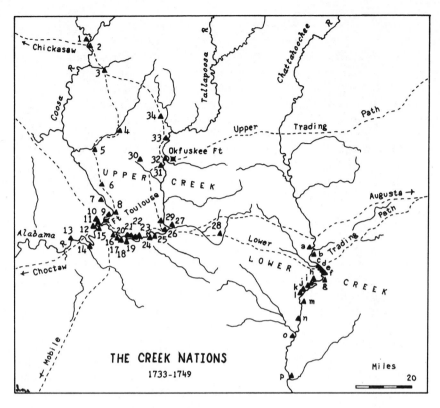

Lower Creek Towns

(Approximately 1,200 Warriors)

a.	Coweta	e.	Chiaha	i.	Apalachicola	m.	Oconee
b.	Kasihta	f.	Okmulgee	j.	Kolomi	n.	Sawokli
c.	Yuchi	g.	Hitchiti	k.	Atasi	o.	Hogologee
d.	Osochi	h.	Westo	l.	Tuskegee	p.	Eufaula Hopai

Upper Creek Towns

(Approximately 1,365 Warriors)

1.	Chickasaw	10.	Old Coosa	19.	Old Tallassee	27.	Tallassee
2.	Coosa	11.	Tuskegee	20.	Kanhatki	28.	Halfway
3.	Abihkutci	12.	Koasati	21.	Kolomi	29.	Yuchi
4.	Wakokai	13.	Autauga	22.	Fushatchee	30.	Okchai
5.	Pakan	14.	Pawokti	23.	Holiwahali	31.	Eufaula
6.	Wiwohka	15.	Pakana	24.	Atasi	32.	Okfuskee
7.	Okchai	16.	Tawasa	25.	Tulsa	33.	Suka-ispoga
8.	Wetumpka	17.	Muklasa	26.	Tukabahchee	34.	Hilibi
9.	Oktcaiutci	18.	Shawnee				

dictable attitude after Britain, Spain, and France had vied for their allegience with presents during the past fifty years. Since their young unmarried women each cohabitated with numerous young men he believed they lacked any virtuous principles, but Mackay apparently did not realize that his virtues were not the same as those of the Creek. He thought the most disgusting thing about the Indians was their "cowardly" method of making war. Mackay's lack of respect for the Indians soon led to a diplomatic break with the headmen of Tustegoes, perhaps a small branch town of Kasihta, or Cussita. He later punished that town by withdrawing their traders.[31]

Captain Mackay completed his business among the Lower Creek during the last week in March 1735 by assembling all the micos and principle warriors at Coweta to listen to him deliver Oglethorpe's written speech advocating continued friendship and trade with the British.[32]

On 30 March the company began its journey to the Upper Creek. By this time Lieutenant Loyer and his eight rangers had apparently joined Mackay. The company must have maintained an apprehensive guard because the French commander of Fort Toulouse, sometimes called Alabama Fort, had threatened to repel them by force if they entered the Upper Creek nation. Mackay was spoiling for a fight and would have welcomed a confrontation; however, the governor of Louisiana chose to limit French reaction to diplomatic outbursts, thereby preventing clashes between Mackay's rangers and the French garrison. Actually, the governor and his Choctaw allies were involved in a costly war with the Chickasaw and were in no position to extend themselves militarily.[33]

Mackay sent orders to all the Upper Creek traders to meet him at Halfway, a small town on Chewookeleehatchee Creek about forty-five miles east-northeast of present Montgomery, Alabama. From there the traders escorted the company to Tallassee near the junction of Uhapee Creek and Tallapoosa River, where Mackay showed the traders his commissions from Oglethorpe, the trustees, and the governor of South Carolina. The governor's commission may have been a fake because Mackay had admitted earlier that he had been unable to obtain such a document, but the illiterate traders were not aware of the difference. He informed them that Georgia now controlled the trade and that they would have to go to Savannah instead of Charles Town to buy their licenses, regardless of what orders they had from South Carolina.[34]

A short time later Mackay met with the headmen of the Upper Creek towns at Okfuskee, a principal town, and bluntly stated his demands. "First, for them to pull down and demolish the French Fort at Albamas. Secondly, if they would not do that, then to let him build a fort wherever he should think convenient. Thirdly, that if they would not consent to do as before proposed that he would withdraw all the Traders from amongst them."[35] The headmen withdrew and debated the problem for a week. The ultimatum was a blow to the Creek whose national policy was the maintenance of neutrality. However, they had become so dependent upon British trade goods that they could not easily exist without them. They reluctantly agreed to allow Mackay to build his fort.[36]

Although the South Carolina Assembly later argued that a fort was never constructed, it is certain that a fortification of some sort was built near Okfuskee, sometimes called Great Okfuskee, located west of modern Dadeville, Alabama, on the west bank of the Tallapoosa River opposite Sandy Creek. The entire site is now under Lake Martin. Okfuskee Fort, probably a log blockhouse surrounded by a stockade, contained the western-most British garrison in North America.[37]

During his stay in the Creek nations Captain Mackay had learned to detest many of the traders. Although some of them were reputable businessmen, many more were scoundrels who sold unlimited rum, cheated with false weights and measures, contracted immense debts, drank to excess, and conducted themselves like stud horses among the Indian women. Although Captain Mackay seemingly made attempts to reform the traders, they generally ignored him. He resolved to make examples of some of them in order to frighten the others into submitting to his authority. Before leaving for the Upper Creek he had ordered four pairs of handcuffs from Savannah.[38]

Nevertheless, several of the traders, Thomas Wiggins in particular, seem to have been in Captain Mackay's favor. They probably helped him formulate his scheme for more orderly control of the trade by organizing the most honest and reliable traders into a monopolistic trading company. After Mackay received permission from the Upper Creek to build a fort, he met with the traders at Okfuskee and proceeded to organize a trading company that consisted of Thomas Wiggins and ten others. They submitted to Georgia's jurisdiction and were the only authorized traders among the Creek. The members of the company seem to have been pleased with the arrangement; they were spared the £50 charge for a license and a tax of six pennies placed on each deerskin by South Carolina, requirements that they detested, and there was less competition. Captain Mackay informed those traders who had not been invited to become part of the company that they must leave the Creek nations, cautioning them not to return with a renewed South Carolina license because that document was no longer valid. In all, he forced five traders to leave the Upper Creek and three to leave the Lower Creek. Some of these men headed straight for Charles Town to inform their merchant backers.[39]

From the very boldness of Mackay's attack on South Carolina's trading system it appears that he expected to receive lawful backing from the Georgia trustees. At Oglethorpe's instigation they had passed an Indian trading act during the previous January, in which they claimed Georgia's jurisdiction over the trade. However, during April and May 1735 Mackay acted without any authority whatsoever in regulating the trade because the trustees' act was not approved by the king and his council until April, and it did not become effective until June.[40]

About the middle of May, just before Mackay left the Upper Creek, a most unfortunate incident occurred. Doctor Hirsh and William Edwards, a servant to a trader named Alexander Wood, had a quarrel for some unknown reason and they may have exchanged blows. When Captain Mackay heard about it he judged that Edwards was in the wrong and ordered him handcuffed and shackled with leg irons. Mackay had found a man to punish as an example for the traders. The next day Ensign Hugh Mackay, Jr., marched Edwards alongside an escort of rangers to the chuncoe pole, the Creek torture stake, in the town square of Okfuskee. Edwards's shirt was stripped off and he was tied to the pole while two rangers cut a bundle of hickory switches. When all was ready Mackay and the traders joined the crowd of curious Indians to watch.

However, One Handed King, the Okfuskee mico, and Lieutenant, a prominent warrior, interceded to prevent the whipping, which they considered a loathsome form of punishment. One Handed King hugged Edwards in his arms and said they would have to whip him too. Lieutenant said Edwards would not be whipped. Mackay said the punishment would be carried out. Lieutenant picked up the bundle of switches and threw them aside. It was a tense moment for Indians and white men alike. Finally, Captain Mackay relented and Edwards was freed.[41]

Anthony Willy, formerly the lieutenant of Fort Moore, South Carolina, was apparently commissioned lieutenant of the company at about that time to replace Adrain Loyer. Willy was the first officer in the company with any experience on the frontier. He and a small party of rangers were left at Okfuskee, probably to build the fort, while Mackay and the remainder of the company returned to Coweta on the Chattahoochee River.[42]

During June the headmen of both the Upper and Lower Creek left for Savannah where a large quantity of presents had arrived from England. Mackay, intending to preside over the distribution, left Coweta with his detachment of the company, arriving in Savannah on 18 June.[43]

As Mackay rode into Savannah a political storm was breaking over his actions among the Creek. The Spanish governor of Saint Augustine had written two letters of protest concerning Licko's raid and would soon write a third. The banished South Carolina traders were arriving in Charles Town and indignant merchants were crying for restitution. Governor Johnson, who might have defended Mackay to some extent, had died the month before. His replacement, Lieutenant Governor Thomas Broughton, was in sympathy with the South Carolina Indian trading faction and pressed the attack against Mackay. Mackay, undaunted by the uproar he had caused, added to the storm by issuing Georgia licenses to those traders who had accompanied him to Savannah.[44]

Because of the outraged complaints from South Carolina and Florida, the Georgia magistrates made an attempt, in appearance at least, to determine whether Mackay had sent Licko and his war party on their raid against the Spanish fort in

Florida. About the first of July they conducted a hearing in the presence of the Creek headmen. They exonerated Captain Mackay and placed the blame on John Barton, the company's South Carolina interpreter whom Mackay had disliked from the beginning. Barton was placed under arrest for inciting Licko to raid Spanish territory, but he was probably released in about a month following a protest by Lieutenant Governor Broughton.[45]

Captain Mackay outfitted the company for further service by having uniform coats tailored to replace the rangers' civilian coats. During the first part of July, after the Indian conference, he prepared to set out with the company on a scouting mission toward Florida. Instead he went to Beaufort, South Carolina, perhaps to recover from a recurrence of his fever.[46]

Throughout July indignant letters were exchanged between Mackay and Lieutenant Governor Broughton and also between the Georgia magistrates and the lieutenant governor. Broughton claimed Mackay had exceeded his instructions, which were only military, but Mackay, with the magistrates backing, said his actions were well within his authority.[47]

The indignation in Charles Town over Mackay's actions against the traders led to direct action. Broughton and the assembly resolved not to pay for the cost of the Independent Company as previously promised. In addition, Broughton sent his Indian commissioner to reside in the Creek nations to insure that traders with South Carolina licenses were not barred from trading. There were rumors that South Carolina would thwart Mackay with military force if necessary. Additional rumors hinted that the Georgia militia would back Mackay. By the end of the summer it was apparent that a physical clash would occur if Captain Mackay returned to the Creek nations with the intention of enforcing his trading laws. He wisely decided to spend the remainder of 1735 with part of his company at Josephs Town, while Lieutenant Willy and his detachment of the company sat quietly at Okfuskee.[48]

Word of Mackay's actions eventually reached the Georgia trustees in London. His provocation of an Indian attack on a Spanish fort was an international incident and his unauthorized banishment of the South Carolina traders had caused a rupture in their relations with South Carolina, a colony that was providing valuable aid to Georgia. In order to avoid further trouble and to placate South Carolina, the trustees ordered Captain Mackay discharged and directed Oglethorpe to investigate his actions and punish him if necessary.[49]

After returning to Georgia, Oglethorpe visited Captain Mackay at Josephs Town on 9 February 1736. There is no record of what they said at that meeting, but it must have been embarrassing for both of them; although Mackay's actions had been highly provocative, he had been attempting to implement an unworkable policy planned by Oglethorpe. Oglethorpe retained the rangers on duty, but he carried out the trustees' order and discharged Captain Mackay.[50]

Patrick Mackay commands a degree of sympathy from modern observers. He was one of the most conscientious officers to serve under Oglethorpe in Georgia; despite sickness, hardship, and extreme misfortune he continued to carry out his instructions with great personal courage. His attempt to improve and regulate the conduct of the traders, although impossible within his limited power, was nevertheless valiant. Unfortunately, he had two primary shortcomings that seriously hampered his effectiveness. First, he had a deep prejudice concerning men who were not of his social stature and culture. Unlike Oglethorpe, he could not tolerate what he believed to be repulsive habits and customs of the traders and Indians. Second, he was a newcomer to America without experience or knowledge of frontier politics and the established relationship of the Indian trade with the South Carolina economy. Nevertheless, he might have succeeded if Governor Johnson had lived, for that British statesman apparently considered Indian affairs from the strategic standpoint. His successor, Lieutenant Governor Broughton, viewed the Indians as one of the financial mainstays of his friends, the South Carolina merchants. Thus, even if Mackay had been a man of exceptional tolerance and great experience he probably could not have secured a portion of the Creek trade for Georgia without incurring the wrath of the South Carolina merchants. The bitter dispute between South Carolina and Georgia concerning jurisdiction over the Indian trade was still far from settled.

IV

Occupation of the Spaniards' Doorstep

January–June 1736

The old Spanish-mission province of Guale, that vast land of seacoast, marsh, and forest between the Georgia settlements and Spanish Florida, had lain virtually uninhabited since 1727 when the British garrison was withdrawn from Fort King George on the Altamaha River. When Oglethorpe returned to England in late 1734 the British flag still flew over the fort, but the outworks were in ruins and the garrison included only two lonely South Carolina watchmen whose existence was centered around a supply boat's periodic visits.[1]

In 1730 the British Board of Trade had ordered South Carolina to establish two "townships" on the Altamaha River and to rebuild Fort King George as a buffer against the Spaniards, but the order was ignored. The project was tabled after the plans for settling Georgia were finalized; however, Oglethorpe's personal strategy called for Georgia to colonize that region before the Spaniards could reestablish themselves there. During March 1735, nine months after his return to England, he began his campaign by inducing the Georgia trustees to ask Parliament for £51,800, half of which would fund the establishment of 880 men in twenty forts on the Altamaha River. According to Oglethorpe's probable expectation, Parliament naturally did not agree to such an outlandish request, but they did provide, without significant question, a budget of £26,000, enough to allow Oglethorpe to continue planning. In June the trustees approved Oglethorpe's more conservative plan for two fortified

towns in the Altamaha River region of old Guale. Scottish Highlanders were to establish a town and garrison the site of Fort
King George, while Englishmen and Salzburgers were to settle
a town and garrison a fort on Saint Simons Island.[2]

The Scottish settlement was the responsibility of Hugh Mackay, Sr., who was a former British army lieutenant, a brother
of Patrick, an uncle of Hugh, Jr., and a Georgian since 1733.
Mackay and John Cuthbert, another Highland gentleman, were
given trustees' commissions as captain and lieutenant, respec-
tively, of the militia. More than 170 people, including a number
of men who indentured themselves as servants, were recruited
from the county of Sutherland in Scotland. They embarked
for Georgia in October 1735 and arrived at Tybee Roads, the
mouth of the Savannah River, in January 1736. Mackay and
part of the men immediately set out for the Altamaha River
and the remainder followed soon afterwards with the women
and children. Their town, Darien, located on the site of the
modern village of that name, initially consisted of some huts,
a small battery of cannons, a guard house, a store house, and
a makeshift church. The Gaelic-speaking Scots were a colorful
addition to the American wilderness with their Highland dress,
consisting of belted plaids, stockings, brogues, and bonnets.
Each man was armed with a broadsword, a target (shield),
and a poorly manufactured musket.[3]

The settlers for Frederica, the proposed town and fort for
Saint Simons Island, were recruited in London. Oglethorpe
left England with two ships containing 257 colonists in December 1735, arriving in Georgia during early February 1736.
Leaving the settlers at Tybee Roads, Oglethorpe continued
upriver to the town of Savannah where he remained for a
week, completing necessary business before sailing southward
for the Altamaha River. He agreed with those Salzburgers who
were already settled at Ebenezer, north-northwest of Savannah,
to move their settlement to a better location on the western
bank of the Savannah River. He also agreed to allow many
of the fifty-nine German-speaking Salzburgers who had accompanied him to settle with their countrymen at New Ebenezer rather than at the proposed town of Frederica.[4]

One of Oglethorpe's first priorities was to establish five
ranger units (a total of fifty men) to provide additional frontier

protection. According to the trustees' order Oglethorpe discharged Captain Patrick Mackay, but he divided the Independent Company into two separate parties: he retained Lieutenant Anthony Willy's detachment at Okfuskee in the Upper
Creek nation, and he ordered the detachment of Ensign Hugh
Mackay, Jr., to prepare for duty in the Altamaha settlements.
A third unit, Captain Aneas Mackintosh's Palachacola Rangers,
was already garrisoning Fort Prince George near the Savannah
River in South Carolina. The two remaining units were probably on duty by June of that year: Oglethorpe drew orders
for Captain Roger Lacy to enlist a party of rangers for the
purpose of building and garrisoning Fort Augusta on the upper
Savannah River and for Lieutenant John Cuthbert to recruit
a party of rangers to defend the immediate northern approaches to Savannah. Not included among the new detachments was Captain James McPherson's Company of Southern
Rangers, which belonged to South Carolina. Oglethorpe ordered Captain McPherson and a detachment of his company
to ride south to the new settlement of Darien and provide
the Highlanders with additional protection until the Frederica
settlers could move to support them. He also ordered Ensign
Mackay and his party of ten rangers and two packhorsemen
to escort two surveyors on a reconnaissance of the wilderness
between Savannah and Darien to find a good route for a road.[5]

Oglethorpe encountered a major problem in moving the
Frederica settlers from Tybee Roads to Saint Simons Island;
the captains of the ships refused to sail southward and enter
the uncharted entrance of Jekyll (Saint Simons) Sound. They
were probably also afraid to venture too far into Spanish-
claimed waters without the protection of a British warship.
A solution was finally discovered when Oglethorpe offered
to purchase the cargo of a merchant sloop named *Midnight*
if the master promised to unload at the Frederica site. The
ships' captains consented to accompany the sloop to reconnoiter
the entrance to the sound. Thirty male settlers boarded the
vessel under the direction of William Horton and John Tanner,
Jr., gentlemen who had accompanied Oglethorpe on his return
to Georgia, and sailed on the evening of 15 February.[6]

The following evening Oglethorpe, with two assistants and
a party of Indians, sailed toward the proposed Frederica settle-

ment in the South Carolina scout boat. Captain William Ferguson, the boat's commander, and his crew of ten Southern Scouts had been on loan from Beaufort, South Carolina, since January 1733. Initially stationed in Savannah, the crew had built a base fort on modern Green Island near the southern end of Skidaway Island by early 1735. South Carolina had been using scout boats almost continuously since the beginning of Queen Anne's War (1701–13) when they were stationed at Port Royal to prevent Spaniards and enemy Indians from entering the settlements via the Inland Passage. The scouts' function was similar to that of the rangers, but instead of patrolling on horseback along paths, they plied the rivers and creeks of the Inland Passage (present Intracoastal Waterway) in their boat. Although they were often rather irresponsible, their performance was excellent under competent leadership; like marines, they could fight from their boat or land and fight on foot. The scout boat, which the Georgians informally named the *Carolina,* had been built about 1728, and was evidently a large, double-ended canoe boat, dug from a giant cypress log, having a length of about thirty-five feet and a beam of about six feet. It probably had two gaff-rigged masts; however, its main propellants were the ten scouts, each of whom pulled a large oar. Three swivel-guns (small cannons) provided enough firepower to engage small boats and to counter ambushes from the river banks. The *Carolina* was valuable for operations in the Georgia tidewater; it was shallow draft, light, rugged, and fast.[7]

They rowed and sailed down the Inland Passage instead of the open sea, which was dangerous for an open boat. Leaving the Savannah River, the swift scout boat entered the Wilmington River and quickly arrived at the Thunderbolt settlement on the western bank where Roger Lacy, one of the new ranger commanders, was a principal settler. During the short visit that followed, Oglethorpe perhaps gave Lacy his commission and instructions on recruiting his men. The first night's camp was made on the north end of Skidaway Island. The next morning they pushed on, passing Captain Ferguson's scout-boat base, and while crossing Ossabaw Sound at the mouth of the Ogeechee River the wind rose and the *Carolina* was nearly swamped. The twists and turns of the channel and the

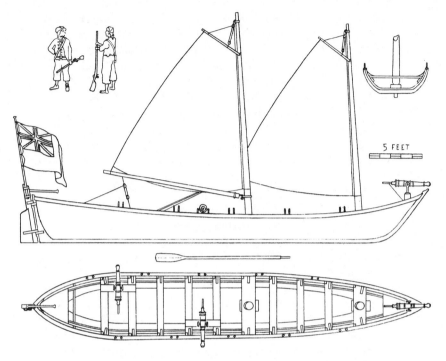

The Scout Boat Carolina, *ca. 1728–1743*
(*Conjectural*)

(*Reproduced from Larry E. Ivers, "Scouting the Inland Passage, 1685–1737,"* The South
Carolina Historical Magazine 73 [*July 1972*], *by permission of The South Carolina
Historical Society*).

many tributaries disappearing into the savannah marsh and
woods made navigation extremely difficult, but Captain Ferguson had scouted this area many times and did not miss a turn,
even during darkness. Oglethorpe was in a hurry and he pushed
the scouts to row day and night. They, like most soldiers who
served directly under Oglethorpe, were satisfied with his leadership and competed for his compliments. Even the Yamacraw
warriors occasionally took the oars. [8]

On the morning of 18 February the *Carolina* moved cautiously down the Frederica River alongside Saint Simons Island.
After the scouts primed their muskets and the boat's swivel-

guns, the Indians were landed on the southern end of the island near the sound to reconnoiter the area for the presence of Spanish patrols. They soon met a hunting party of Yamacraw who informed them that a strange ship was anchored in the sound. A stealthy observation by Oglethorpe and the scouts identified the vessel as the sloop *Midnight.* Later that same day they disembarked at present Fort Frederica National Monument and built a few "booths," or temporary huts, constructed of pole frames that were sided with palmetto leaves, to serve as shelters for themselves and their supplies. During the next few days Oglethorpe traced the outline of Fort Frederica and taught the men a few techniques of fortification.[9]

On 22 February, Oglethorpe took the scout boat and began the return trip to Savannah. During the journey he visited Darien and earned the Highlanders' respect by disdaining a soft cot and a tent, choosing instead to spend the night on the ground wrapped in a Highland plaid. Oglethorpe and the scouts reached Tybee Roads on 25 February and were followed the next day by the two ships' captains who still refused to sail their vessels into Saint Simons Sound from fear of uncharted waters and Spanish men-of-war. However, the settlers agreed to a request by Oglethorpe to make the journey in open piraguas despite the hardships that would result.[10]

A little fleet of piraguas departed for Frederica on 2 March. Piraguas were constructed from large cypress or cedar logs, but they were larger than canoes, their close relatives. In order to achieve a length of forty to fifty feet or more, a beam of seven or eight feet, and a depth of four or five feet, the following construction technique was utilized: a long dugout log was cut in half lengthwise, a large plank and fitted end-pieces of timber were fixed between the two halves, and sideboards were placed atop the gunwales. The square stern was decked with a cabin beneath, and another small deck was built in the sharp bow. Those cargo craft were normally driven by two gaff-rigged masts and a couple of oars, but additional oars were provided on this occasion to enable the new settlers to speed their progress to Frederica. Oglethorpe kept the men hard at work on the oars by placing all of the beer in one of the lead piraguas.[11]

Upon arriving at Frederica the settlers began building huts

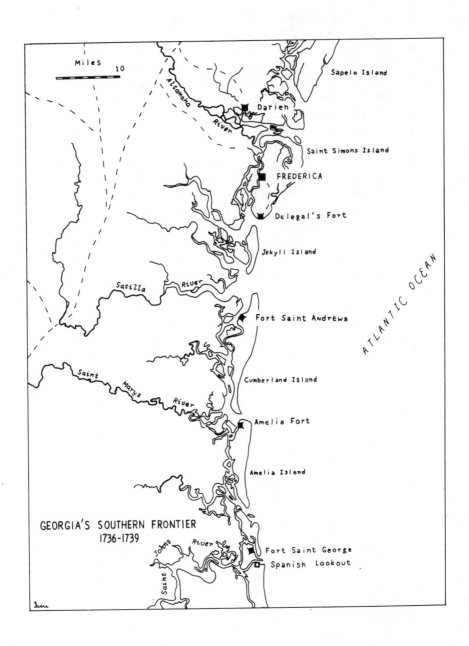

Miles
10

Altamaha River

Sapelo Island

Darien

Saint Simons Island

FREDERICA

Delegal's Fort

Jekyll Island

Satilla River

Fort Saint Andrews

Saint Marys River

Cumberland Island

Amelia Fort

Amelia Island

GEORGIA'S SOUTHERN FRONTIER
1736-1739

Saint Johns River

Fort Saint George
Spanish Lookout

Saint

ATLANTIC OCEAN

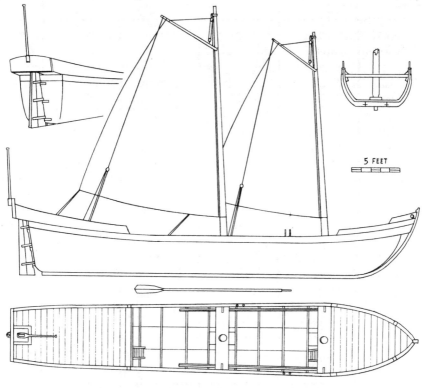

A Small Piragua

and earned trustees' pay by assisting in the construction of the fort. Fort Frederica was a square-shaped fortification, 124 by 125 feet on the inside with a regular bastion at each corner and a spur battery that jutted beyond the fort on the river side. Sod-faced earthen walls and a row of palisades planted in a moat surrounded a storehouse, powder magazine, well, and blacksmith shop.[12]

Hugh Mackay, Jr., and his party of rangers arrived in Frederica on 15 March after a ninety-mile road-surveying journey from Savannah to Darien. The horses were transported to Frederica in piraguas and were lent to the settlers for use in plowing the small fields that were prepared for planting potatoes, corn, and other crops. The rangers then returned to Darien to help protect that settlement.[13]

On 16 March Oglethorpe boarded Captain Ferguson's scout boat *Carolina* and began a hasty reconnaissance of the Inland Passage to the south, looking for a site upon which to build an outpost for the additional protection of the Frederica and Darien settlements. He decided that a fort with a garrison on Cumberland Island, twenty miles to the south, could effectively block the Inland Passage. A month later, on 18 April, Oglethorpe set out with a party to establish the fortification and conduct a more thorough reconnaissance of the Inland Passage. Accompanying him were the scout crews of the *Carolina* and a new sister scout boat named the *Georgia,* recently purchased in South Carolina and commanded by John Ray, one of Ferguson's scouts. Forty Yamacraw warriors under Tomochichi accompanied the party in their canoes. The next morning they rendezvoused with a piragua from Darien containing Captain Hugh Mackay, thirty Highland indentured servants, and Ensign Hugh Mackay, Jr., with his party of ten rangers. That afternoon the boats landed on the northwest side of Cumberland Island where Oglethorpe traced the outline of Fort Saint Andrews on a hill overlooking the Inland Passage, a location now known as Terrapin Point. Captain Mackay directed the trustees' Scotch servants in the construction of the fortification while his nephew's rangers protected them.[14]

Fort Saint Andrews was built in a configuration called a "Star-Work," the shape of which was a four-pointed star, each of the points being a bastion. The northern points were short; the two southern points were long. Excluding the bastions, the inside dimensions of the fort were about 65 by 130 feet. In order to construct a wall from the loose sand, the only earthwork material in the area, it was necessary to cover a layer of limbs and brush with a layer of sand, which was covered, in turn, by a layer of limbs, etc. This was merely an expedient; not long afterward a wooden form was constructed to contain the sand walls. A palisade of logs was planted in the moat into which natural springs flowed, providing fresh water. A single-story plank-sided frame house was constructed with a powder magazine and store house in the cellar under-

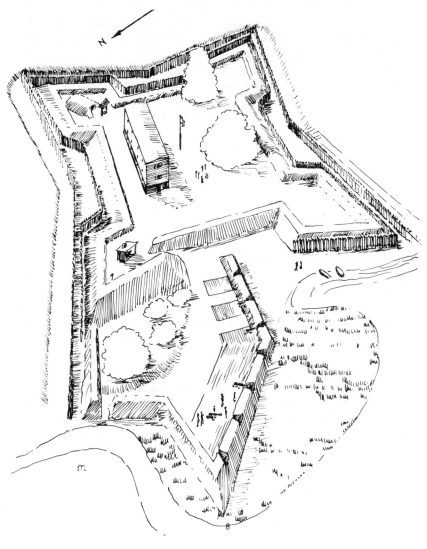

Fort Frederica, 1736
(Conjectural)

(Reproduced from Albert C. Manucy, The Fort at Frederica *[Tallahassee, 1962],*
by permission of The Department of Anthropology, The Florida State University).

neath. A triangular earthen battery surrounded by a palisade was soon built at the bottom of the hill for cannons covering traffic on the Inland Passage.[15]

While the fort was under construction Oglethorpe continued his journey southward to the Spanish outposts on the south side of the Saint Johns River to inquire about a British diplomat who was conducting negotiations with Florida's governor. The British secretary of state, the Duke of Newcastle, realizing that the settlements at the Altamaha River's mouth would cause added tension, had dispatched his personal representative, Charles Dempsey, to Florida in order to attempt a negotiated settlement with the Spaniards. An escort under Major James Richards, a Swiss settler from Purrysburg, South Carolina, had conducted Dempsey from Savannah to Florida two months before, but no word had been received from them since.[16]

During the reconnaissance Oglethorpe underwent his first experience in the utilization of Indian allies in a combat situation. Tomochichi was determined to kill some Spaniards or their Yemassee Indian subjects in retaliation for the ambush of one of his hunting parties the year before. Oglethorpe left the Indians on the north side of the Saint Johns River, under the watchful eye of William Horton with one of the scout boats, while he crossed the Saint Johns River looking for Spaniards who could provide information about Dempsey. After an unsuccessful attempt to make contact with the Spaniards he returned to the northern bank where he found that Tomochichi had taken most of his Indians and disappeared. Oglethorpe was left with the terrible apprehension that Tomochichi was about to create a disastrous incident by attacking a party of Spaniards. That night, following hours of worrying, one of the Indians' boats returned containing a handful of seemingly crazed warriors who nervously jumped about and "foamed at the mouth." Tomochichi had discovered a camp of Spaniards nearby and was preparing to attack them. Fortunately, Oglethorpe quickly joined the old mico and was able to induce him to wait until daylight before initiating his attack. The next morning the force of scouts and Indians cautiously approached the camp that was located less than a mile away. Just before initiating an attack they discovered that the camp actually consisted of Major Richards and the crew of the boat that had escorted Dempsey to Saint Augustine.[17]

The governor of Florida, Francisco del Moral Sánchez, had sent letters to Oglethorpe in care of Richards in which he complained of an attack by Creek Indians on one of his outposts during the previous month. Verbal reports from Richards indicated that Governor Moral was preparing to attack the Altamaha River settlements. Oglethorpe's reaction to the letters and reports was at the same time conciliating and aggravating to Governor Moral. Upon returning to Frederica he ordered the *Colony Piragua,* having four swivel-guns and twenty oars, and the *Marine Boat,* a new eight-oared scout boat, to patrol the Saint Johns River from a base fort that was to be built on Saint George Point (modern Fort George Island). Oglethorpe's written excuse to Governor Moral for this action was to prevent Creek war parties from crossing the Saint Johns River into Florida. As proof of his good intentions he sent Indian runners to the mainland to ask Creek hunting and war parties not to molest Spanish outposts. However, Oglethorpe was actually occupying land that he believed rightfully belonged to England, in spite of the Georgia charter that limited the colony to the land between the Altamaha and Savannah Rivers. He also was not opposed to the idea of eventually appropriating Florida, and there is evidence indicating that some officials within the British government maintained similar convictions.[18]

During May, while the militia and boats were being outfitted for operations on the Saint Johns River, meager British military contingents began arriving in Georgia. A detachment of the Independent Company of Foot transferred to Frederica from Fort Frederick, South Carolina. Not to be confused with the disbanded Independent Company of Rangers, this was an infantry company of the British regular army which had been in South Carolina since 1721 and had garrisoned Fort King George near Darien from 1722 to 1727. Oglethorpe had received permission for their use before leaving England and had ordered their transfer immediately after his arrival in Georgia. After refreshing the detachment with beer he settled them on the southern tip of Saint Simons Island where they began building Delegal's Fort to guard the entrance into the sound. A month later the remainder of the company followed under its acting commander, Lieutenant Philip Delegal, Sr. The sloop-of-war *Hawk* also arrived during May. Captain James Gascoigne, the commander, was an experienced hand, having previously served as a lieutenant on the Carolina station during the period 1728–34. He carried a trustees' grant for five hundred acres of land on Saint Simons Island, a location still known as Gascoigne Bluff.[19]

Captain Christian Hermsdorf, a Salzburger settler, proceeded southward on 13 May in command of the *Marine Boat* and the *Colony Piragua,* intending to build Fort Saint George while Major Richards and Horton carried Oglethorpe's letters to Governor Moral in Saint Augustine. Two weeks later Oglethorpe sent Captain Ferguson and his scout boat *Carolina* to support Captain Hermsdorf, but in the early morning hours of 2 June, Ferguson returned hurriedly with news of a setback in Oglethorpe's plans. Because of Captain Hermsdorf's fort-building activity on the Spaniards' doorstep, Major Richards and Horton had been made prisoners in Saint Augustine, and Spanish soldiers were reputed to be maneuvering on the southern bank of the Saint Johns River. Captain Hermsdorf had been forced to withdraw his apprehensive force of English and Salzburger milita to Cumberland Island when they became mutinous.[20]

Oglethorpe immediately set out for Fort Saint George with the scout boat *Georgia* and a yawl from the sloop-of-war *Hawk,* whose crews he reinforced with Highland militiamen from Fort Saint Andrews. After quieting the fears of Hermsdorf's men, whom he met at the southern end of Cumberland Island, Oglethorpe rowed on to Fort Saint George. They continued the construction of the fort on the northeast side of modern Fort George Island on present Mount Cornelia, a hill about sixty feet high, where the southern entrance to the Inland Passage could be easily guarded. A fort had been built there in times past enclosing a hill about forty-five feet high on the immediate eastern slope of Mount Cornelia. The old moat and earthen walls were repaired and palisades were planted, connecting the fort with the top of Mount Cornelia where cannons commanded the island. Captain Mackay was soon brought down to replace Hermsdorf and take command of Fort Saint George, leaving Ensign Mackay, Jr., in command of Fort Saint Andrews.[21]

Governor Moral, viewing Oglethorpe's activities with alarm, believed the defenses of Florida were too weak to withstand an immediate assault by the Georgians. He decided to enter into negotiations and released Dempsey, Richards, and Horton, accompanied by a Spanish officer to act as an intermediary. Subsequent negotiations between Oglethorpe and the Spanish officer took place in Saint Simons Sound aboard the sloop-of-war *Hawk* during the latter part of June 1736. The Spaniards wanted the English to withdraw from the area settled by Georgia, to control the depredations of the Creek Indians, and to abandon Fort Saint George, obviously leaving room for future compromise by qualifying the unacceptable demand to evacuate Georgia with a reasonable demand to abandon only the military complex on Florida's doorstep. The conference lasted seven days, but no agreement was reached.[22]

Oglethorpe was under considerable political pressure during that period. In April the trustees had written him that Parliament had granted only half of the money that had been requested to subsist the colony during the approaching year. In order to keep expenses within the limited budget they ordered Oglethorpe to discharge the rangers and scouts, to temporarily disregard his plans for building the new towns of Darien and Frederica, and to resettle the colonists on the Savannah or Ogeechee Rivers. However, Frederica and Darien were well established by the time Oglethorpe received the orders. He unquestionably engaged in considerable self-debate over the instructions, but since he believed that Georgia had to expand her defenses or be eventually destroyed by the Spaniards and the French, he boldly decided to ignore the trustees and continue the establishment of the two settlements. In June the trustees relented, perhaps because of pressure from sources within the British government. They wrote Oglethorpe that they were still of the opinion that Frederica and Darien ought to be abandoned because of the shortage of funds, but since withdrawing the colonists might signify British weakness he could proceed in building the towns if he believed they were necessary. They warned him to keep spending to a minimum,[23] but this was another order he decided to ignore.

During October, Oglethorpe and Governor Moral finally reached an agreement. Both parties agreed to hold their Indians in check, Oglethorpe abandoned Fort Saint George and Moral agreed not to occupy the site afterward, and all future disputes were to be submitted to their respective governments for settlement. Not long afterward the agreement was rendered effectively void when the Spanish government in Madrid relieved Moral of his governorship because of its dissatisfaction with his compromise. But Moral had only been buying time; two and a half weeks before signing the treaty he had requested a reinforcement of fifteen hundred regular Spanish soldiers to enable him to conduct a surprise attack on Georgia.[24]

During his occupation of the Spaniards' doorstep Oglethorpe had displayed his principal strength and his primary weakness regarding his military ability. He was highly respected by his contemporaries, for his ability to exert leadership over men in his immediate presence, expecially during crises periods, was exceptional. However, he was sometimes extremely reckless, a trait that was becoming increasingly obvious. Although the Spaniards were understandably angered and frightened by the British settlement of the Altamaha River area, his provocative actions, such as his unauthorized construction of Fort Saint George and the establishment of patrols on the Saint Johns River, pushed them to the brink of armed conflict. A war at that time would probably have resulted in Georgia's destruction. No permanent diplomatic settlement of border issues was possible while Oglethorpe continued in personal command of Georgia's defenses.

V

The Coveted Indian Trade
June–November 1736

Oglethorpe was still determined that Georgia should assume jurisdiction over the Indian trade within Georgia's chartered boundaries, despite Captain Patrick Mackay's previous failure in carrying out that mission. The trade in deer skins was far too lucrative to ignore; it could provide Georgia with the stable economic base that it needed in order to achieve self-sufficiency. Probably more important to Oglethorpe was the Indian trade's potentiality as a bargaining lever that could be utilized to assure the Indians' allegiance to Georgia in the event of war with Spain or France. Georgia's claim for jurisdiction over the trade was logically based on the fact that the Creek and Chickasaw resided within Georgia's chartered boundaries. However, South Carolina had maintained a monopoly of the trade for forty years and would not quietly yield such a prize to Georgia. The Charles Town merchants had weathered Oglethorpe's first crude assault by his agent, Captain Mackay, and they were more than prepared to continue the fight and appeal to the British government if necessary.

During early 1735 the trustees had appointed Oglethorpe as Georgia's commissioner of the Indian trade. His powers were enumerated in "An Act for maintaining the Peace with the Indians in the Province of Georgia," which specified the following: all traders operating in Georgia must procure a trustees' license and post a £100 bond to guarantee good conduct; a £100 fine was established for trading without a license; traders who disobeyed the orders of Commissioner Oglethorpe were subject to arrest by a constable supported by a detachment from the nearest military garrison; traders traveling to and from the Indian nations must report to a designated garrison whose commander would monitor their activities; and Commissioner Oglethorpe was to establish a monopoly by distributing the traders among the towns. Since Oglethorpe and the trustees mistakenly believed that the Cherokee lived within the boundaries of Georgia, they attempted to extend their jurisdiction to include those nations in addition to the Creek and Chickasaw. The British government approved the act and the secretary of state wrote a letter in care of Oglethorpe, ordering South Carolina to abide by its provisions. Ironically, the act was based on South Carolina's trading act of 1731.[1]

In February 1736, less than a week after discharging Captain Mackay for his indiscretions among the Creek, Oglethorpe set in motion his new campaign to wrest control of the Indian trade from South Carolina. He sent a copy of the trustees' trading act to Lieutenant Anthony Willy, who commanded Georgia's garrison of rangers at Okfuskee Fort, to show to the Upper Creek traders, and another copy was dispatched to South Carolina's Fort Moore, near which many of the traders maintained storehouses and homes. All traders were ordered to appear in Savannah during the period between March and June to procure Georgia trading licenses.[2]

During June, Oglethorpe began to enforce the act in earnest after discovering that many of the traders had not obeyed his summons to purchase Georgia licenses. Noble Jones, the colony's surveyor, was sent to Fort Moore as his personal representative to order the traders to conform to the Georgia trading act. Oglethorpe designated Roger Lacy, a new ranger captain, as the agent to the Cherokee, and John Tanner, Jr., a young gentleman from Frederica, as the agent to the Creek. Oglethorpe instructed both men to ride to their appointed Indian nations and enforce the trustees' trading act by seizing the trading goods and property of those traders who did not have a Georgia license.[3]

Captain Lacy had arrived in Georgia in February 1734 and had been given a five-hundred-acre grant of land at Thunderbolt near Savannah. Some thought he was an epileptic, but it was also rumored that his periodic fits were psychological, caused by his rather irresponsible wife, Mary. Others said that his sickness was caused by a nervous condition, resulting from heavy drinking.[4]

On 11 June Oglethorpe wrote orders for Lacy, requiring him to send constables and some of his rangers to arrest the offending Cherokee traders and to confiscate their property. At the same time Oglethorpe wrote a letter to ten Cherokee traders, who evidently had secured trustees' licenses, appointing all of them constables to assist Lacy. Three days later he granted each of those men five hundred acres of land in Georgia across the Savannah River from Fort Moore, South Carolina.[5]

Lacy decided to accomplish the mission himself and began the journey up the Savannah River with the ten allied traders and ten of his rangers. During July, after stopping for a short visit at Fort Moore, the party apparently took the trade route along the west bank of the Savannah River, the Upper Cherokee Trading Path, to the Lower Settlements, the nation of Cherokee at the heads of the Chattooga and Keowee Rivers in present South Carolina. Then they probably turned northwest and rode through the Middle Settlements at the headwaters of the Little Tennessee River in present North Carolina. There the party apparently turned southwest and rode around the southern slopes of present Great Smoky Mountains National Park, passing through the Valley Settlements. The last nation of Cherokee the party visited was the Over Hills Settlements to the north along the upper Tennessee and French Broad Rivers in the vicinity of present Knoxville, Tennessee. Captain Lacy and his party were probably impressed by the terrain that they rode through during that summer. The rugged tree-covered Smoky Mountains with their perpetual haze were a drastic change in scenery and temperature from the swamps and tidelands of the Savannah region. However, the rangers' horses, which had lately belonged to Captain Patrick Mackay's Independent Company of Rangers, were quite familiar with the terrain, as they had originally served as pack animals for a Cherokee trader.[6]

As Lacy and his party moved from town to town they seized the trading goods and deer skins from the stores of those South Carolina traders who did not possess a Georgia license.[7] This greatly confused and disturbed the Cherokee; after all, "they were all Englishmen that traded amongst them and they did not concern themselves where they came from."[8]

The traders in the Over Hills Settlements had five days advance warning of Lacy's approach and were waiting for him. He arrived at the town of Great Tellico near present Tellico Plains, Tennessee, on 4 August where he confronted the trader John Gardiner who apparently served as spokesman for the others. Lacy informed Gardiner that he was acting according to instructions from Oglethorpe to discipline traders who did not possess a lawful Georgia trading license. When Gardiner asked him what he proposed to do about the Virginia traders operating among the Cherokee, Lacy replied that his orders from Oglethorpe were not to interfere with them. Lacy advised Gardiner to sell his trading goods to one of those traders who had a Georgia trading license (one of the constables) and then take his deer skins to Savannah and sell them after procuring a Georgia license. Gardiner refused, obviously thinking that Lacy was bluffing.[9]

Three days later Captain Lacy, his rangers, and the trader-constables visited Gardiner at his store in Tennessee, a small town a few miles northeast of Great Tellico on the south bank of the Little Tennessee River. When Gardiner refused to open his storehouse door Lacy had a constable break it down. He gave Gardiner a receipt for the confiscated items and ordered him out of the Cherokee nations. Similar incidents were repeated in town after town.[10]

In general, the Indians became incensed at Lacy for evicting the traders, some of whom were well liked. When the headmen of Great Tellico asked Caesar, a principal chief, if Lacy and his men were Frenchmen, he replied, "No, but . . . they were all one as Enemies."[11] The Over Hills Cherokee would apparently have assassinated Lacy and his men if the South Carolina traders had requested it.[12]

About 1 September, after confiscating the possessions of most of those traders who had South Carolina licenses, Captain Lacy and his rangers wisely departed from the mountains of the Cherokee and returned to Savannah.[13]

John Tanner, Jr., agent to the Creek, had set out for the Creek nations about June. He apparently established his headquarters at the house of trader Thomas Wiggins in the Lower

Creek town of Kasihta on present Lawson Army Airfield, Fort Benning, Georgia. Most of the South Carolina traders in the Creek towns had purchased a Georgia trading license in order to avoid further trouble with Georgia agents; however, on the last day of August, two South Carolina traders, who had earlier been removed from the Creek nations by Captain Patrick Mackay, arrived and reopened their trading stores for business. Jeremiah Knott was licensed by South Carolina to trade at Tukabahchee in the Upper Creek nation and Thomas Johns was licensed for Kasihta in the Lower Creek, Tanner's headquarters. Before a week had passed Tanner sent for both men and ordered them to leave the Creek nations within ten days. Knott apparently departed, but Johns ignored the instructions and continued to trade. Ten days later Tanner visited his store and repeated his warning, again with no response. A week afterward, on 27 September, Lieutenant Willy and three rangers surprised Johns, confiscated all his property, and evicted him from the town.[14]

It appears that Tanner, who was only about twenty years old, was not respected by the Creek, who considered him a child. The Creek were as confused and angered as the Cherokee over the seizure of the South Carolina traders' property. The warriors of one Lower Creek town actually applied war paint in preparation for killing Tanner, but they were prevented by the pleadings of a trader. Hobohatchey of Abihkutci, a principal mico of the Upper Creek, declared that "no Goods should be seized in his Towns."[15] Even Tanner's host, Ellick, a mico of Kasihta, warned him to return Johns's trading goods and informed him that he was no longer welcome. Reacting to a timely order from Oglethorpe, Tanner left the Creek nations for Savannah on 27 October, escorted by Lieutenant Willy and his Okfuskee garrison of rangers.[16]

While Lacy and Tanner were bullying their way among the Indian towns, the commander of South Carolina's Fort Moore had considerably complicated matters by refusing to allow anyone to enter the Creek or Cherokee nations without a South Carolina trading license.[17]

Meanwhile, unknown to any of the front-line participants, Oglethorpe had been forced to give ground to the South Carolina trading interests. South Carolina's Lieutenant Governor

Thomas Broughton and his merchant friends had been in a quandary since the British secretary of state had informed him that the Georgia Indian trading act had the king's approval and must be obeyed. To conform with the secretary of state's orders and give up the profitable Indian trade was unthinkable; however, to ignore the British government was not without its dangers. They decided to attempt a compromise. By this time they had secured the sympathy of most of the South Carolina government. A committee from both houses of the assembly met with Oglethorpe in Savannah during the last week in July and proposed, quite reasonably, that the Indian trade be jointly conducted and regulated. Wording a reply in the guarded polite terms of a diplomat, Oglethorpe in no way conceded South Carolina's right to any portion of the trade with those Indians inside Georgia's boundaries;[18] nevertheless, he knew that South Carolina could and probably would mount a considerable campaign to retain control over a share of the Indian trade. In addition, it was obvious that Georgia would soon have to fight Spanish Florida, and without South Carolina's help disaster would be almost certain. Therefore, the last part of his reply to the committee stated that since the exact boundaries of Georgia were unknown, South Carolina's traders would not be molested "until the Boundary Lines are settled or his Majesty's Pleasure known concerning the same."[19] In one sentence he had declared that he would thereafter place the Indian trading problem in the laps of the Georgia trustees and the British government.

During the spring and summer of 1737 the British government considered a petition from the South Carolina Assembly which asked for continuation of their monopoly of the Indian trade. Relying on Oglethorpe's testimony, the resulting decision of the attorney general and the solicitor general recognized Georgia's jurisdiction over the trade; however, the Privy Council's review modified the decision by requiring Georgia to license all traders who were certified by South Carolina.[20] In effect, both colonies were deprived of any real authority to regulate the trade or to control the conduct of the traders. Their only logical recourse was cooperation, but by then neither colony was in a mood to share authority.

The Indians and their traders would have noticed few

changes in the operation of the trading system. Even though Georgia had won the right to issue licenses and to maintain a commissioner for those Indian nations within her boundaries, the trading business was still monopolized by the Charles Town merchants and most of the trade's economic benefits continued to flow to South Carolina. The traders continued their abuse of the Indians, seldom controlled by either Georgia or South Carolina. Thus, Britain's relationship with the southern Indians was less than satisfactory during the ensuing war with Spain and France.

Oglethorpe's plans to assume jurisdiction of the Indian trade had been faulty and ill-timed from the beginning. He had misjudged the impact of the Indian trade on South Carolina's economy, tradition, and pride, and he had not expected the entire South Carolina Assembly to support the interest of only thirty-one Charles Town merchants who were engaged in the trade. In early 1734 he might, with Governor Robert Johnson's help, have reached some type of compromise with the merchants which would have given Georgia a little profit and a measure of disciplinary authority over the traders. Instead, he chose to employ provocative measures in an attempt to capture the entire trade. Such tactics infuriated Lieutenant Governor Broughton, who had assumed the acting governorship upon Johnson's death in May 1735. Broughton and the merchants, already opponents of the colonization of Georgia, were able to promote a feeling of resentment for the new colony among a growing number of South Carolinians. In early 1737, in retaliation for Oglethorpe's tactics, the assembly discharged Captain James McPherson's Company of Southern Rangers and Captain William Ferguson's scouts of the boat *Carolina,* the discharge being retroactive to September 1736. Oglethorpe continued both units in service, but they were now paid by the Georgia trustees. Attitudes became more amiable after Broughton died in November 1737 and William Bull, Oglethorpe's friend and advisor, assumed the acting governorship; however, the close family relationship between the two colonies had been damaged beyond repair.[21]

VI

Preparations for War
1737–1739

Ships arriving in Charles Town and Savannah from the Caribbean Sea in January 1737 brought reliable rumors that the Spaniards were preparing to attack. By the following month an invasion appeared so imminent that the South Carolina government raised a company of soldiers, a portion of which formed the crews of two scout boats, and stationed it in Fort Frederick near Beaufort, an anticipated Spanish objective. In addition, handfuls of men were placed along the coast as lookouts, and Indians were ordered recruited under South Carolina officers to scout in Georgia along the Savannah and Altamaha Rivers.[1]

The Georgia militia remained in a state of alert throughout the late winter and spring of 1737. At Savannah the men spent a month building a fort near the trustees' garden as a refuge for the women and children. It was a large well-built structure about two hundred feet square, consisting of a stockade wall, two timbers thick, with two bastions on the land side and two half bastions facing the river.[2] The Georgia trustees disapproved of the fort, astutely observing that "The real Defense of the Town is the Woods and Swamps, and a few Men who know the Country assisted by the Indians might have made a much better Defense in the Woods than in the Fort; Since thereby; they could have prevented an Enemy from coming to the Town which they could not by defending the Fort."[3]

At Darien, Lieutenant John Mackintosh and his Highland militia rushed work on the fort that Oglethorpe had traced during the previous September. The fortification, located on or near old Fort King George, had two bastions on the land side and two half bastions facing the marsh. One night during the spring, when the sentries thought they saw a group of strange men near the fort, the entire settlement became excited and a number of volleys were fired into the darkness.[4] Several weeks of alert were unfavorably affecting the Georgians' nerves.

When a Spanish invasion force still had not appeared by the spring of 1737, the South Carolina provincial company was discharged and tensions began to ease on both sides of the Savannah River. But the real danger had just begun. Relations between Spain and Britain concerning commercial issues, depredations against English shipping, and the settlement of Georgia had steadily worsened since late 1736. Finally, in April 1737, while Georgia and South Carolina were relaxing their guard, the king of Spain became exasperated with Britain's refusal to abandon Georgia and secretly ordered the governor of Cuba to begin preparations to destroy that entire British colony. The Cuban governor spent the remainder of the year 1737 collecting soldiers, ships, and provisions. In October he informed the Spanish king that the attack could be launched as early as the following spring.[5]

Despite her preparations for war, Spain continued to negotiate for Britain's withdrawal from Georgia. By January 1738 both countries were considering the organization of a commission to discuss seriously the settlement of the boundary issue between Georgia and Florida. Believing that Britain was considering the abandonment of its towns near the Altamaha River, the king of Spain dispatched a message to the Cuban governor ordering him to cancel the planned invasion of Georgia. The royal messenger was almost too late. When he arrived in Cuba during March the invasion force of more than one thousand men had already loaded their ships and were prepared to sail in a few hours. The commission to settle the Georgia-Florida boundary dispute was never organized, principally because Spain, miscalculating Britain's determination to retain the colony of Georgia, demanded the abandonment of the Altamaha settlements and forts before discussions could begin.[6] Spain lost the best opportunity she ever had to destroy Georgia.

Ignorant of the fact that they had barely escaped destruction, the Georgia militia had returned to scratching a living out of the soil. In 1737 the delay in planting the crops, caused by the fort-building activity, plus the lack of rain until late summer were responsible for a miserable yield.[7]

Previously, during the year 1736, Oglethorpe had administratively divided Georgia into the southern and northern military divisions, separated by the Ogeechee River. Frederica and Darien were located in the southern division; Savannah was in the northern division.[8]

Practically all the rangers, about two-thirds of the Georgia trustees' tiny army of approximately one hundred provincial soldiers, were stationed in the northern division, perhaps to replace Savannah's ring of fortified villages that were largely depopulated because of death and desertion. Captain James McPherson's Company of Southern Rangers, now in the trustees' pay, remained in garrison at Fort Argyle near the Ogeechee River. William Elbert had resigned as lieutenant in the spring of 1735 and Arthur Ogle Edgecomb had been commissioned in his place. In the fall of 1736 Edgecomb left the colony, reportedly dissatisfied with Georgia because rum was not allowed. Apparently, a replacement lieutenant was not appointed. The company's strength varied from nineteen to twenty-five men. Fort Argyle was in ruins by the spring of 1738; decay had damaged the palisade and rains had eroded the earthen wall.[9]

Captain McPherson spent a large amount of his time purchasing beef cattle in South Carolina and driving then to Georgia where they were butchered for the settlers. Oglethorpe and the trustees were well satisfied with his performance of duty and showed their appreciation by presenting him with a silver watch. However, he did not get along well with Thomas Causton and William Stephens, the trustees' officials in Savannah. During March 1738, when McPherson threatened to disband the company unless he and his men received an increase in pay, Causton and Stephens readily agreed to his demand because of their fear of a Spanish invasion. Nevertheless, Stephens, the trustees' secretary, reported that McPherson had been remiss in his duties, accusing him of sitting idly in Fort Argyle instead of patrolling the frontier.[10]

Lieutenant John Cuthbert commanded a party of six rangers which had been raised during the summer or fall of 1736.

Cuthbert was a Scottish gentleman and a dependable officer who had initially served as the lieutenant of Darien's Highland militia under Captain Hugh Mackay. He and his men were stationed on his plantation at Josephs Town where they screened the northwest approach to Savannah.[11]

During May 1737 Thomas Jones and two men, all skilled South Carolina woodsmen, entered the trustees' service as a party of rangers and were stationed near Savannah. Jones's father was an Indian trader and his mother was an Indian, probably Creek. His South Carolina home was near Pon Pon (modern Jacksonboro), but he had owned a lot in Savannah since 1734. "Tommy" had been a trader among the Creek since at least 1723 and he had recently made an unsuccessful attempt to trade among the French-allied Choctaw Indians.[12]

Captain Aneas Mackintosh's garrison of Palachacola Rangers at Fort Prince George in South Carolina continued to range the country north of Purrysburg and protect the major Savannah River crossing site. Except for preventing South Carolina settlers from encroaching upon the Uchee Indian land just across the river and capturing runaway indentured servants, the garrison's existence was uneventful.[13]

Previously, in early 1736, Oglethorpe had instructed Captain Roger Lacy and his party of rangers to build and garrison a fort named Augusta on the upper Savannah River. The project was an intregal part of Oglethorpe's scheme to assume control of the Indian trade. The intended fort site was located at the crossroads of the principal trading paths that led to the Creek and Cherokee nations, and it overlooked the head of navigation on the Savannah River. A garrisoned fortification at that location could protect a Georgia storage center and traders' settlement, provide a refuge for traders during an Indian war, and serve as a lifeline to Lieutenant Anthony Willy and his three rangers at Okfuskee in the Upper Creek nation. The fort and its garrison would not have been necessary if Georgia and South Carolina had cooperated in administering the Indian trade; the latter colony concurrently maintained a garrison in Fort Moore at Savannah Town, or New Windsor township, only four and one-half miles to the southeast on the eastern bank of the river.[14]

Lacy had intended to begin building Fort Augusta in late

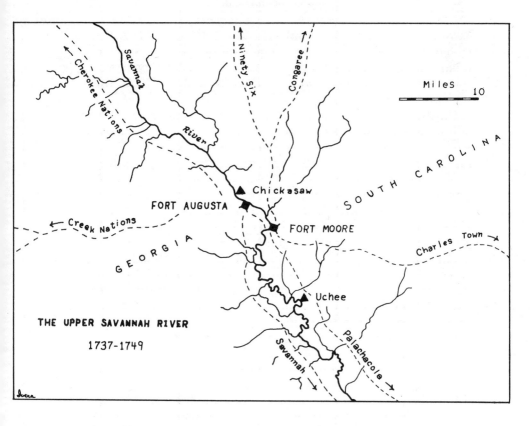

THE UPPER SAVANNAH RIVER

1737-1749

1736 after returning from the Cherokee nations; however, because of the difficulty in gathering provisions and delays caused by the Spanish alarm, he did not leave Savannah until 19 May 1737. Lacy and fourteen men arrived at Kinyans Bluff, the site of modern Augusta, in their garrison boat named the *Augusta* on 29 May. Lacy's assistant, Lieutenant Richard Kent, and a half-dozen workers joined them during the latter part of July. They set to work on the construction of a stockade of puncheons (logs that were split in half and planted upright with the round side facing out), which was probably about nine feet high. They may have built a banquette, or platform walkway, along the inside of the stockade. The fort was 110 feet square with a projecting bastion at each corner containing small one-pounder cannons. There were no earthworks and apparently no moat since Fort Augusta's principal danger was from Indian raids and a stockade was adequate protection against a war party's musket balls. Houses for the two officers, barracks for the rangers, a stable, a powder magazine, a store-house, a corn crib, and a well were probably constructed within the enclosure formed by the walls. Farming, patrolling, and inconveniences, such as the instance of one of the men suffering an alligator bite while on a boat trip from Savannah, delayed completion of the fort until April 1738.[15]

Lacy became too sick to perform his duties during December 1737 and returned to his home at Thunderbolt where he was expected to die. However, after a long illness he recovered and resumed his duties at Augusta during the latter part of April 1738. Mary Lacy never joined her husband at Augusta. During July 1738 she was indicted in Savannah for having knowingly purchased stolen beef. After being informed of his wife's trouble Lacy arrived in Savannah, extremely ill. Two days later, on 3 August, the ranger captain died.[16]

The garrison of fifteen rangers at Augusta was placed under the command of Lieutenant Richard Kent, who continued in that capacity for the ensuing ten years. Kent, whose father was a former member of Parliament and a good friend of Oglethorpe's, was one of several young gentlemen who arrived in Georgia on Oglethorpe's coattails. He developed into an outstanding ranger officer and, of all the soldiers in Georgia, he apparently became Oglethorpe's favorite.[17]

The only rangers stationed in the southern military division of Georgia were Ensign Hugh Mackay, Jr., and his party of ten men who garrisoned Fort Saint Andrews on Cumberland Island. They patrolled the island's woods and dunes on horse-back and scouted the Inland Passage as far south as the Saint Johns River in an eight-oared scout boat called the *Saint Andrews*.[18]

Most of the trustees' soldiers stationed in the southern division were scouts. The two principal scout boats were the *Georgia,* still commanded by John Ray, and the *Carolina,* now commanded by John Latter following Captain William Ferguson's return to South Carolina. Ray's and Latter's scouts continued to patrol the Inland Passage between the Savannah and the Saint Johns Rivers. A third crew of scouts, perhaps under the command of Francis Brooks, manned the scout boat *Amelia* and garrisoned Georgia's southernmost outpost located on the northwestern portion of Amelia Island. Amelia Fort had apparently been built in October 1736 by the militiamen who had been withdrawn from Fort Saint George according to the agreement between Oglethorpe and Governor Moral of Spanish Florida. The crude fortification consisted of a large clapboard house surrounded by a stockade. Five small cannons commanded Saint Marys Inlet and the Inland Passage.[19]

Oglethorpe had departed for England during November 1736, arriving there in January 1737 after his ship narrowly escaped disaster in a storm. One of his first tasks was to placate the trustees who were incensed over his vast expenditures and their lack of information regarding his activities in Georgia. Oglethorpe, an excellent speaker and showman, won the trustees' gratitude after only two conferences.[20]

The primary reason for Oglethorpe's return to England was to secure adequate defensive measures for Georgia. He correctly surmised that Spain was fully prepared to undertake military action, if necessary, to eliminate the Georgia settlements. During a frank converation with Prime Minister Sir Robert Walpole in February 1737, he argued that the southern frontier could best be defended by regular British soldiers, pointing out that Georgia could field only about three hundred militiamen. During that month Walpole offered Oglethorpe the position of "General of the Forces of South Carolina and Georgia," but Oglethorpe refused unless a regular regiment of British soldiers was raised under his command for the defense of those colonies. Walpole apparently also offered Oglethorpe the governorship of South Carolina, but he reportedly refused because he would have had to give up his seat in Parliament. Walpole sensibly questioned whether British soldiers should have been stationed on the southern frontier for fear of further agitating Spain; however, knowledge of the Spaniards' preparations for attacking Georgia overcame his reluctance. In June, Oglethorpe received a commission as "General & Commander in Chief of the Forces in South Carolina & Georgia" and a promise of British soldiers. On 25 August, Oglethorpe was given an additional commission as colonel of a regiment to be raised for service in Georgia, and after a successful audience with King George II in September he began recruiting his soldiers.[21]

The establishment, or table of organization, of General Oglethorpe's infantry unit, the Forty-second Regiment of Foot, authorized a total strength of 684 officers and men. The regimental staff included an adjutant, quartermaster, chaplain, surgeon, and two surgeon's mates. There were six companies, each of which included a captain, lieutenant, ensign, four sergeants, four corporals, two drummers, and one hundred private men who enlisted for seven years. A company was composed of four platoons of twenty-five men each, led by sergeants who were assisted by corporals. The Forty-second Regiment's companies were authorized more men than companies of other regiments of foot, probably because they were designed to be scattered among the forts of Georgia and South Carolina, thereby operating like independent companies.[22]

Two hundred and fifty men were drafted out of the Twenty-fifth Regiment of Foot that was stationed at Gibraltar. These men, combined with the soldiers of the Independent Company of Foot that were already stationed in Georgia, were divided into three companies. The remaining three companies were recruited in northern and central England.[23]

According to tradition, General Oglethorpe received a commission as captain of the first company, but the actual labor of command was accomplished by a captain lieutenant, a position filled by Albert Desbrisay. Likewise, Lieutenant Colonel James Cockran and Major William Cook, the second and third ranking officers, also received commissions as captains; however, their companies were commanded by their lieutenants. The remaining three companies were commanded by Captains Richard Norbury, Alexander Heron, and Hugh Mackay, Sr.[24]

The War Office allowed General Oglethorpe to select some of his own officers, but Lieutenant Colonel Cockran, Major Cook, Captain Norbury, and Captain Heron received commissions because of their connections within the British government. All were experienced soldiers, but the first three eventually caused the regiment considerable trouble. Oglethorpe appointed some of his Georgia militia officers to regimental positions. Besides Captain Mackay were John Tanner and William Horton who received commissions as ensigns, and Hugh Mackay, Jr., who became regimental adjutant. About twenty young gentlemen volunteers accompanied the regiment as cadets who hoped to eventually obtain commissions.[25]

The regimental uniform was in sharp contrast to the drab civilian clothing worn by the trustees' rangers and scouts. Men of the Forty-second Regiment wore a black cocked-hat with their long hair tucked underneath, a red loose-fitting coat with green lapels and lining, a red waistcoat, red knee breeches, and white spatterdashes (brown for field duty) to cover the lower legs. Corporals wore a white worsted knot on the right shoulder as a badge of rank. Sergeants were designated by a crimson sash with a green stripe around the waist, silver lace on the hat, and a silver-hilted sword. Beyond wearing red coats, the officers' uniforms seem to have been designed according to individual taste.[26]

Each private and corporal carried a ten-pound, long land musket, commonly known as the "Brown Bess." This was a reliable smooth-bore weapon without sights, having practically no accuracy beyond one hundred yards. Cartridges were carried in a leather box on the right side, suspended by a strap that passed over the left shoulder. A bayonet and a short infantry sword were worn on the left side in a carrier attached to the waist belt. Sergeants carried a halbred, a spear-ax weapon, instead of a musket.[27]

On 6 May 1738 two transport ships carrying Lieutenant Colonel Cockran and some of the soldiers from Gibraltar anchored in Tybee Roads at the mouth of Savannah River. A third transport arrived six days later after mistakenly steering course for South Carolina, a place that Oglethorpe had ordered the transports to avoid because he feared that the soldiers might desert for the delights of Charles Town. A large quantity of supplies and about thirty ailing soldiers were brought up river to be housed in Savannah. Three weeks later Captain Mackay embarked his company in five piraguas and moved them via the Inland Passage to Fort Saint Andrews on Cumberland Island where Adjutant Hugh Mackay, Jr., had supervised the trustees' seventeen Highland indentured servants in the construction of Barrimacke, a small village of huts, to house the regulars. On 29 May, Lieutenant Colonel Cockran sailed in a transport and a brigantine with his company to the south end of Saint Simons Island where they assumed garrison duties at Delegal's

The Forty-Second Regiment of Foot, 1737–1749
Private in a Battalion Company and a Private in a Grenadier
Company

(*Drawing by Bill Drath*)

Fort and began constructing adjacent Fort Saint Simons. During early June the Independent Company of Foot was transported from Delegal's Fort to Fort Frederick near Beaufort, South Carolina, its new station. Reinforced with the soldiers who had recovered from their illness in Savannah, the Independent Company was integrated into the regiment as Captain Norbury's company.[28]

The three companies that were recruited in England conducted a public parade in London during early March 1738 and were ready for embarkation at Portsmouth by the middle of May. Unfortunately, the ships did not sail until midsummer because of contrary weather that kept them wind-bound in the harbor. On 18 September five transports carrying General Oglethorpe, about three hundred soldiers, and a like number of women and children arrived at Saint Simons Island. Oglethorpe's company was stationed at Fort Saint Andrews with Captain Mackay's company, Major Cook's company apparently garrisoned the south end of Saint Simons Island with Lieutenant Colonel Cockran's company, and Captain Heron's company was probably stationed at Fort Frederica. William Horton, the commander of Frederica's militia during the previous two years, was commissioned ensign in the latter company. The entire regiment consisted of 629 officers and men present for duty.[29]

Six weeks after his arrival Oglethorpe inspected his and Captain Hugh Mackay's companies at Fort Saint Andrews. Members of Captain Mackay's unit, men who had been transferred from Gibraltar, were in a surly mood. They were disappointed with their primitive surroundings, they were not receiving extra pay for food as they had in Gibraltar, and they had not yet received the traditional extra pay for the sea journey to Georgia.[30] Many were probably heartbroken because of leaving their Spanish mistresses, and Oglethorpe's prohibition against rum was undoubtedly a severe disappointment. However, these dissatisfactions should not have, by themselves, precipitated a mutiny. The underlying cause of the rebellious attitude was probably one that adversely effects commanders of many newly organized military units. When the commander of the Twenty-fifth Regiment at Gibraltar selected 250 of his men for assignment to Oglethorpe's Regiment, he obviously "unloaded" his misfits. Captain Mackay's company therefore contained a large part of an entire regiment's most undesirable men—the slow-witted, the physically and psychologically ill, and the malevolent, and this last group apparently intended to test the courage and tenacity of their new officers.

Oglethorpe observed a dawn reveille ceremony outside on the parade ground and then walked into the fort. A large number of soldiers from Captain Mackay's company followed him, stood outside the house where he was eating breakfast, and loudly demanded to be heard. In order to entice the mob of soldiers out of the fort, Oglethorpe calmly left the house and walked out the gate. The mob tumbled after him. Once all were outside he stalled for time by listening to their shouted grievances while the fort was secured. After voicing the mob's demands, a ringleader suddenly yelled for action. Oglethorpe immediately grabbed the man and dragged him into the fort. Another soldier then took over leadership of the mutiny, and he was apprehended by Captain Lieutenant Desbrisay, Oglethorpe's assistant company commander. The soldiers attempted to pursue Oglathorpe and Desbrisay into the fort, but Captain Mackay and Adjutant Mackay, blocked their path at the moat bridge. A brief struggle ensued and a soldier named Ross seized and broke Captain Mackay's sword, wounding Captain Mackay in the hand. Some Highlanders, who were present in the fort, came to the officers' rescue with broadswords drawn. The frustrated mutineers ran to Barrimacke, their camp of huts below the fort, in order to get their weapons.[31]

Desbrisay quickly visited the camp and returned to the fort where he reported that the mutineers were loading their muskets. After ordering the few Highlanders and scouts who were present to procure their weapons and follow him, Oglethorpe and some of his officers ran down to the camp where they found the men of Captain Mackay's company assembling in the street. As they drew near, one soldier, about five yards distant, pointed his musket at them. Oglethorpe ordered "down with your arms,"[32] but the rebellious soldier answered, "No, by God, I'le down with you."[33] Almost simultaneously Oglethorpe charged forward with his sword drawn, the soldier fired his musket, and Captain Mackay, who had previously wrenched a musket from another mutineer, fired at Oglethorpe's assailant. Captain Mackay's bullet struck and wounded the soldier whose own bullet buzzed harmlessly over Oglethorpe's shoulder. The soldier attempted to use his empty musket as a club, but Oglethorpe tore it from his hands, contemptuously refusing to use his sword. At about the same moment Desbrisay narrowly escaped death when another soldier attempted to shoot him and his musket misfired. A third soldier pointed his musket at Oglethorpe and pulled the trigger, but it also misfired. Oglethorpe rushed him, seized his musket, recocked it, and threatened the other soldiers who were then crowding into the street. He offered to pardon those who dispersed and to shoot those who would not. They dispersed, cowed by his ferociousness and his apparent invincibility.[34]

Oglethorpe walked along the streets of the camp, ordering the sergeants to keep the men in their huts. His officers conducted a search of each hut and found twenty-five loaded muskets. The young "new raised men" of Oglethorpe's company had been influenced by the veteran "Gibraltar men" of Captain Mackay's company; however, after observing their officers' courageous actions they began obeying orders. A short time later Oglethorpe had both companies assembled. He sternly reprimanded them, but he pardoned all except five of the ringleaders. That night he wisely talked to each man individually and ascertained that their only justifiable complaint was the lack of sea pay, and this he ordered paid.[35] His prompt and skillful actions averted a blow to Georgia's defenses, for had the mutineers been successful their best recourse would have been to cast their lots with the Spaniards in Saint Augustine.

Dissension within the regiment was not confined to rebellious enlisted men. Lieutenant Colonel Cockran and Captain Mackay began quarreling and, by early March 1739, a mutual hatred had developed. General Oglethorpe, obviously disgusted by their conduct and fearing violence, ordered a court-martial to be conducted in order to determine who was at fault. Since there were not enough British officers in North America who outranked Lieutenant Colonel Cockran, both he and Captain Mackay were arrested and separately escorted to Charles Town from where they were transported to England to stand trial. Captain Mackay was the vindicated party. He was ordered back to the Forty-second Regiment, arriving in Georgia during October 1739. Lieutenant Colonel Cockran was "removed," or transferred, to the Fifth Marine Regiment.[36]

The arrival of the regiment significantly increased the military strength in Georgia; therefore, the trustees refused to pay any more expenses for rangers, scouts, or fortifications after 1738. Oglethorpe reluctantly began discharging the trustees' military units. The party of rangers headed by Ensign Hugh Mackay, Jr., which had been recently transferred from Cumberland Island to Amelia Island, was disbanded in early October 1738. Mackay remained at Amelia Fort with the trustees' sixteen Highland indentured servants who provided a militia garrison for the fortification and a crew for the scout boat *Amelia*. Captain James McPherson and his Southern Rangers, now a mixed company of Georgians and South Carolinians, were discharged in mid-November and McPherson returned to his Saltcatchers plantation in South Carolina. Two rangers remained in Fort Argyle as caretakers. Captain Aneas Mackintosh's garrison of Palachacola Rangers was disbanded in December, but he was kept on the payroll until the end of May to assist in rounding up the trustees' cattle which ranged free in the woods. Thomas Jones and his party of rangers were retained until June 1739, then they were also discharged.[37]

Oglethorpe did not disband the remaining ranger units and the scout-boat crews because he considered them too essential to Georgia's defense. He did dispatch a fifteen-man detachment of Captain Norbury's regimental company from Fort Frederick, South Carolina, to garrison Fort Augusta; however, after the boat carrying the regulars capsized in Daufuskie Sound— drowning ten soldiers, three wives, a boy, and two South Carolina Negro boatmen—he decided to retain Lieutenant Richard Kent's garrison of Augusta Rangers, now reduced to ten men. Likewise, Lieutenant John Cuthbert's small party of rangers was retained at Josephs Town. Lieutenant Anthony Willy remained at Okfuskee Fort with one man to watch French movements among the Creek nations, and another officer, perhaps the trader Samual Brown, and one soldier were placed in the Cherokee nations. Oglethorpe considered the two scout boats under John Ray and John Latter absolutely necessary and refused to disband their crews. Defending Georgia against Spanish and French threats and British criticism had been Oglethorpe's passion for some time. Now he proved his commitment by assuming payment of those remaining Georgia provincial rangers and scouts out of his own pocket.[38]

In June 1739 a message arrived from the secretary of state, informing Oglethorpe that England and Spain had finally agreed to stop their preparations for war and begin serious discussions. Oglethorpe decided to take advantage of the enforced lull in military preparations and seek the assured assistance or, at the very least, the neutrality of the Creek Indians in the event of a war with Spain. Although he was not particularly worried about the loyalty of the Cherokee or the Upper Creek, he was concerned about the possible actions of the Lower Creek who bought English trade goods but continued to send delegations to Saint Augustine. Having failed earlier to achieve jurisdiction over the Indian trade, which would have given him a powerful lever for use in demanding the loyalty of the Lower Creek, he was forced to use the less effective tactic of rendering them the diplomatic courtesy of his personal visit.[39]

On 8 July 1739 he left Frederica accompanied by a few officers of the Forty-second Regiment and some Scottish gentlemen including Lieutenant George Dunbar, Adjutant Hugh Mackay, Jr., and Aneas Mackintosh. After traveling by boat to Ebenezer they transferred to horseback and rode north to the Uchee town where Lieutenant John Cuthbert and his party of six rangers were waiting to act as the expedition's escort. The rangers had just finished blazing a trail from Augusta to the Uchee town along the west bank of the Savannah River. The expedition now consisted of Oglethorpe, twelve officers and gentlemen, Cuthbert and his rangers, about five servants, and an unknown number of Indians who served as hunters and guides. Oglethorpe also hired an additional ranger, probably Thomas Hunt, to accompany him as a bodyguard-servant. He apparently continued to serve Oglethorpe during the ensuing four years.[40]

They left the Uchee town on 24 July, probably following the trail that Patrick Mackay's company had traveled five years earlier. On 8 August the expedition arrived at Coweta and received a very cordial welcome from Chigelley, the principal

mico of the Lower Creek. Chigelley was a warrior to be reck-
oned with. Twenty-four years earlier he had led a war party
of several hundred Creek and Apalachee to within twelve miles
of Charles Town, South Carolina, leaving ashes and death behind him. During the next two and a half weeks Oglethorpe
was treated as a very important guest of the towns of Coweta
and Kashita where he held several councils during which he
passed out presents and exchanged speeches with the headmen
of both Creek nations. Even the men of his expedition served
as diplomats. On one occasion while they were watching the
Indians dance, traders' rum or the primitive beat of the drums
induced some of them to compliment the Indians by joining
in the rhythmic stomping.[41] The visit was extremely timely
and may have been partially responsible for the Creek maintenance of neutrality during the subsequent war with Spain and
France. The results were probably disappointing to Oglethorpe,
however, for he had hoped that the Creek would provide him
with large war parties for use in raiding Florida.

On 25 August Oglethorpe and his expedition began their
return to the coast, initially setting out on the Lower Trading
Path toward the Savannah River, arriving at Augusta eighteen
days later. Even though Oglethorpe became sick with a fever
he inspected Fort Augusta, which was under the command
of Lieutenant Richard Kent, visited with Captain Daniel Pepper
of South Carolina's nearby Fort Moore, and talked with several
Cherokee headmen who came down from their nations to receive presents.[42]

On 13 September, a rumor arrived at Augusta that war had
been declared against Spain. Four days later, after Oglethorpe
and his expedition had started down river toward Savannah,
they met a trading boat whose crew was carrying the terrifying
news that some Negro slaves in South Carolina had revolted
a few days before. South Carolinians, outnumbered by their
slaves and living in fear of a revolt for more than a quarter
of a century, had taken elaborate but ineffective measures over
the years to keep the slaves unarmed, uneducated, and unor-
ganized. The slave insurrection took place west of Charles
Town on Stono River where Angola-born Negro slaves who
lived in that neighborhood had banded together, armed them-

selves, and killed twenty-three people. The local militia quickly cornered them, killed about forty, despite their brave stand, and scattered the remainder in the swamps.[43]

The threat of a number of slaves escaping to Florida via Georgia and rumors of war with Spain gave Oglethorpe the excuse he had been looking for to increase the size of his ranger force. On 18 September, while he and his expedition continued down the Savannah River, he wrote a captain's commission for John Cuthbert and ordered him to expand his small party of rangers into a company. Captain Cuthbert and his men apparently disembarked at the Uchee town, and within a few days he and his new lieutenant, Richard Scroggs, rode to Charles Town to buy horses for the company.[44]

When Oglethorpe arrived at Fort Prince George, or Palachacola Fort, across the river from the Uchee town he found thirty South Carolina militiamen from Purrysburg in garrison. The obvious objective for the rebellious slaves was Saint Augustine—the Spanish governor had promised freedom for all slaves who escaped to Florida—and the principal route to Saint Augustine crossed the Savannah River at Palachacola. In fact, some of Captain James McPherson's slaves had recently escaped on stolen horses from his Saltcatchers plantation, crossed the river at Palachacola, and ridden nearly unhindered through Georgia to Florida. Oglethorpe ordered Captain Aneas Mackintosh, the former commander of the fort and a member of the expedition, to recruit and command a new ten-man garrison of rangers for Fort Prince George. He also bargained with some Indians to patrol along the river. Oglethorpe had a personal interest in that area. Unable as a trustee to own land in Georgia, South Carolina had earlier granted him a twelve-thousand-acre barony in and around Palachacola.[45]

On 27 September 1739, three days after arriving in Savannah, Oglethorpe received a letter from King George II, informing him that the final attempt at negotiations with Spain had broken down and ordering him to "annoy the Subjects of Spain, and to put the Colonies of Carolina and Georgia in the best posture of Defence."[46] Oglethorpe, obviously delighted, interpreted the instructions as his authority to invade Florida even though war had not been declared. He wrote a letter to Lieutenant Governor William Bull of South Carolina that same day, acquainting him with the king's instructions and requesting assistance in laying siege to Saint Augustine. He also dispatched requests to the various Indian nations, asking them for warriors and giving them his permission to raid Florida.[47]

A week later Tomochichi, the ancient mico of the Yamacraw, died after a long illness. Oglethorpe paid his old friend the honor of giving him an elaborate military funeral and burying him in one of Savannah's town squares with a monument erected over his grave.[48]

After remaining in Savannah and making war preparations for a month, Oglethorpe set out for Frederica, arriving there on 8 November. War was just a few days away.[49].

VII

Beginning of the War of Jenkins's Ear

1739–1740

Before dawn on 13 November 1739 about a dozen Yemassee Indians silently beached their dugout canoes on the west side of Amelia Island. The warriors cautiously advanced through the woods and thickets to the northwestern end of the island until they were looking across a space of cleared ground at the silhouette of Amelia Fort's stockade and house. The war party concealed itself inside the woods near the path that led from the fort and hoped a man would stray into their ambush.[1]

Garrisoning Amelia Fort were sixteen Highland indentured servants who belonged to the trustees and served as scouts aboard Francis Brooks's scout boat *Amelia,* a sergeant's guard of twelve men from Ogelthorpe's Forty-second Regiment, and about ten women and children. Adjutant Hugh Mackay, Jr., the commander, was temporarily at Frederica. After sunup two Highlanders, John Mackay and Angus Macleod, left their warm beds to gather wood for the breakfast fire. Although neither man was feeling well they had not shirked their duty. Unarmed and unsuspecting, they walked out of the fort's gate and up the sandy path into the pines where the war party was hidden. They probably had little time to react before they were shot down by a volley from the Indian's trade muskets. The war party hacked off the Highlanders' heads and carried them off, scalping them as soon as time permitted. Startled from their slumber by the gunshots, the Highlanders and regulars attempted to pursue the Indians, but they were too late.

The Indians escaped in their dugouts and paddled safely toward Saint Augustine with their trophies.[2]

Five days after the raid Oglethorpe surrounded Amelia Island with several small boats while he and a detachment of soldiers searched the woods, thickets, and dunes for skulking Indians. They found no one. An officer and a platoon of regulars reinforced the fort and Oglethorpe returned to Frederica to continue preparations for the invasion of Florida.[3]

Two weeks after their first raid on Amelia Fort, Spanish Indians repeated their performance and may have killed two more men. Oglethorpe was angry and confused. Spanish allied Indians were moving at will against his southern frontier and he had no definite information about Spanish military preparations in Florida. He was sure that Florida's Governor Manuel de Montiano did not yet have the means to mount an invasion of Georgia, but preparations for a major raiding effort to destroy Amelia Fort or Fort Saint Andrews might be underway. In the style that became typically Oglethorpe, he gathered about two hundred regulars, rangers, militia, and Indians under his personal command for a raiding and reconnaissance thrust into Florida.[4]

The rangers who were ordered to accompany the raiding force were members of a new unit, the Troop of Highland Rangers, which had been raised on 19 November 1739. The troop numbered about a dozen men commanded by Adjutant Hugh Mackay, Jr., who thus held commissions in both the Forty-second Regiment and the Georgia provincials. The rangers had been recruited from the Highlanders at Amelia Fort and Darien.[5]

The raiding party embarked in fourteen boats on 1 December 1739. During the ensuing two and a half weeks they inflicted very little material damage on the Spaniards; two lookout huts were burned, several cattle were destroyed, and one man was killed. However, Oglethorpe and his officers did familiarize themselves with the terrain immediately south and east of the Saint Johns River and they gained confidence as a result of the Spaniards' timid reaction. On 11 December, when the raiding party sighted a Spanish column, the Spaniards retreated so fast that the Indians, stripped for the chase, could not catch them.[6]

While Oglethorpe was returning to Frederica on 18 December he placed a small party of men in garrison at old Fort Saint George, which he had abandoned three years before. In order to continue the reconnaissance and keep the Spaniards on the defensive, he sent Lieutenant George Dunbar and two platoons of the Forty-second Regiment up the Saint Johns River (south) in two scout boats to continue harassing the Spaniards. In a short while Lieutenant Dunbar encountered two small forts. Fort Picolata sat on the east bank of the river near the present town of that name, seventeen miles west-north-west of Saint Augustine. Fort San Francisco de Pupo, which had suffered from minor attacks by Creek Indian war parties during the years 1735, 1736, and 1738, was located across the river, one and one-half miles to the northwest. Both structures had been built in late 1734. Their positions were strategic because they protected the ferry crossing in the path that led from Saint Augustine to Fort San Marcos de Apalachee, located one mile west of present St. Marks, Florida. Another path that led north from Fort Pupo had been used by Yemassee raiders to penetrate the South Carolina frontier since 1716. Lieutenant Dunbar attempted a surprise night attack on Fort Picolata, the weaker of the two forts, but after being repulsed, with the loss of a sergeant, he returned to Frederica on 25 December.[7]

Oglethorpe was determined to capture Fort Pupo as soon as possible. A strong British garrison there would hinder communications between Saint Augustine and Apalachee, it would command the principal Spanish war path into the British colonies, and it would secure that path for the passage of Georgia rangers into Florida during the planned invasion.[8]

At Frederica on 1 January 1740 Oglethorpe embarked 180 men for the attack on Fort Pupo. Included were a detachment of the regiment, the Highland Rangers, a small train of field artillery, and a mixed party of Creek, Chickasaw, and Uchee Indians. Upon arriving at Fort Saint George on 3 January they were joined by a British privateer sloop that had been standing off the mouth of the Saint Johns River, looking for an easy Spanish prey. With the onset of a favorable wind three days later, they set sail up the Saint Johns River, quietly landing about five miles downstream (north) from Forts Picolata and

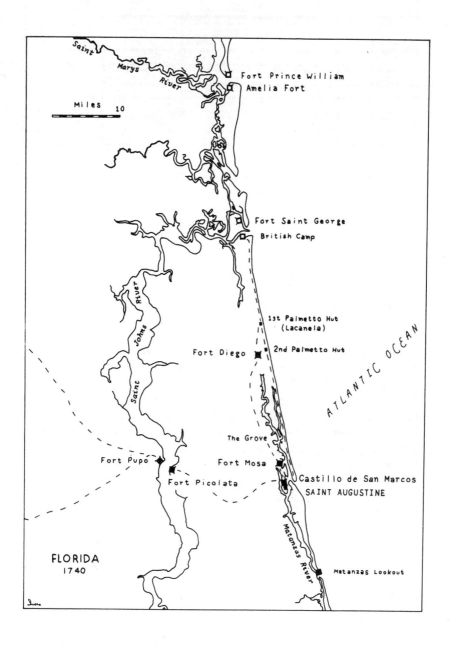

Saint Marys River

Fort Prince William
Amelia Fort

Miles 10

Fort Saint George
British Camp

Saint Johns River

1st Palmetto Hut
(Lacanela)

Fort Diego

2nd Palmetto Hut

ATLANTIC OCEAN

The Grove

Fort Pupo

Fort Mosa

Castillo de San Marcos
SAINT AUGUSTINE

Fort Picolata

Matanzas River

FLORIDA
1740

Matanzas Lookout

Pupo at four o'clock in the afternoon. About two o'clock the next morning, 7 January, the Indians and their white officers approached Fort Picolata and laid an ambush on the path leading from the fort to Saint Augustine in order to prevent the Spanish garrison's escape or reinforcement. At daybreak the Indians burned Fort Picolata after finding that it had been abandoned since Lieutenant Dunbar's abortive attack three weeks before.[9]

At Fort Pupo the Spanish garrison saw Oglethorpe's Indians near Fort Picolata and thought they were a party of Yemassee Indians coming to reinforce them. A few soldiers of Fort Pupo's garrison manned the oars of their boat and started across the Saint Johns River to ferry the Indians over. They almost rowed too far before they discovered their mistake. Churning the water with their oars, they came about and returned to Fort Pupo.[10]

The Indians immediately followed the Spaniards across the river. Oglethorpe landed the regulars about a mile downriver and began unloading four cannons. Mackay's Highland Rangers and the Indians fired on Fort Pupo, diverting the garrison's attention, while the detachment of red-coated regulars struggled with the small but heavy cannons, pushing and pulling them unnoticed through the woods toward the fort. Oglethorpe ordered the cannons divided into two batteries for placement in concealed positions inside the woods a little more than three hundred yards from the fort. A shallow flat-bottom trench was dug for each battery and the loose dirt was thrown up, creating breastworks to protect the gunners from the Spanish cannons. The rangers and Indians kept the garrison's attention diverted all afternoon, but about five o'clock the Spaniards discovered the red-coat activity among the trees and began concentrating their cannons' fire in that direction. It was too late, for the batteries' breastworks were complete. The trees and brush in front of the guns were hastily chopped away, exposing Fort Pupo to the British cannons.[11]

Fort San Francisco de Pupo was a strong outpost probably lately strengthened because of the Creek Indians' raids. The fort consisted of a plank blockhouse about thirty feet tall with a projecting upper floor, surrounded by an earthen breastwork and a stockade twelve feet high.[12]

The carriages of the British cannons were turned until Ensign Sanford Mace, the artillery expert, had the barrels aimed at the blockhouse. He then supervised the placing of wedges under the breech ends of the barrels until they attained the proper elevation. Just before sunset a slow-burning rope was applied to the touch holes of the freshly loaded cannons, causing each cannon, in turn, to buck and roar. Most of the iron balls must have been fairly accurate because the Spaniards immediately ceased fire. Oglethorpe sent a drummer to the fort with a flag of truce to ask the garrison to surrender. They haughtily refused and resumed firing. A cannon ball narrowly missed General Oglethorpe. Ensign Mace realigned the cannons and fired a second volley. The garrison quickly changed its mind and surrendered just at dusk. A Spanish sergeant, ten soldiers, one Indian, and six small artillery pieces were captured.[13]

The resulting victory was not impressive, but it was exhilarating. The sweat of fear and labor, the smell of burned gunpowder, the sight of captured enemy soldiers, and only a small amount of blood and torn flesh can make a battle seem like a glorious adventure. After six years of preparations the British and Spaniards had finally crossed swords.

Two days later a detachment of regulars and Indians crossed to the east bank of the Saint Johns River to look for Spaniards. A troop of Spanish dragoons, on their way to discover what had happened at Fort Pupo, saw the British detachment and fled.[14]

On 11 January 1740, four days after the battle, Oglethorpe began his return to Frederica in order to continue preparations for laying siege to Saint Augustine. He assigned fifty men, including the Highland Rangers, a few regulars, and a crew of scouts, to remain behind as a temporary garrison for Fort Pupo. They were later reinforced with thirty-six men and an armed sloop. Hugh Mackay, Jr., was placed in command with the title of fort major and received orders to dig a better moat and build a more effective earthen breastwork around the fort. Within a few days they captured an unsuspecting messenger party that was bound from Apalachee to Saint Augustine.[15]

On 8 November 1739 Lieutenant Governor William Bull

officially informed the South Carolina Assembly of General
Oglethorpe's five-week-old request for assistance in capturing
Saint Augustine. Committees of the commons and council debated the request for another five weeks. The delay may appear
to have been inexcusable and suggests that South Carolina's
machinery of government was clumsy. Their debate was ration-
al, however, for several reasons: Oglethorpe was viewed with
distrust because of his inept handling of the Indian trade issue,
the ever present danger of a slave revolt made them reluctant
to transfer a large number of men out of the province, the
colony's financial situation had been quite unstable since the
Yemassee War, and there was also some pessimism concerning
the possibility of a successful invasion; they remembered too
well the colony's failure to capture Saint Augustine in 1702.
Nevertheless, the possibility of eliminating South Carolina's traditional enemy was worth considering. The venture just might
succeed; General Oglethorpe was an experienced officer with
a regiment of regular troops, and the royal navy had the king's
orders to support him. On 12 December the assembly asked
Oglethorpe to send them his plan of attack for their consider-
ation.[16]

Three days before moving south to attack Fort Pupo, Oglethorpe answered the assembly's request and sent one of his
officers to Charles Town to represent him. In a letter Oglethorpe stated that he intended to lay siege to Saint Augustine
and he asked South Carolina to provide siege artillery, eight
hundred pioneers (laborers), transport boats, a troop of
rangers, pay for two hundred Georgia provincials, a company
from Purrysburg, and provisions for everyone including one
thousand Indians, the Georgians, and the Forty-second Regiment.[17]

On 24 January, after returning from Florida, Oglethorpe
sent South Carolina a new expanded "shopping list." It included
a South Carolina regiment of 600 men, 105 rangers, 800 Negro
slave laborers with 160 white guards, and 58 white officers
for 2,000 Indian warriors. In addition, he still wanted the
artillery and boats that he had previously asked for.[18] The
request was unrealistic, but this was not the first time that
Oglethorpe has used this tactic of asking for the unreasonable
in order to get what he needed.

A committee of the commons computed that those items

would cost South Carolina more than £200,000, an impossible amount, but they thought the province could affort an expenditure of £120,000 if Oglethorpe could assure them of a victory. That amount of money would provide six months pay and provisions for a South Carolina regiment of 490 men, 49 rangers, 300 white or 400 Negro pioneers, presents and weapons for 1,000 Indians, 20 boats, and 12 siege cannons.[19]

Oglethorpe was undoubtedly becoming discouraged. If he were to conduct a successful siege of Saint Augustine it would have to begin soon, because the small British fleet available for the venture could provide assistance only until the beginning of the hurricane season about five months away, then they would have to withdraw to the haven of the northern colonies' ports. Also, the Spaniards in Saint Augustine were presently weak; they were short of food, they had few armed craft with which to guard the harbor and prevent landings, the town was poorly fortified (although Fort San Marcos was very strong), and the citizens of the underpopulated colony were terrified following Oglethorpe's recent raids. However, the Spaniards were doing everything possible to improve their defenses; fortifications were being strengthened, indentured servants were freed and enlisted as soldiers, and armed half-galleys full of men and provisions were en route from Cuba.[20]

The Spaniards were not as timid as the British officers had imagined. At least one of their patrols in a launch had bypassed the forts and scout boats on the Inland Passage and was operating deep in Georgia. About the middle of February, Lieutenant Dunbar with a detachment of the Forty-second Regiment in the *Colony Piragua* and the scout boat *Amelia* were reconnoitering the mouth of the Altamaha River when the soldiers in the scout boat disobeyed his orders and went ashore to pick oranges. Suddenly they were attacked by a party of Spaniards and Indians who had obviously been lying in wait near the tempting orange grove. The soldiers managed to board their scout boat and shove off, but as they pulled away from the shore the Spaniards and Indians fired a volley, killing a soldier who was manning an oar and Francis Brooks, the boat's commander. The British had some small compensation; they discovered and captured the Spaniards' launch, forcing them to walk back to Florida.[21]

The incident had a embarrassing and chilling effect in Georgia. On 23 March, Oglethorpe arrived in Charles Town to instill personally a sense of urgency in South Carolina's politicians. By now he had abandoned hope of conducting a siege that spring; within four or five months easterly winds would begin blowing, foretelling the possible arrival of ship-smashing hurricanes. Actually, he did not think a siege was necessary. Not long after arriving in Charles Town he informed Lieutenant Governor Bull that there were three alternatives remaining. First, immediate assault on Saint Augustine with those forces that could be quickly gathered to frighten the Spaniards into surrendering without the necessity for a siege. Second, South Carolina could provide him with the means to conduct hit-and-run raids into Florida, keeping the Spaniards off balance until the end of the hurricane season next fall when a siege could be initiated. If South Carolina would not assist him in carrying out either of these alternatives he would be forced to undertake the third and least desirable course of action, which would involve gathering all his regular and provincial soldiers at Frederica to await a certain Spanish attack. He finished by stating bluntly that he needed a quick answer so that he could return to his soldiers who were dangerously dispersed.[22]

The commons committee asked that Bull require Oglethorpe to outline his needs for a immediate assault. On 29 March Bull gave them Oglethorpe's requirements, which included a provincial regiment of four hundred men and a small troop of rangers for three months, five hundred Indians for four months, boat transportation, and a small train of field artillery. Oglethorpe endeavored to add a note of urgency by saying that if the above were not readied within two weeks he could not guarantee success.[23]

The commons decided it was impossible to gather the men and provisions within two weeks and inquired what Oglethorpe would need to harass Florida until a siege could be undertaken in October. Oglethorpe obviously had not been expecting that answer; he was appalled. He could not understand why they did not have confidence in him. His two penetrations into Florida had greatly increased his contempt for the Spaniards' courage and he was so certain of a quick victory that he had already written to the British government suggesting that Havana, Cuba, could be the next objective if he were only provided with a couple of thousand additional regular soldiers.[24]

General Oglethorpe reacted quickly. That same day he and Commodore Vincent Pearse, commander of the Royal Navy vessels assigned to the area, met with the combined committees of the council and commons. Oglethorpe skillfully argued for an attack against Saint Augustine as soon as possible even though there might be a delay in raising men and supplies. He boasted that he would quickly overrun the small outlying settlements and the town of Saint Augustine, driving the inhabitants into Fort San Marcos. A few explosive shells thrown into the fort among the closely packed refugees would cause the garrison to quickly surrender. Commodore Pearse reinforced Oglethorpe's argument by promising the navy's full assistance, assuring the South Carolinians that he would establish a perfect blockade of Saint Augustine. The personal presence of General Oglethorpe, newly arrived from successful combat with the Spaniards, and Commodore Pearse, a ranking officer of His Majesty's Navy, erased most of the pessimism concerning the invasion. If any doubtful voices remained they were probably quieted when Oglethorpe offered to loan South Carolina £4,000 sterling from his own estate at 8 percent interest, 2 percent lower than the colony's legal rate. The sum of £4,000 sterling was worth more than £30,000 in South Carolina's inflated currency. The loan was accepted to the extent of £2,000, and one week later, on 5 April, the assembly passed an act into law authorizing men and material for Oglethorpe's attack on Saint Augustine.[25]

General Oglethorpe returned to Frederica and began putting his own forces in readiness. He was attempting to recruit and equip two troops of rangers, but he was experiencing difficulty. Captain John Cuthbert and Lieutenant Robert Scroggs had ridden to Charles Town in late September or early October 1739 to purchase horses for their company. In November, Lieutenant Scroggs returned to Georgia with news that Captain Cuthbert had died. Scroggs assumed acting command of the company, which was named the Troop of English Rangers. Nothing is known about his background although he had probably been one of John Cuthbert's rangers. A handfull of men were recruited into his troop and were stationed at Fort Argyle under the command of Lachlan Mackintosh, a ranger who had already spent considerable time there. Six more rangers were recruited under a man named Danner, or Darmer, who was commissioned a quartermaster. Not all the Troop of English Rangers were English; the troop included a few Salzburgers from the settlement of Ebenezer.[26]

From January to June 1740 Captain Hugh Mackay, Jr., garrisoned Fort Pupo in Florida with part of his Troop of Highland Rangers. His lieutenant, Robert McPherson, a young gentleman from Darien, was in Georgia recruiting men at Darien and capturing horses on Amelia Island, the range of a small herd that had been under the care of the trustees' Highland indentured servants.[27]

Each ranger troop was authorized a captain, lieutenant, cornet (ensign), two quartermasters (officers whose primary function was to have been the procurement of troop supplies, but who were actually utilized as line officers), a trumpeter, and twenty-nine privates. Their pay was very good and officers were given allowances for servants and extra horses; however, in the tradition of the ranger service, the men were required to provide their own clothing, weapons, horses, saddles, bridles, and food. Oglethorpe had horses, saddles, and weapons purchased in bulk, outfitting new rangers as necessary and deducting the cost from their wages. The Highland rangers carried traditional Scottish claymores, dirks, and pistols. Their principal weapon was probably a long land musket, which had the barrel sawed off short for easy handling on horseback. The troop was probably initially dressed in bonnets and plaids in the Highland tradition, but in June 1740 they were newly outfitted with English checked shirts, breeches, shoes, stockings, hats, and blankets. The English Rangers' uniforms and weapons were similar, except that they carried swords or hatchets rather than traditional Highland weapons.[28]

Oglethorpe sent Scroggs back to South Carolina to buy enough horses for both troops. During a brief stop in Savannah someone stole his lettercase containing the money with which to purchase the horses. Oglethorpe tried to raise a third troop of rangers before the invasion of Florida, but it was impossible. There were not enough men or horses to complete two troops. By the time the rangers rode to Florida, each troop included no more than twenty-five men, and possibly half of them did not yet have horses.[29]

General Oglethorpe had intended to combine all of the scout boats and their crews into a company of boatmen, but he changed his mind and each craft remained independent under the command of a cockswain. By late April, Georgia had several "Armed Row Boats," including the *Colony Piragua,* which was a well-armed converted cargo boat, and the scout boats *Cutter, Carolina, Georgia, Savannah, Amelia, Saint Andrews, Darien, Agencourt, Frederica,* and *Speedwell.* In addition, there were three sloops, a schooner, and three cargo piraguas.[30]

It was intended that a small independent company of foot be recruited from among Georgia's English settlers, but the unit was never raised. Instead, Oglethorpe allowed volunters from Savannah and Ebenezer to join the South Carolina Regiment. In April about thirty Georgians under Lieutenant Noble Jones joined the company commanded by Captain Peter Laffite of Purrysburg.[31]

On 2 May, Oglethorpe ordered John Mackintosh, commonly called John Mohr (Big John), the forty-year-old commander of the Darien militia, to recruit the Highland Independent Company of Foot. Captain Mackintosh returned to Darien from Frederica on 6 May and recruited his company of warlike Highlanders within about five hours. The company was authorized 115 officers and men, but only 70 men could be recruited; there were not enough Highland men to fill up a 35-man ranger troop, a 115-man foot company, and still have enough left to protect the women and children of Darien. The men of the Highland Independent Company were dressed and armed in the Highland fashion. Their skirt-like plaids were wool tartans about ten to twelve yards long, part of which was gathered and belted around the waist, making a knee-length kilt. The remainder of the material was draped over the left shoulder and fastened with a brooch. It was a practical garment that also served as a blanket. Some of the men probably wore little kilts (similar to modern kilts). Scotch plaids were sold in the trustees' store and seem not to have been any particular pattern.[32]

Although Oglethorpe was paying the cost of the Georgia provincial soldiers from his private funds, he was confident that the British Parliament would soon assume the responsibility for their maintenance. After all, the king had ordered him to organize provincial units. He made appeals to the Georgia trustees to approach Parliament about the matter, but he received only a negative response.[33]

General Oglethorpe had initially hoped for one thousand Indians to accompany him and he later increased the requirement to two thousand. Finally, he decided to settle for five hundred. Even this last figure was too optimistic. Of approximately five thousand warriors who accepted British presents and bought British trade goods, only a little more than two hundred, more than half of whom were Cherokee, chose to assist the British against Saint Augustine. Oglethorpe had counted on the assistance of the Lower Creek because of the exuberant welcome that he had received there during the previous summer, but he had overlooked their traditional policy of neutrality in relations with Europeans. Chigelley, the principal mico, discouraged all but a few of his warriors from participating in the campaign, and while Oglethorpe was gathering forces the Lower Creek were holding talks with the Louisiana French. In addition to the Cherokee and a small number of Creek the expedition included a few Uchee, Chickasaw, and a handful of Yamacraw, most all of whom lived near the Savannah River. Squirrel King's Chickasaw from near Augusta were the best warriors, and even though they numbered only about thirty, their reputation placed their value equal to a hundred. The Indian auxiliaries had white officers, mostly traders, but they usually served as interpreters rather than leaders. The Indians were too independent and too proud to accept commands from white men, and they did not often obey their own micos. The only officer who had any control whatever over them was Thomas Jones, the ranger, but he was half-Indian.[34]

Four hundred soldiers of the Forty-second Regiment were readied for combat in Florida. The remaining two hundred men continued to garrison Fort Frederica and its outlying forts. In April they finished a new outpost, Fort Prince William, on the southern tip of Cumberland Island.[35]

Previously, in early 1738, British warships on the American and Jamaican stations had received explicit instructions to protect Georgia. During October 1739 the king ordered Commodore Pearse to use those men-of-war that were on the American station to assist Oglethorpe in capturing Saint Augustine. In late March 1740 Pearse promised the assistance of four twenty-gun ships and a sloop, with three more ships on the way. It was imperative that a tight sea blockade be drawn around Saint Augustine to prevent its being resupplied and reinforced. Just as important was the requirement to shield Oglethorpe's troops from the guns of Spanish men-of-war. In addition to the royal ships, several privateers were authorized by letters of marque from Oglethorpe and Lieutenant Governor Bull to plunder the Spaniards.[36]

The Spanish soldiers and citizens of Florida awaited Oglethorpe's certain attack. Saint Augustine had never consisted of more than a few hundred persons. Its primary purpose was to protect the Spanish colonies further to the south, shield Spanish ships cruising between Spain and the Americas, rescue shipwrecked sailors, and serve as a base for missionary activities among the local Indian tribes. In early 1740 the Spanish fighting force in Florida numbered a little more than six hundred men stationed in a number of outposts scattered along the northern portions of the colony. The principal fortification was Castillo de San Marcos, a massive well-built stone fort protecting the town of Saint Augustine. Two and a quarter miles to the north was Fort Mosa, built to protect a village of runaway South Carolina Negro slaves. About eighteen miles north of Saint Augustine was Fort Diego, sitting on a large plantation. Seventeen miles to the west of the town were Fort Picolata, which had been burned in January, and Fort Pupo, which now contained a British occupation force.[37]

The occupation of Fort Pupo by Hugh Mackay, Jr., was an effective harassment. The fort's British garrison and armed boats had turned the Saint Johns River into a British waterway, severing land communication between Saint Augustine and the eighty-man Spanish garrison at Fort San Marcos de Apalachee in western Florida. Governor Montiano considered the recapture of Fort Pupo, but he did not dare remove the necessary troops from their important defensive positions since a counterattack on Fort Pupo would undoubtedly prompt a vigorous reaction from Oglethorpe.[38] Montiano had no intention of confronting Oglethorpe in open battle.

Saint Augustine's military situation was suddenly and remarkable improved during April. The governor of Cuba dispatched more than two hundred men and a large quantity of provisions in a convoy of two sloops and six half-galleys. The *Tarter,* a twenty-gun British warship, was cruising near Saint Augustine in a position to intercept the convoys. She was scheduled to be relieved of the blockade duty by the *Squirrel,* a sister ship, but three days before the relief was expected the *Tarter's* captain abandoned the station and sailed north. Before the *Squirrel* arrived to renew the blockade the Spanish convoy slipped into Saint Augustine. It was a major blunder. Each of the Spanish half-galleys rowed with twenty oars, mounted very effective nine-pounder cannons in bow and stern, and maintained a crew of thirty-two men who also functioned as marines. When the *Squirrel* unsuspectingly arrived off Saint Augustine the half-galleys charged out of the harbor and immediately attacked her. After exchanging cannon fire the courageous Spaniards ran their little craft back into the harbor where the water was too shallow for the *Squirrel* to follow.[39]

Oglethorpe now had some doubts about the possibilities of a quick victory, but the planning and commitments had progressed too far to cancel. During the previous October the British government had declared war on Spain—the War of Jenkins's Ear. The conflict was named for an English ship captain who appeared before the British Parliament and displayed his severed ear, the result of an encounter with a Spanish search party on the high seas. King George II ordered Oglethorpe to capture Saint Augustine, one of Britain's first objectives of the war. Oglethorpe's planned adventure was thus legalized.[40]

VIII

The British Invasion of Florida
May-June 1740

South Carolina continued recruiting soldiers and gathering supplies while General Oglethorpe waited impatiently at Frederica. Finally, on 3 May 1740 all was ready and he moved to the designated rendezvous site at Fort Saint George with the advance party of the expedition, which included a few men of his regiment, some rangers, and one hundred Indians. He landed on the south bank of the Saint Johns River on the night of 8 May near present Mayport, Florida, to reconnoiter and secure a landing site for the main army. Before dawn the next day a large party of Cherokee scouted the immediate countryside, surprising seven men and capturing one, a Negro slave. The remaining Spaniards escaped into Fort Diego, the northernmost Spanish fortification. Later that day about 200 regulars of the Forty-second regiment and 125 provincials of the South Carolina Regiment arrived. A camp was laid out and tents were pitched on the southern bank of the Saint Johns River.[1]

Early on 10 May, Oglethorpe left about fifty men at his camp and marched the main body south along the seabeach with the intention of capturing Fort Diego. After that night's camp was made at a Spanish lookout called Lacanela, about nine miles south of present Jacksonville Beach, a picked party of regulars, provincials, and Cherokee was sent ahead to attempt to capture Fort Diego by surprise attack. The attempt went awry. After quietly surrounding the fort during the night someone set fire to a nearby house, signaling their presence. The alerted Spaniards easily repulsed a dawn attack. Oglethorpe arrived before noon with the main body and surrounded the fort.[2]

Fort Diego, located about a mile and a half south-southeast of modern Palm Valley, was the private fortification of a plantation owner named Diego Spinosa. It consisted of a house surrounded by a square-shaped stockade fifteen feet high with two bastions at opposite corners. Including Diego Spinosa's household and a detachment of Spanish soldiers, the garrison numbered about fifty men.[3]

On the morning of 12 May, Oglethorpe sent a Spanish prisoner, who had been captured at Fort Pupo during January, to ask the garrison to surrender. His testimony of good treatment and their hopeless situation convinced them to ask for terms. After being promised that the Cherokee would not harm them or plunder their possessions, the garrison surrendered.[4] Oglethorpe had won another easy victory.

George Dunbar, recently promoted to captain lieutenant of Oglethorpe's company, was left at Fort Diego in command of a garrison of fifty regulars. Oglethorpe rode back to the Saint Johns River, later followed by the remainder of his soldiers. He was escorted by a small detachment of rangers who seem to have acted as his personal servants and bodyguards throughout the campaign.[5]

By 13 May most of the Forty-second Regiment and the Highland Independent Company had arrived at Fort Saint George. Two days later all the soldiers were moved to the new camp on the south bank of the Saint Johns River. In the cool of that evening Oglethorpe set out with a detachment of regulars and the Highland Company to resupply his garrison at Fort Diego seventeen miles to the south-southeast. The following morning, as the tired soldiers pulled the supply carts within sight of Fort Diego, an ambush was suddenly triggered by a party of Yemassee Indians. Gabriel Baugh, a Salzburger serving as an English Ranger and one of Oglethorpe's servant-bodyguards, was immediately killed. The Spanish allied Indians took advantage of the confusion to cut off Baugh's head and escape through the woods. Oglethorpe began an immediate pursuit of the Yemassee toward Saint Augustine through thickets and swamps. The regulars and Highlanders probably fell behind, but Oglethorpe and his rangers continued a hot pursuit on horseback for several miles, causing the Indians to drop Baugh's head. During the chase Oglethorpe had a horse shot from under him and his coat was reportedly torn by the Indians' musket balls. That night the weary pursuers returned to Fort Diego, having rounded up thirty badly needed Spanish horses.[6] The most effective result of the pursuit was the Yemassee Indians' refusal to ambush Oglethorpe again.

Oglethorpe returned to the Saint Johns River camp on 18 May. During the following morning he met with Commodore Pearse to discuss tactics for the attack on Saint Augustine. Their information about Saint Augustine's defenses was very limited; nevertheless, they agreed to approach Saint Augustine—Pearse by the sea, Oglethorpe overland. Pearse would supply Oglethorpe and transport his cannons in ships' boats via the harbor entrance and the Diego (Tolomato) River. When all was ready Pearse was to assault the town across the harbor with seamen in ships' boats while Oglethorpe attacked the town's land defenses with his army. The object was to drive the inhabitants into the fort, occupy the town, and then bombard the closely packed people until the garrison surrendered.[7]

Oglethorpe was forced to begin moving sooner than planned when scouting Indians arrived and reported that Fort Diego was under attack. After a hard forced march the general and his relief force arrived at the fortification on May 20, only to discover that they had reacted to a false alarm. A new camp was established for the army around Fort Diego.[8]

The following day Oglethorpe and some of his officers reconnoitered the beach south to Point Quartell, a narrow peninsula one and a quarter miles northeast of Saint Augustine. Accompanying him were Colonel Alexander Vanderdussen (commander of the South Carolina Regiment), a detachment of the Highland Company, and a party of Indians. Oglethorpe and his officers, on horseback, set such a fast pace that the independently minded Indians and already tired Highlanders, on foot, dropped behind. Two of his officers also had to turn back because of the heat. Oglethorpe never traveled anywhere leisurely; whether by boat, horse, or on foot, he drove his men. However, long, fast marches through deep sand under a hot sun with full equipment is extremely exhausting, even for soldiers in excellent physical condition, and death by sunstroke was not uncommon during the campaign. Oglethorpe, Vanderdussen, and another officer continued the reconnaissance unescorted. At two o'clock in the morning of 22 May they returned to Fort Diego on foot, having exhausted and abandoned their horses.[9] Oglethorpe's disregard for personal safety was often so foolhardy and reckless that one must suspect that he deliberately encountered dangerous situations.

General Oglethorpe conducted a more leisurely reconnaissance of the road leading from Fort Diego to Saint Augustine with a strong escort during 27–29 May. Two Negroes were captured and reported that Governor Montiano was planning to attack the British army when it approached the town. Oglethorpe and his officers were delighted with that information.[10]

During the night of 31 May, Oglethorpe moved his army against Saint Augustine. Three hundred regulars and Georgians marched south along the road to the town, followed by four hundred South Carolinians. On the previous day a small detachment of regulars had moved south along the beach to occupy Point Quartell in order to establish communications with Pearse. On 2 June, Oglethorpe and Vanderdussen established a temporary camp at Fort Mosa, a deserted earthen walled fort located north of Saint Augustine. All the companies' drummers were placed into one formation and, escorted by a detachment of regulars, they approached the town, mockingly beating the "Grenadiers' March" on their drums. It had no effect. Governor Montiano could not be shamed into the open. Oglethorpe and Vanderdussen determined that the town was too strongly fortified on the land side to be attacked without cannons. The only practical way to bring cannons and rations to the Fort Mosa area was by ships' boats, but that was not possible because the six Cuban half-galleys had chased the detachment of regulars off Point Quartell and were preventing the British men-of-war's boats from entering the harbor. Any hope Oglethorpe had of quickly occupying the town was forgotten. The tired and hungry army marched the twenty miles back to Fort Diego on 3 June.[11]

A few men of the expedition, a group of South Carolina gentry, were expressing their disgust with Oglethorpe's conduct of the campaign. These well-born gentlemen, several of whom had extensive Indian fighting experience, had joined the expedition as a company of volunteers without pay. Most of them were accustomed to voicing their opinions and making decisions by virtue of their social and financial positions. The most difficult military unit to command and control is one composed of experienced leaders. Disregarding military etiquette, individual volunteers frequently approached Oglethorpe with suggestions and advice on the tactical conduct of the campaign. Oglethorpe had initially angered them by using all the captured Spanish horses to mount the rangers instead of carrying their baggage. Other irritants were Oglethorpe's policies of paying a Spanish farmer for slaughtered cattle, forbidding the burning of Spanish buildings, and his exceptionally humane treatment of prisoners of war. Their Indian-fighting experience had not prepared them for a general officer who thought ahead to the subjugation of a cooperating rather than a hostile Spanish population. While the army stood before Saint Augustine on 2 June some of the volunteers wanted to attack the town immediately, but Oglethorpe refused. They later hinted that he lacked the necessary courage. It is obvious from a study of Oglethorpe's character that he would have personally led an attack on the town, but he believed too many men would have been needlessly killed.[12]

On 5 June, Commodore Pearse warned General Oglethorpe that, because of the approaching hurricane season, the eight ships of the Royal Navy must leave the area on 5 July, only a month away. He recommended that a siege be initiated and he offered to assist Oglethorpe in attacking and occupying Anastasia Island, half a mile east of Saint Augustine across the harbor. He believed that batteries of cannons placed there could blockade Saint Augustine until his ships could return after the end of the hurricane season. Oglethorpe agreed with the occupation of Anastasia Island; however, he did not intend to initiate a siege. The basic plan remained unchanged; he intended to attack and capture Saint Augustine and bombard Fort San Marcos into submission. However, the Cuban half-galleys would have to be destroyed before the harbor side of the town could be attacked. Oglethorpe decided that part of the Forty-second Regiment and a force of seamen would capture Anastasia Island and establish batteries of cannons there while a detachment of the Forty-second Regiment and the en-

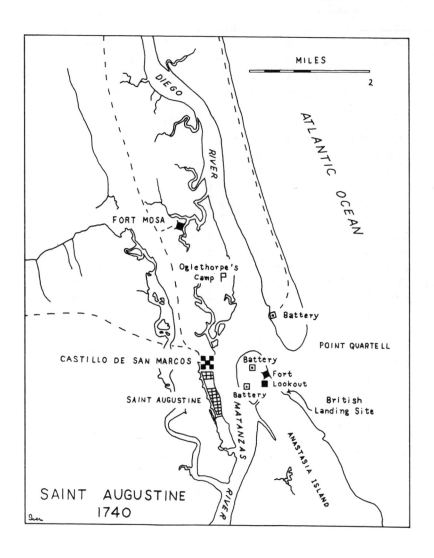

MILES

2

ATLANTIC OCEAN

DIEGO RIVER

FORT MOSA

Oglethorpe's Camp

Battery

POINT QUARTELL

CASTILLO DE SAN MARCOS

SAINT AUGUSTINE

Battery

Fort Lookout

Battery

British Landing Site

MATANZAS RIVER

ANASTASIA ISLAND

SAINT AUGUSTINE
1740

tire South Carolina Regiment prepared a battery on Point Quartell. After the batteries destroyed the half-galleys or drove them permanently into the Matanzas River, Oglethorpe and his regiment were to be transported to the mainland near Fort Mosa. On a prearranged signal the seamen and South Carolinians would attack the harbor (east) side of Saint Augustine in small boats while the Forty-second Regiment and Georgia provincials assaulted the north side of the town by land.[13]

Most accounts of the Florida campaign describe Oglethorpe's marching aimlessly up and down the seacoast until he finally decided to conduct a siege. During the ensuing "siege" Oglethorpe is pictured as clumsily violating most of the principles of war. In actuality the marches were each conducted for a purpose and a siege was never initiated. Oglethorpe's strategy deviated little from the basic plan that he and Pearse had formulated, but confusion resulted during the campaign and afterwards because he did not always keep all his principal officers informed of those changes in tactics that he did initiate.[14] Oglethorpe was most comfortable while leading a charging detachment of rangers or Highlanders; however, that was a task for a company officer. A general was supposed to plan and direct the tactical movements of the entire army with the advice and assistance of his staff and subordinate commanders. During the spring and summer of 1740 Oglethorpe was still learning to be a general.

On 6 June, Colonel Vanderdussen's South Carolina Regiment occupied Point Quartell. A detachment from the Forty-second Regiment joined him a week later and the joint force began establishing a battery. Fortunately, the government of South Carolina had provided some unrequested but badly needed siege artillery, the principal pieces being large mortars and eighteen-pounder cannons. On 11 June a mobile force of rangers, Highlanders, and Indians arrived at Fort Mosa on the north side of town. Their mission was to prevent Spanish foraging parties from rounding up cattle and horses for use in feeding the inhabitants of Saint Augustine. On 12 June, Oglethorpe and two hundred men of the Forty-second Regiment, two hundred seamen, and about two hundred Indians conducted an unapposed landing on Anastasia Island. Typically, Oglethorpe was the first man ashore. His intentions were

to secure the island, destroy the half-galleys, and then transport
the regulars and Indians to Fort Mosa by 17 June in preparation for an assault on the town. The total British force now
numbered about fifteen hundred men.[15]

By 14 June, Oglethorpe's revised plan was progressing well.
The hastily improvised battery on Point Quartell had begun
lobbing a few shells across the harbor at the half-galleys and
into the town and fort. The small provincial boats were anchored safely in the entrance of the harbor. Three weeks remained before the men-of-war would withdraw. And the Spaniards inside the town were terrified. All this changed in the
pre-dawn of 15 June. Sentries on Point Quartell and Anastasia
Island suddenly came wide awake as volley after volley of musket fire rattled from the direction of Fort Mosa.[16]

IX

The Battle of Fort Mosa
June 1740

During May 1740 Robert McPherson, lieutenant of the Highland Rangers, gathered detachments of his troop and the English Rangers at a temporary camp about thirteen miles northwest of Darien on the Altamaha River. They waited several days for the arrival of a troop of rangers from South Carolina, but, unknown to them, that unit had not been recruited. During the latter part of May, McPherson tired of waiting for the nonexistent troop and led the rangers south along an old war path to Florida. About 1 June they reached Fort Pupo on the Saint Johns River and rendezvoused with Captain Hugh Mackay, Jr., the senior officer of the Georgia rangers. By 7 June most of the Highland and English Rangers had gathered in the British camp at Fort Diego.[1]

The rangers arrived just in time to participate in the tactical maneuver that was designed to prepare the way for an assault on the town of Saint Augustine. Most of the army was preparing to occupy Anastasia Island and Point Quartell for the purpose of establishing batteries of cannons to destroy the Cuban half-galleys and bombard the town. However, with the removal of most of the British army from the mainland the Spaniards could safely leave Saint Augustine and forage the deserted farms for food. Colonel Vanderdussen advised General Oglethorpe to blockade the north side of the town with a force stationed at Fort Mosa until the half-galleys were destroyed and the Forty-second Regiment was transported back to the mainland for the assault on the town. Oglethorpe determined that the Spaniards could best be deterred from leaving the town by the presence of a highly mobile "flying party."[2]

On 9 June, Oglethorpe assembled the flying party and gave its officers their orders. The Troop of Highland Rangers, commanded by Captain Hugh Mackay, Jr., took ten men on the mission, half of whom were officers. The Troop of English Rangers, under Lieutenant Robert Scroggs, counted only eight men. Each troop was short handed because of detachments made to the remainder of the expedition. The Troop of Carolina Rangers, composed of South Carolina volunteers who had been recruited and were paid by General Oglethorpe, mustered nine men. This troop, commanded by Captain William Palmer, had been formed after landing in Florida. The Highland Independent Company of Foot, under Captain John Mackintosh, included only fifty-seven men since several were sick and left behind. Thirty Uchee Indians served under a white trader named James Hewit, and ten Yamacraw and Creek followed the leadership of the half-Indian, Thomas Jones. The latter party had served as Indian Rangers for the past month. In order to provide a disciplined core around which the party could be bolstered during battle, a regular red-coated detachment including a sergeant and twelve privates was added from the Forty-second Regiment of Foot. The entire flying party apparently consisted of 137 men of all ranks.[3]

General Oglethorpe gave the ill-defined operational control of the party to Colonel John Palmer (Captain William Palmer's father), a South Carolina volunteer, but actual command of the soldiers was retained by Captain Mackay. Colonel Palmer did not possess a provincial or a regular military commission; therefore, under the tradition of that period, he could advise but he could not command the soldiers of the flying party. Palmer was apparently well qualified for the assignment; he was one of South Carolina's most experienced Indian fighters. In 1715, as an impetuous young scout-boat captain, he had led his crew of about sixteen scouts in a brave and successful assault on a well-fortified Yemassee town, located north of Beaufort, South Carolina. During the ensuing four months he participated in at least two well-planned and superbly executed ambushes. He subsequently served as a militia officer, and in 1728 he organized and led a large waterborne raiding force that destroyed three Yemassee towns located near Saint Augustine. During the latter action he gained important first-hand knowledge of the terrain in which the flying party was to operate. Unfortunately, Palmer was an egotistical man of short and violent temper who was convinced that he possessed a superior knowledge of military tactics. Previously he had attempted, unsuccessfully, to persuade Oglethorpe to conduct the campaign according to his tactics, which were based on laying waste the countryside. Even as he was given the operational control of the flying party he insisted again and again that their numbers were too small, accepting the assignment only after Oglethorpe threatened to offer the position to another.[4]

General Oglethorpe had unwittingly set the stage for the only defeat his soldiers would suffer in a man to man encounter with the Spaniards during the campaign—the Battle of Fort Mosa. It is extremely difficult to determine the details of the British defeat at Fort Mosa. The subject became such a heated issue between Georgia and South Carolina that each side covered their own mistakes while emphasizing the mistakes of the other. Depositions of Georgia soldiers are in direct opposition to those of South Carolina soldiers on many issues. It is possible, however, to discover considerable inconsistency in the accounts of both Georgia and South Carolina participants. A reasonably complete account can be pieced together through critical analysis of these inconsistencies.

The flying party left Fort Diego on 10 June and marched to a place between Saint Augustine and Fort Diego called the "Grove," where they camped the first night. They arrived at Fort Mosa about noon the following day.[5] The fortification was described as "four Square with a Flanker at each Corner, banked round with Earth, having a Ditch without on all Sides lined round with prickly Palmeto Royal and . . . a Well and House within, and a Look Out."[6] The British had partially demolished the structure during their previous visit a few days before. The gate had been carried off, a large breach had been battered in each of two walls, and the house within had been burned, making the structure no longer useful as a fortification.[7]

General Oglethorpe had instructed the flying party to range

west and east across the narrow strip of land between the Diego and Saint Johns Rivers, taking advantage of their mobility. The soldiers had been stripped of all unnecessary equipment for lighter and faster movement. They were to spend no more than one night in any one location, hiding in the thickets by night and moving into the open during the day to intercept Spanish foraging parties. If a superior force appeared they were to withdraw to Fort Diego. Oglethorpe estimated that they would only have to employ their hit-and-run tactics for about a week, for as soon as the Spanish half-galleys were destroyed the Forty-second Regiment and the remainder of the Indians were to come from Anastasia Island and join them in preparation for an assault on the town. Nevertheless, most of the officers chose to ignore the general's instructions by establishing a semipermanent camp at demolished Fort Mosa.[8]

Diplomacy between the colonies of Georgia and South Carolina had been somewhat strained during the past five years because of the rivalry over the bountiful Creek and Cherokee Indian trade. Some bickering between the officers of the two colonies had been evident from the initial days of the invasion. Now an actual breach opened in the relations between the Georgia and South Carolina officers of the flying party which eventually led to their destruction. The basis of the discord seems to have centered around a personality conflict between Colonel Palmer and Captain Mackay. Colonel Palmer seems to have used no tact whatever in his dealing with Mackay. Mackay, possessing both regular and provincial commissions, considered himself superior in status to Palmer who carried only honorary rank based on former service in the South Carolina militia. He refused to follow the colonel's orders and advice without a show of defiance.[9]

Georgia officers later stated that Colonel Palmer ordered the following disposition of soldiers that first night. The Highland Company, Highland Rangers, regulars, and Indians were to camp inside Fort Mosa; the English and Carolina Rangers were to camp outside in the dry moat around the fort. Depositions of South Carolina officers disagreed. They stated that Mackay and Mackintosh disobeyed Colonel Palmer's orders to camp on the plain and moved into the fort. Regardless of whose idea it was, those soldiers moved inside the demolished structure and began constructing temporary quarters of thatched palmetto.[10]

The first real argument between Palmer and Mackay concerned the number and location of the guards. Colonel Palmer and Captain Mackintosh began placing sentries at musket-shot distance (approximately two hundred yards) from the fort, but Mackay objected, saying that the Indians would only destroy them. He wanted several corporal-guards (about half a dozen men each) placed out at critical locations, rather than single sentries. Because of this argument the guard plan was never complete and adequate sentries were never posted outside the fort.[11]

The second disagreement arose that evening when Colonel Palmer assembled the unit commanders to discuss the disposition of the party in camp and the conduct of their mission. Captain Mackay began by brazenly suggesting that the party forsake the vicinity of Fort Mosa and camp in the thickets according to Oglethorpe's orders. Colonel Palmer retorted that his previous experience rendered him more capable of determining the Spaniards' fighting ability. He did not believe they would dare attack his force and he thought that Saint Augustine could be easily watched if the party remained "at, or in Sight of, Fort Mosa."[12]

Although the issue is clouded it appears that either at that meeting or soon thereafter the colonel began insisting that the Georgia soldiers move out of the demolished fort and camp just outside with the Carolina and English Rangers. His reason was that they were easily observed from Fort San Marcos as long as they remained inside Fort Mosa. He may have been changing his former orders concerning the disposition of the party or perhaps he had never intended that they actually build shelters and sleep within. Both Mackay and Mackintosh are said to have stubbornly refused to move out, probably believing if they had to camp in the vicinity of Fort Mosa they might as well camp inside.[13]

It is evident that Captain Mackay began usurping Colonel Palmer's operational control of the party. He did not refuse to obey Palmer's tactical directives; he merely ignored Palmer and acted only on those orders that he deemed were necessary. Except for the nine Carolina Rangers the party was composed of regulars, Georgians, and Indians, and most, if not all, of those soldiers and their officers followed Mackay's example.

Colonel Vanderdussen, stationed on Point Quartell, had seen the colors flying from Fort Mosa. One of his soldiers swam the Diego (Tolomato) River and made contact with the flying party.[14]

According to Colonel Palmer's orders the drummer beat "to arms" at three o'clock the next morning.[15] Palmer required the English and Carolina Rangers to stand near the moat with their weapons ready. The colonel had fought the Yemassee Indians frequently enough to know their favorite time of attack. After seeing to his son's rangers he walked into the fort to inspect the readiness of the soldiers camped inside. What he found enraged him. Some of the men were sitting in their makeshift huts of palmetto, lazily pulling on clothing. Most remained wrapped in blankets and tartans. Colonel Palmer "fell into a Passion with them . . . telling them . . . that they lied like Dogs to have their Throats cut."[16] This scene was repeated in essentially the same manner during the next three mornings.[17]

By 12 June the "grounded" flying party had settled into a routine. At three o'clock each morning the long roll of the drums sounded "to arms." Soon afterward, at daybreak, Colonel Palmer delivered his loud and timely lecture to the soldiers inside the fort. Later in the day the Carolina Rangers rode out of the camp to round up Spanish horses, sometimes accompanied by English and Highland Rangers. The Indians also spent most of their time ranging back and forth across the narrow peninsula looking for horses. Oglethorpe had promised a reward of £40 for each stallion and £30 for each mare in order to increase the size of his ranger force, authorizing Captain Palmer to hunt for horses "wherever he thought proper."[18] More than one hundred captured horses were corralled around Fort Mosa by 14 June.[19]

During the evening of 12 June, Captain Mackay led the first of the nightly harassing patrols. Rangers from all three troops, in company with the Indians and about half of the Highland Company, patrolled as far as Saint Augustine and fired on the town in order to frighten the inhabitants.[20]

The next day Captain Mackay wrote a letter to Colonel Vanderdussen requesting beef and rice to supplement his soldiers' ration of bread that would be gone by the next day. He also asked for a surgeon because several men of the flying party were sick with dysentery. Cornet Kenneth Baillie, of the Highland Rangers, and two men paddled an old canoe across the Diego River to Point Quartell and delivered the letter. That same evening they returned to Fort Mosa with only half a barrel of rice and a letter addressed to the commanding officer. Mackay opened it. Colonel Vanderdussen was also low on provisions.[21]

Colonel Palmer had begun to talk aloud about a disaster that was about to befall them. More than once the men heard him say that "the General had sent him there for a Sacrifice."[22] Palmer did have cause to worry. No word had been received from Oglethorpe and their rations were running out. But justified as he may have been in his fears, Palmer only increased the apprehension and ill feeling that already existed when he expressed himself in front of the men.

During the evening of 14 June a Creek mico bolstered the party with between five and seven warriors and reported that thirty more were on the way. Later that night Captain Mackay led a ranger patrol to the town of Saint Augustine in order to burn a particular house close to the gate, but the night was so dark they could not find it. Arriving back at Fort Mosa between midnight and one o'clock, the handful of Carolina Rangers who had accompanied the patrol reported to Colonel Palmer that they had heard the Indians inside the town dancing the war dance. Palmer had probably been expecting this. He ordered everyone to sleep while they could because there would be "a Brush before Day."[23]

The daily bombardment of the Spaniards in Fort San Marcos had caused little loss of life or material damage, but the psychological impact was pronounced. There was also a real danger that Saint Augustine would run out of provisions. Governor Montiano reported that "it is impossible to express the confusion of this place . . . [without relief] we must all indubitably perish."[24] The Spaniards needed a victory, no matter how small, to boost sagging morale. With good planning and luck a small victory might be possible. The selected target was the British force camped at Fort Mosa. On Saturday, 14 June, three hundred Spanish infantry, dragoons, militia, and Yemassee Indians were assembled and briefed. Captain Antonio Salgado was appointed as the commander and ordered to conduct a predawn assault.[25]

At about eleven o'clock that night the Spanish raiding force quietly moved out of Fort San Marcos and began a cautious advance toward the sleeping camp. The ranger patrol and the Spanish raiders apparently missed making contact by only a few minutes. Salgado's force arrived near Fort Mosa at about two o'clock on Sunday Morning, 15 June. A small reconnaissance party was sent forward to ascertain the positions of the British, and the dragoons were dispatched in a half circle around the fort to station themselves astride the route of escape to Fort Diego. An hour later the reconnaissance party returned with information concerning the British positions and strength. Their details of the British flying party's unpreparedness bolstered Spanish confidence.[26]

About three o'clock, when Colonel Palmer had the drums beat "to arms," the majority of the Carolina and British Rangers left their blankets and dressed. Palmer then walked into the fort and found most of the soldiers asleep. After he berated them for their laziness and inefficiency nearly all got up and dressed; however, after standing to arms for a few minutes most of the soldiers within the fort and some of those outside crawled back into their bedrolls.[27]

Captain Salgado's soldiers deserve praise for their stealth and discipline. They were divided into three parties and apparently attacked from as many directions. They were able to move unseen to within almost one hundred yards of the fort before one of the sentries, a Carolina Ranger, discovered them moving forward in the first light of dawn. The frightened sentry ran back to the fort crying that Spaniards were upon them.[28]

Colonel Palmer and Thomas Jones were standing in the gateway talking when they heard the sentry's warning. Palmer immediately called out for everyone to stand to their arms and to hold their fire until the Spaniards had fired first. No sooner had he spoken than a detachment of the Highlanders stationed in the nearest bastion opened fire. With curses Palmer ordered the Carolina and English Rangers into the moat. The Spaniards began pouring volleys on the fort.[29]

Jones ran inside to assemble his Indians who were just waking from a sound sleep. He found the entire party in a state of confusion. Half-dressed soldiers were searching frantically for weapons. Shouting officers and sergeants were vainly trying to gather their men in their appointed bastions.[30]

Captain Mackay had probably been wakened by the commotion. He was dressed only in a shirt, a pair of linen breeches, stockings, and was carrying a small sword and a musket. Mackay ordered the officer of the guard, Cornet Baillie, to defend the gate with his guard of eighteen men, but within a short time the Spaniards began pushing them back. Mackay then ordered his cousin, Ensign Charles Mackay of the Highland Company, to support the guard with twelve men.[31]

Outside in the moat the rangers were holding their own. Lieutenant Scroggs and the English Rangers were separated from Captain Palmer's Carolina troop. Captain Palmer had just finished pulling his boots on and buckling his spurs when he heard the warning shouts. He grabbed his brother and another ranger and ran to the moat about twelve yards away, believing they were in more danger from the Highlanders' fire to the rear than from the Spaniards' fire to the front. A short distance away Colonel Palmer, William Steads, and another ranger kept firing at the Spanish party that was trying to enter the gate. The rangers outside the fort do not appear to have been in much danger at that moment; the Spaniards were more interested in getting inside.[32]

Inside the fort Captain Mackay and Jones met while moving from bastion to bastion, each trying to rally the men and improve their dispositions. Jones reported he had killed the Spanish officer who had led the first assault. He suggested that Mackay reinforce those Highlanders who were trying to hold the gate.[33]

The Highlanders repulsed the first two charges, but a considerable body of Spaniards finally forced their way in by sheer weight of numbers. Captain Mackay hurriedly dispatched what men he could find to reinforce the gate, but it was too late. The fighting became hand to hand. The Spaniards had the advantage in that their numbers were greater and they were using their bayonets to cut the British to pieces. The Highlanders had left their bayonets and targets (shields) behind to make them lighter of foot. Without a target a broadswordsman was no match for a trained soldier with a bayonet. They began to give way. Spaniards from the other two assault parties were now hacking their way into the fort through the two breaches in the walls.[34]

Colonel Palmer was loading his gun when he was hit by a musket ball. Bleeding at the mouth, he finished loading his gun and died.[35]

Two thirds of the men of the Highland Company were casualties. The detachment of regulars were all dead, wounded, or captured. Almost half of the Highland Rangers had been killed or taken prisoner. One fourth of the English Rangers were dead. The majority of the Yamacraw and Creek were dead or captured.[36]

Captain Mackay scrambled to the top of the earthen wall and called to those below to follow. He and William Mackintosh, the fourteen-year-old son of Captain Mackintosh, jumped off the wall into the moat below.[37]

Shortly afterward Jones and everyone who was able also climbed over the wall. Jones met Captain Palmer and his brother near the moat and, in the company of six Indians, they began to force their way through the Spaniards under the cover of thick clouds of gunsmoke. A Yemassee Indian lunged at Jones, but Captain Palmer turned and shot him. Jones and Palmer broke through and ran to the stream near the fort, wading down to its junction with the Diego River where they met Captain Mackay, Lieutenant Scroggs, and the men they had been able to bring from the fort. The appearance of Scroggs suggests that he had also been caught napping. He wore only a shirt and was armed only with a pistol. Mackay had a wound across two fingers and two other wounds, "in his Breech and the Top of his Yard."[38] He said he had been wounded while defending the gate, but the Carolina officers suspected he must have received his wounds from the prickly palmetto royal that had been planted in the moat around the fort.[39]

The remains of the party were in a perilous state. At any moment the Spaniards might find them and add them to the list of casualties. One man was ordered to swim across the river to Point Quartell and ask Colonel Vanderdussen to send over a boat. A short time later the scout boat *Georgia* was sighted coming down the river. The boat was hailed and twenty-five thankful survivors boarded and were taken to Point Quartell and safety. Other survivors made their way to safety by ones and twos.[40]

At Fort Mosa the Spaniards were surveying their victory in the early Sunday morning sunlight. Their prisoners included Captain Mackintosh and about a dozen men of the Highland Independent Company, Cornet Baillie and Quartermaster James McQueen of the Highland Rangers, four or five men of the Forty-second Regiment, and an unknown number of Indians. The Spaniards stripped them, bound their hands behind their backs, and began marching them to Saint Augustine. Two prisoners who were too badly wounded to walk were killed and their heads and genitals were chopped off. One of the severed, dripping heads was sadistically rubbed in the face of Edward Lyng, a soldier of the Forty-second Regiment. A total of sixty-three British dead, including both whites and Indians, were left lying in and around the fort. Determining Spanish casualties is difficult. British estimates placed Spanish losses at between sixteen and three hundred. Governor Montiano admitted losing ten men.[41]

Obviously, no one individual can take full responsibility for the British defeat at Fort Mosa. Each of the principal officers involved must share a portion of the blame. General Oglethorpe probably should not have given operational control of the party to Colonel Palmer without also giving him full command. He should also have been aware that Palmer's personality would surely cause a clash. It is easy to argue that if Oglethorpe's orders had been followed the flying party would have maintained its mobility and would never have been caught in Fort Mosa. Captain Mackay protested repeatedly that he was the only officer who wanted to follow Oglethorpe's instructions (it seems likely he was). However, it is extremely difficult to hide the camping place of 140 men and 100 horses. Yemassee scouts would have located them easily, and with only a little more difficulty the Spaniards could therefore have attacked the flying party almost anywhere in the area.

The principal reason that the Spaniards were able to destroy an elite force of British and provincial soldiers was the inefficiency of two men, Colonel John Palmer and Captain Hugh

Mackay, Jr. Had sizable outposts been established they would have been able to fight a delaying action that might have enabled the party to escape to Fort Diego; Colonel Palmer posted single sentries despite Captain Mackay's suggestion of placing several corporal-guards at critical locations. Conversely, if Captain Mackay had assisted Colonel Palmer in rousing the soldiers they would have been standing to their arms, ready for the surprise attack. The morale of the men in the ranks is easy to imagine. Their two principal officers were constantly bickering within full view and earshot. Colonel Palmer even accused General Oglethorpe openly of wanting them killed. The Spaniards could not have picked a better time to attack; the British party was psychologically prepared for defeat.

X

Defeat and Withdrawal
June–July 1740

The defeat at Fort Mosa marked the turning point in the campaign. Two days before the attack Governor Montiano seemed ready to capitulate, but four days after his victory at Fort Mosa he arrogantly refused General Oglethorpe's call to surrender. Spanish morale had received a tremendous boost. Conversely, morale among the British regular soldiers and seamen began sinking. Oglethorpe grew ill tempered and, on one occasion, lost his self-control, angering his best fighting Indian allies, Squirrel King's Chickasaw from near Augusta. The Indians had swum across the narrow part of the harbor, ambushed a Yemassee Indian, and cut off his head, but when they attempted to present the horrible trophy to Oglethorpe, he lost his temper and dismissed them.[1]

Despite the spreading gloom, Colonel Alexander Vanderdussen's excellent leadership served to maintain efficiency and discipline among the South Carolina provincial soldiers. His regiment of foot included about five hundred men divided into ten companies, one of which consisted of grenadiers.[2] They probably wore their own civilian clothing, drab in comparison to the Forty-second Regiment's red coats with green facings; however, as events were shortly to prove, Vanderdussen's provincials were better disciplined and more efficient than Oglethorpe's regulars. Vanderdussen, believing that victory was still possible, informally assumed responsibility for preparing the expedition's battle plans and began trying to convince the British army and navy officers that they should take offensive action against the Spaniards.

Colonel Vanderdussen's Dutch accent and his military skill suggested the colorful background that he later recounted to one of Oglethorpe's officers. As a young man in Holland he had fallen in love with his cousin, but her father prevented them from eloping. During the resulting struggle young Vanderdussen secured a pistol and shot a servant in the arm with a bullet intended for his uncle. Before arriving in South Carolina, several years later, he was presumably employed by the Spaniards in the Philippine Islands and in South America. He apparently left their employ when he married a Spanish woman against a local governor's wish.[3]

It was evident to Colonel Vanderdussen that the half-completed improvised batteries of British cannons on Point Quartell and Anastasia Island did not have the capability of inflicting any appreciable damage on the Cuban half-galleys or on Fort San Marcos. Some of the cannons' barrels were laid on dunes and fired because of the lack of carriages, and the resulting recoil dug the barrels into the sand. Even those cannons that were mounted on carriages were difficult to employ, since recoil caused the wheels to shift and sink in the loose sand, necessitating a time-consuming realignment after each shot. Ideally, the carriages should have been placed on solid platforms constructed of heavy planks, but even under ideal conditions the sustained rate of fire for an eighteenth-century cannon was only about eight rounds per hour. Only two of Oglethorpe's officers were experienced gunners.[4]

The Cuban half-galleys still controlled the harbor and the British had to destroy them before an attack could be initiated against the harbor side of the town. On 16 June, Vanderdussen made a bold recommendation that his South Carolina Regiment, supported by a force of seamen in the men-of-war's long boats, conduct a surprise night attack against the half-galleys. Captain Peter Warren, commander of the naval forces on Anastasia Island, agreed to assist. Oglethorpe quickly approved the suggestion and ordered Vanderdussen to move his regiment to Anastasia Island and prepare to attack the half-galleys while the Forty-second Regiment moved to the mainland near Fort Mosa to regain gound lost by the flying party. Despite the movements, the original plan of attack on the town was still basically unchanged.[5]

Captain Warren and his seamen had apparently been very deeply affected by the defeat at Fort Mosa. On 16 and 17 June, Vanderdussen visited Anastasia Island and found Warren and his seamen making senseless complaints and refusing to do further work on the batteries. Warren was undoubtedly having second thoughts about his agreement to help engage the Cuban half-galleys in close combat. Vanderdussen skillfully played the role of mediator by arranging a meeting among General Oglethorpe, Commodore Pearse, Captain Warren, and himself. During the meeting Vanderdussen recommended the following: first, to complete the batteries quickly; second, to attack and destroy the half-galleys; third, to transport half the army and the Indians to the mainland; and fourth, to attack the town. Everyone present agreed to carry out his recommendations.[6]

Commodore Pearse and Captain Warren had no intentions of abiding by their agreements because they greatly feared the Spanish half-galleys. On 25 June, after several days delay, Vanderdussen boarded Pearse's flagship and again argued that it was necessary to destroy the half-galleys. Pearse relented, but by the next day he was again doubtful of the possibilities for successs and informed Vanderdussen that the navy would assist only if he received some assurance against the possibility of failure. Vanderdussen and Warren met and again agreed to attack the half-galleys, but Warren stipulated that the water around the Spanish boats had to be deep enough for the attacking boats to maneuver. Pearse and Warren had quite obviously been trying tactfully to tell Vanderdussen that they wanted no part of an attack on the half-galleys. Finally, on 26 June, Pearse bluntly wrote Vanderdussen that the navy would not assist.[7] Without the navy's men and boats there could be no attack.

The navy dealt the campaign another blow that same day. A nasty easterly wind began blowing and Pearse signaled the men-of-war to rendezvous with him and sail out to sea to prevent their being beached. One ship had been assigned to blockade the entrance to the Matanzas River thirteen and one-half miles to the south, a route used by small shallow-draft Spanish boats when moving between Cuba and Saint Augustine. As the British ship was sailing from Matanzas to join Pearse seven Cuban supply boats were sighted, but instead of attacking them the British captain continued toward his rendezvous with Pearse. Between 27 June and 2 July, while the British men-of-war were at sea, the Cuban supply boats lay safely in the shelter of Matanzas River. On 3 July they delivered their cargo of desperately needed food to Saint Augustine.[8]

On 26 June, Oglethorpe and his soldiers landed on the mainland and established a camp. The next day they visited the battlefield at Fort Mosa where half of the British dead, butchered and headless, still lay unburied.[9] The bloated putrid corpses would already have been partly eaten by scavengers. The exhilaration that the officers and men had felt after capturing Fort Pupo four months earlier was gone. As they buried the bodies they undoubtedly became sick with the sight and smell, the reality of war.

Vanderdussen had been occupying Anastasia Island with his regiment since 24 June. Although there was no longer any hope of quickly capturing the town Vanderdussen was determined that the campaign should not fail. He wanted Oglethorpe to leave the army in position after the men-of-war's scheduled departure on 5 July and conduct a siege until fall when the navy would return and the town could be attacked. Vanderdussen, believing it was absolutely necessary to blockade the mouth of the Matanzas River where the Cuban supply boats had entered, asked Pearse to station two of his sloops there after the remainder of the ships departed. Pearse agreed, provided that the water in the river was deep enough to float the sloops. The sloops' pilots sounded the mouth of the Matanzas on 2 July and returned to Pearse with their opinion that the water was not deep enough, there was no cover from hurricane winds, and there was no room for them to maneuver. Although the lieutenant of one of the sloops disagreed and said it was practical to station the sloops in the river, Pearse followed the pilots' advise and refused to leave the vessels behind.[10]

Vanderdussen believed the second best solution would be to build a battery on the southern tip of Anastasia Island near the Spaniards' old lookout and station all the provincial boats there to blockade the Matanzas River. However, the two hundred seamen on Anastasia Island would be needed to remain there during the summer to assist in manning the batteries and defending the island. Oglethorpe agreed with Vanderdussen's siege plan and personally requested Pearse to leave his seamen on Anastasia until he and his ships returned in the fall. But Pearse had no intention of leaving his ships short-handed or of destroying the morale of his fleet by the appearance of abandoning two hundred of his men in Florida. All hope of further assistance from the Royal Navy was lost.[11]

Vanderdussen, optimistic to the last, was convinced that a siege could be conducted even without the navy's help. On 4 July he recommended to Oglethorpe that he move the Forty-second Regiment from the mainland back to Anastasia Island, that a battery be built on the southern tip of the island, that the provincial boats be stationed in the mouth of Matanzas River, and that additional soldiers and vessels be requested from South Carolina.[12]

Oglethorpe was forced to consider the situation realistically. The odds were heavily against his and Vanderdussen's regiments being able to maintain a siege around Saint Augustine until October when the navy would return. Fifty men of the Forty-second Regiment were already too ill with dysentery and other summer ailments to perform duty. Saint Augustine had been resupplied twice during the naval blockade and it was reasonable to assume that the town would continue to be resupplied. The Cuban half-galleys would certainly break out of the harbor and begin raiding the batteries as soon as the British men-of-war left, and it was highly possible that the blockading forces on Anastasia Island and Point Quartell might themselves become blockaded. The Indians had become bored and were preparing to go home; their concept of war was to ambush and raid, not to sit inactive in a sickly camp. If a withdrawal were to be safely executed it would have to be conducted before the navy withdrew.[13]

On 4 July, Oglethorpe ordered a retreat. Two men-of-war stayed to cover Vanderdussen's withdrawal from Anastasia Island, but the remainder of the ships departed on 5 July. The army's retreat began on 9 July when Vanderdussen conducted a skillful predawn withdrawal from Anastasia Island to Point Quartell. There he found a detachment of the Forty-second Regiment hurriedly burning their provisions and extra equipment instead of carrying it off in the provincial boats. The operation was poorly supervised and confused. A loaded musket was thrown into a fire and discharged, wounding Ensign Sanford Mace, the officer in charge. The next day Vanderdussen continued his withdrawal north along the seabeach while Oglethorpe marched his regiment defiantly toward Saint Augustine. When Governor Montiano refused to offer battle, Oglethorpe turned and marched north along the road to Fort Diego. By 15 July the entire army had assembled at the old camp on the southern bank of the Saint Johns River.[14]

The day after the Battle of Fort Mosa, Oglethorpe had written Lieutenant Governor Bull of South Carolina, asking for more assistance. Letters from Bull arrived at the Saint Johns River camp on 16 and 17 July, informing Oglethorpe that a schooner, a company of infantry, and more cannons were on the way. Oglethorpe, his morale suddenly improved, informed Vanderdussen that they were going to return to Saint Augustine as soon as they had rested, hoping to surprise and demoralize the Spaniards with his quick return and the initiation of a siege.[15]

By 19 July the soldiers of the Forty-second Regiment had learned that they were going to return to Saint Augustine. Oglethorpe did not realize that they had already been pushed too far. The regulars had been recruited in the countryside and in the cities of England from the lower stratum of society. They did not possess the patriotic feelings of the middle and upper classes, but under good leadership or enforced harsh discipline they were capable of excellent performance. However, there was a limit to their loyalty to leaders and to their fear of punishment. When the regulars became disgusted with their plight and could bear it no longer they deserted. The companies of the Forty-second Regiment had been scattered among the various Georgia and South Carolina forts since 1738, and they had probably never identified with the regiment or Oglethorpe, its commander. Until then only a few men had deserted to the Spaniards during the campaign, but on 20 July the situation grew dangerous. A sergeant, a corporal, and six men deserted. The next day Oglethorpe lost most of his control over the regiment when many of the men threatened to desert in a body unless they were returned to Georgia. General Oglethorpe, realizing that they were not bluffing, transported most of the regiment across the Saint Johns River to Fort Saint George that same evening. They began moving to Frederica the following day.[16]

By comparison the Georgia and South Carolina provincial soldiers seem to have maintained a large measure of loyalty. This was possibly because of Colonel Vanderdussen's exceptionally good leadership and probably because they had more at stake. The Spaniards had long been a real threat to their families and homes. However, the threat of severe punishment did play a large part. The second man to desert from the South Carolina Regiment had the misfortune to be captured by one of South Carolina's most able soldiers, July, a free Negro who commanded a party of Negro and Indian scouts. After the deserter was shot in front of the entire regiment there were no more desertions.[17]

General Oglethorpe waited at the Saint Johns River camp with the South Carolina Regiment while Captain Lieutenant Dunbar and a company of regulars (Oglethorpe's) returned from Fort Pupo with the small British detachment that had been in garrison there. On 26 July the remainder of the British soldiers, regular and provincial, departed Florida. About 152 men were left behind. Of these 122 were buried in the sandy earth, about 16 were prisoners, and 14 had cast their lots with the Spaniards. Oglethorpe and the rear guard arrived at Frederica on 28 July, sick with dysentery and failure.[18]

Oglethorpe should have studied South Carolina's deplorable 1702 campaign against Saint Augustine, for he made the same principal mistake: he underestimated the strength of Castillo de San Marcos and the courage of its Spanish garrison. Consequently, he had neither plans nor special equipment for the conduct of an assault on the fort's walls. In fact, he would not have had any large cannons if South Carolina's Lieutenant Governor Bull had not provided them.

Overconfidence was not Oglethorpe's only shortcoming. His primary fault as the commander of a field army was his extremely poor utilization of subordinate officers. He conducted his own reconnaissance, prepared his own plans, effected his own coordination, and was involved in the forefront of almost every skirmish. There were two negative results. First, planning was often incomplete as evidenced by the fiasco at Fort Mosa where the flying party operated under a confusing command structure, received inadequate supplies, did not fully understand its mission, and had almost no contact with the remainder of the army. Second, he stifled the talents of certain subordinate officers. He certainly should have utilized Colonel Vanderdussen from the beginning, for he was an excellent leader and coordinator and he obviously possessed the knowledge and common sense required for tactical planning.

Of course, Oglethorpe should not share the total blame for the defeat. He had no real command or control of the British naval contingent. Commodore Pearse's captains were disappointing; their failure to maintain a tight blockade was the result of extreme carelessness, and their refusal to engage in close combat suggests a lack of courage.

XI

On the Defensive
1740–1742

During August and September 1740 General Oglethorpe isolated himself in his house at Frederica. Long marches, lack of sleep, bad water, and tainted food had sickened him. His most serious illness, however, resulted from the psychological shock that his extraordinary pride and self-confidence had suffered because of his defeat in Florida.[1]

About October, Oglethorpe overcame his fever and the shame of his failure and began thinking about his responsibilities to Georgia. During the following twenty-one months he worked unceasingly to bolster Georgia's defenses with the knowledge that Florida's Governor Montiano would invade Georgia and South Carolina as soon as he could amass enough men and ships. Oglethorpe could expect little assistance from South Carolina; relations between the two colonies had never been worse. The South Carolina Assembly rescinded the £2,000 that he had previously loaned them for the conduct of the Florida invasion, and, after a year-long investigation followed by a lengthy report, they charged that he had been incompetent. He, in turn, charged the South Carolinians with a lack of courage and cooperation. Only minor help could be expected from mother England because Georgia was far down on the priority list during the War of Jenkins's Ear. Oglethorpe was very much alone.[2]

Oglethorpe ordered the Forty-second Regiment of Foot to undergo drastic changes in disposition. The Indian raids of November 1739 had shown him that Amelia Fort was in a vulnerable location. Although that fort maintained a small reg-

133

ular garrison for a time and was used as a temporary rest stop for scout-boat crews, it was no longer an important part of Georgia's defenses. Fort Prince William, a new and better positioned fortification, had been finished in April 1740 just before the invasion of Florida. Located on the extreme southern tip of Cumberland Island, it was a weak structure consisting of a plank-sided house, a stockade with bastions at each corner, and eight cannons. A small detachment of regulars provided its garrison.[3]

A small detachment under the command of Lieutenant William Tolson (Captain Dunbar's company) garrisoned Fort Frederick, South Carolina. Either the conditions there were very bad or the temptations were irresistible because desertions from that post were common.[4] Part of the fort still stands at the U.S. Navy Hospital near Beaufort.

Oglethorpe concentrated most of the regiment on Saint Simons Island for better defense against a Spanish invasion. He transferred his company and that of Hugh Mackay, Sr., to Fort Frederica, leaving only a detachment at Fort Saint Andrews on Cumberland Island. The defenses of Fort Frederica and the town were strengthened. He stationed the greater part of the four remaining foot companies on the southern end of Saint Simons Island. That area developed into Georgia's most heavily fortified and garrisoned complex. Delegal's Fort, a tabby blockhouse surrounded by a horseshoe-shaped earthen wall, sat on the southeastern tip of the island. Nearby was a field battery of three cannons. About four hundred yards to the west was Fort Saint Simons, a large square earthen-walled fortification containing seven large cannons. Between the two forts was another battery of five cannons. Infantry trenches near Fort Saint Simons completed the defenses. Several nearby rows of clapboard huts served as barracks for the soldiers and their families.[5]

Captain Hugh Mackay, Sr., still commanded his company; however, the other five companies had newly promoted commanders, as a result of James Cockran's transfer and the deaths of two captains. In early 1742 General Oglethorpe's company was commanded by Captain Lieutenant James Mackay. The previous captain lieutenants of that company were Albert Desbrisay, George Dunbar, and Raymond Demere. Lieutenant

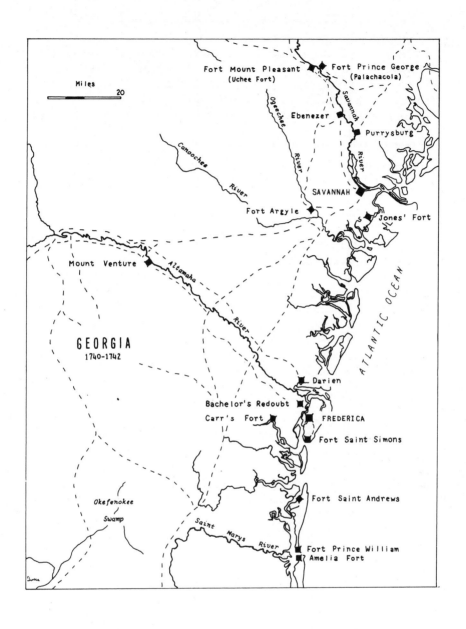

Miles
20

Fort Mount Pleasant
(Uchee Fort)

Fort Prince George
(Palachacola)

Ogeechee River

Ebenezer

Savannah River

Purrysburg

Canooches River

SAVANNAH

Fort Argyle

Jones' Fort

Mount Venture

Altamaha River

GEORGIA
1740-1742

ATLANTIC OCEAN

Darien

Bachelor's Redoubt

Carr's Fort

FREDERICA

Fort Saint Simons

Fort Saint Andrews

Okefenokee
Swamp

Saint Marys River

Fort Prince William
Amelia Fort

Colonel William Cook commanded the company formerly belonging to James Cockran. Cook's former company was commanded by Major Alexander Heron. The company formerly commanded by Richard Norbury, now deceased, was commanded by Captain George Dunbar. Captain Raymond Demere commanded the company initially belonging to Heron and later to Desbrisay, the latter of whom was deceased. Disease, desertion, and combat had severely depleted the companies until the regiment could field only 384 officers and men, a little more than one-half of its authorized strength.[6]

Before the invasion of Florida, Oglethorpe had sent Lieutenant William Horton to England to request funds from the British government for the maintenance of the provincial units and additional soldiers for the regiment. The government turned a deaf ear to the provincials' maintenance, but it surprisingly agreed during June 1740 to enlarge the regiment. It authorized an additional lieutenant for each company and added a grenadier company, increasing the regiment's authorized strength to 804 officers and men. Grenadiers were considered elite soldiers whose special skill was throwing the primitive fuze hand grenades of that period. They were uniformed and equipped like the regular footmen except for the miter-shaped caps that they wore. William Horton received the king's commission as captain of the grenadiers in December 1740, but he spent more than a year recruiting his men and did not arrive in Georgia until June 1742.[7]

The officers of the regiment had unfortunately developed a penchant for quarreling among themselves. A feud had developed between General Oglethorpe and Lieutenant Colonel Cook in Florida over a disagreement concerning tactics. Their personal conflict grew in intensity and by early 1741 Cook was openly disobeying Oglethorpe's orders. In June 1742 Cook took a leave of absence and sailed for England with the excuse of poor health, probably at Oglethorpe's suggestion.[8] Although Cook was apparently a malicious and spiteful man, one can sympathize with his frustrating position as Ogelthorpe's lieutenant colonel. Oglethorpe was too energetic to use his staff; he acted as colonel, lieutenant colonel, major, captain, lieutenant, and at times he even performed the duties of a sergeant. An intelligent ambitious lieutenant colonel would have been bored and frustrated while serving as his second in command.

Other feuds within the regiment had more serious consequences. In late December 1739, just before the invasion of Florida, Ensign John Leman and Patrick Sutherland, a cadet who was in line for a commission, fought a duel and Leman was shot in the leg. The wound quickly infected and his leg was amputated. Fitted with a wooden peg, he was unable to function as an infantry officer, and a year later he sailed to England to seek other employment. In June 1742 he was appointed fort major of the British fortifications at Annapolis in Nova Scotia.[9] Sutherland was unharmed and lived on to become a captain and a hero of the Forty-second Regiment.

Two duels were fought during May 1740 at the Saint Johns River camp in Florida. Ensign William Tolson, who would be denounced as a coward while under fire two years later, killed a man named Eyles who was evidently a civilian volunteer surgeon. A few days later Cadet Peter Grant goaded another cadet named Shannon into a sword duel and was killed by him.[10]

In May 1741 two company commanders, Captains Richard Norbury and Albert Desbrisay, settled their differences with a sword duel and Norbury, an ill-tempered old man, was killed. Within a year Desbrisay was also dead, perhaps of his wounds. General Oglethorpe's reaction to these senseless duels is unclear, but he surely recalled the time when, at the age of twenty-six, he had killed a man under similar circumstances.[11]

The disposition of the Georgia provincial military units also underwent several changes upon their return from the Florida invasion. Lieutenant Robert Scroggs and about six men of his Troop of English Rangers established a camp approximately four miles northwest of Frederica on the mainland. The location, called White Post, or Carteret's Point, at the head of Grant Creek, guarded the land approach to Frederica. Scroggs constructed a small fortification there named Bachelor's Redoubt, which was probably a blockhouse inside a small square stockade. They maintained communications with Oglethorpe's headquarters at Frederica in their small boat named the *Bachelor's Redoubt*.[12]

Between four and eight English Rangers garrisoned Fort Argyle under Lachlan Mackintosh. He and his rangers were careless in the performance of their duties, for during the middle of September 1740 all the men were gone from the fort, leaving two indentured servants, a man and a woman, alone and unprotected. William Shannon, a disreputable character who had been drummed out of the Forty-second Regiment, and a Spanish doctor, both of whom had recently escaped from the Savannah jail, visited the fort during the rangers' absence. After plundering the huts the fugitives attacked the man servant, cutting off his head and throwing his body into the Ogeechee River in an attempt to make the Georgians believe it was the work of Yemassee Indians. The woman servant was carried off into the forest where she was eventually murdered. Mackintosh reported the murders to the Savannah magistrates who immediately offered a reward and sent a three-man posse in pursuit. The fugitives were caught in a hut at the Uchee town where they had fled to escape a driving rain. Both men were tried and hanged at Savannah six weeks later. Shannon received special treatment. According to Oglethorpe's order his rotting corpse was hung in chains at the mouth of the Ogeechee River as an example to other potential criminals. Oglethorpe attempted to enlarge the Fort Argyle garrison, following the murder, but men and horses were hard to find and by early 1741 the fort was guarded by only four rangers.[13]

Another handful of English Rangers was stationed on Saint Simons Island, carrying messages between Fort Frederica and Fort Saint Simons and probably serving as Oglethorpe's servant-bodyguards. A youth named Thomas Hunt, formerly Oglethorpe's servant, was commissioned quartermaster about August 1741 and was given the command of that detachment.[14] In all, the Troop of English Rangers was about half strength, averaging between fifteen and twenty men.

The Troop of Highland Rangers was also serving at half strength. Lieutenant Robert McPherson had been killed in Florida. Cornet Kenneth Baillie and Quartermaster James McQueen were prisoners of war in Spain. Baillie seems to have been the most enterprising of the Spaniards' prisoners, for after a year and a half he escaped from his prison and slipped out of Spain, arriving in England by March 1742. He was very bitter about the defeat at Fort Mosa and refused to continue his service with the Highland Rangers.[15]

Captain Hugh Mackay, Jr., and four Highland Rangers were

stationed at Fort Saint Andrews on Cumberland Island where they apparently occupied space in two houses and a stable that had been constructed a short distance north of the fort. Mackay's detachment probably carried messages between Fort Saint Andrews and Fort Prince William and patrolled the island's beach on the lookout for raiding Spanish ships. Oglethorpe sometimes employed the detachment to carry messages overland to Charles Town and to drive horses and cattle from South Carolina to Georgia.[16] Mackay, who still retained a commission in the Forty-second Regiment, had been transferred, on paper, as an ensign to the company commanded by Captain Hugh Mackay, Sr., his uncle, and in December 1740 he was promoted to lieutenant. For some unknown reason he transferred to the Third Regiment of Marines in August 1741; however, he never left Georgia to join his marine regiment and continued to command the Highland Rangers.[17]

The remainder of the Highland Rangers were stationed at Darien under the troop's only other officer, Quartermaster Hugh Morrison. This detachment numbered only ten men, varying in age from sixteen to fifty, who patrolled and carried messages between Darien and Fort Argyle on horseback and scouted the Altamaha River in the *Saint Andrews* scout boat.[18]

Eight new widows and twenty-three freshly orphaned children tearfully met the Highland Independent Company of Foot when it returned to Darien from Florida in July 1740. The company's commander, Captain John Mackintosh, and eight of his men were prisoners of the Spaniards and about thirty men were buried in Florida. The company's strength continued to dwindle until May 1741 when there were only sixteen men left, the youngest of whom was fifteen years old. They were commanded by the only remaining officer, Charles Mackay, recently promoted to lieutenant, who was assisted by the one remaining noncommissioned officer, a sergeant. Although the few Highlanders could not function as a company they did provide effective service as a scouting force by manning a large scout boat, the *Darien,* which had fourteen oars and six swivel guns. Fortunately, the unit soon regained its capability as an infantry company with the addition of fifteen new recruits from Scotland.[19]

Lieutenant Richard Kent's Fort Augusta garrison of rangers

had not participated in the invasion of Florida, for the fort on the upper Savannah River was too important, commercially and strategically, to leave unguarded. Augusta was also a tough frontier town. Its population included the rangers, South Carolina Indian traders, packhorsemen, loitering warriors representing most of the southern nations, and the white men's Indian wives, mistresses, and numerous children. Although slavery was probibited in Georgia a few Negro slaves lived there with their South Carolina masters. Augusta's toughness and remoteness from Savannah required the presence of a peace officer. At first Kent had no authority over civilians, but in November 1741 the trustees in London appointed him a conservator of the peace, granting him authority to sit in judgement over breaches of the peace and small civil actions such as minor debts. He was also promoted to captain in June or July of that year. The garrison of rangers was originally authorized a captain, a lieutenant, and fifteen private men; however, by 1741 it had been reorganized similar to a troop of dragoons. The new organization included a captain, two sergeants, two corporals, a drummer, and between twelve and fifteen privates for a total authorized strength of twenty men.[20] Although the garrison may have been authorized a lieutenant, the position seems never to have been filled.

During the late summer of 1741 the inhabitants of Augusta suffered a terrible flash flood. Although the town and fort, located on a bluff, escaped the waters, large numbers of livestock were drowned and an exceedingly good corn crop was destroyed. The Chickasaw Indian town, a few miles upriver, was washed away and the Indians, taken unaware, escaped only by clinging to floating logs and brush.[21]

Captain Aneas Mackintosh, commander of the Palachacola Rangers at Fort Prince George, South Carolina, had returned to Scotland in February 1740. His older brother, the "Laird of M'intosh," was dead or dying and Aneas returned to his homeland to inherit the chieftainship of his clan and the family estate. Aneas's younger brother John, a Palachacola Ranger since at least 1737, was promoted to captain and assumed command of the garrison. The subsequent history of Fort Prince George is confusing. The last reference to a garrison there was in June 1742. There are no records to indicate that the rangers were ever paid by Oglethorpe, the trustees, or the South Carolina Assembly from the time of their reactivation in late 1739. However, the garrison probably numbered fewer than half a dozen men whose primary duty was the operation and protection of the Palachacola ferry across the Savannah River which the South Carolina government had authorized Oglethorpe to establish beginning in June 1740. The rangers' subsistence was perhaps dependent upon the receipts from ferrying passengers, livestock, and freight.[22]

Realistically, there was little need for the Palachacola Rangers after November 1740. During that month Oglethorpe ordered a fort built and a garrison of two officers and twelve rangers stationed near the Uchee Indian town three miles to the west of Palachacola across the Savannah River in Georgia. Thomas Wiggins, who had long owned a trading house there, was commissioned captain of the garrison. Wiggins, a good friend of Oglethorpe's was a capable officer who had a great influence among the Creek and Uchee Indians. His lieutenant was Anthony Willy, former commander of Okfuskee Fort in the Upper Creek nation. By the spring of 1741 a small fort, called Mount Pleasant, had been constructed near the Uchee town. The fortification was probably a stockade surrounding Wiggins's trading house, a few barracks huts, and a stable. The Indian town was practically uninhabited by 1741, although a few Uchees occasionally returned to the area to hunt and a few lived further up river at Silver Bluff in South Carolina.[23] Fort Mount Pleasant, also called Uchee Fort, was strategically located, commanding the Savannah River from a bluff one hundred feet high from which the rangers patrolled to the west of the river, screening the northern approach to the Ebenezer and Savannah settlements.

Two disasters befell Fort Mount Pleasant during the summer of 1742. During the latter part of June, Lieutenant Willy crossed the Savannah River and visited Captain John Mackintosh at Fort Prince George. After both men retired for the night Willy killed himself with one of his pistols for reasons unknown. About two weeks later Captain Wiggins became ill and went to Savannah where he died shortly afterward. John Barnard, another Indian trader, was then commissioned captain of the Mount Pleasant Rangers.[24]

Oglethorpe ordered a number of other new provincial military units raised during the fall of 1740. One of these was a garrison of rangers for Mount Venture, an isolated trading post on the upper Altamaha River. In 1736 Oglethorpe had reconnoitered a considerable distance up the Altamaha in a scout boat and decided that some sort of defense had to be established to hinder Yemassee war parties from crossing the river into the Georgia settlements. Later that year or early the next he persuaded Jacob and Mary Mathews to establish the trading post of Mount Venture, which was probably located on the south bank of the Altamaha River between present Tenmile and Fivemile Creeks, about fifty miles northwest of Darien.[25]

Mary Mathews's ancestry was part English and part Lower Creek. She had been educated and baptized a Christian in South Carolina, apparently at the insistence of her Indian-trader father, but she maintained close ties with her Indian mother's family in Coweta. In 1740 she was about thirty to forty years old and possibly a good-looking woman who possessed a regal bearing. But in an age when women exercised their influence unobtrusively she conducted herself like an outspoken man. Her Indian name was Cowsaponakeesa, and as the niece of Chigelley, the principal mico of the Lower Creek, she was pampered by Oglethorpe and she, in turn, served him well as interpreter and mediator. Unfortunately, many other Georgians never quite considered her as anything but part savage and she often responded in kind.[26]

Oglethorpe intended that some of Mary's Lower Creek kinsmen would always be camped at Mount Venture in a position to counter Yemassee war parties; however, the Indians never established a permanent town there and their presence could not be relied upon. Mary's husband, Jacob, requested that a detachment of the Forty-second Regiment be stationed at Mount Venture for the post's protection. Oglethorpe was reluctant to spare any regulars from the understrength regiment, and, besides, heavy-laden foot soldiers were not suited for patrolling long distances along the thicket-covered banks of the Altamaha River looking for hostile war parties.[27]

In October 1740 Oglethorpe commissioned Jacob Mathews

a provincial captain and ordered him to recruit a garrison of twenty rangers to be stationed at Mount Venture. To Oglethorpe's chagrin Mathews was an inefficient officer. He had immigrated to Georgia as an indentured servant to John Musgrove and after Musgrove died his widow, Mary, had freed Mathews and married him. Mathews used his wife's money and influence with the Indians to his advantage. He was a poor imitation of gentry; his dress was too flashy, his speech and manners were too crude. He was a big spender and was consequently surrounded by some of Savannah's most disreputable citizens who served as his drinking companions.[28]

Mathews did not immediately go to Mount Venture after receiving his commission. For several months he lay sick at his cowpen (cattle ranch) about six miles northwest of Savannah. By April 1741 Mathews had recovered but he was reluctant to leave Savannah and organize his garrison because he and William Francis, his lieutenant, were in Savannah having a good time. Lieutenant Francis had been formerly employed as a messenger and more recently as an English Ranger at Fort Argyle. His partying was rudely interrupted when he learned that his mistress, a German servant girl, was pregnant. Francis agreed to marry her, but after he and Mathews drunkenly reflected on the problem they complained loudly of being duped. Francis married the girl, nevertheless. During the latter part of April, Oglethorpe finally grew exasperated with Mathews and ordered him to repair to Mount Venture.[29]

During July 1741 Lieutenant Francis was again in Savannah with a few rangers and, a month later, he was joined by Captain Mathews. Together they conducted a long drinking spree at the Savannah house of Mathews. At all hours of the day and night small groups of Mary's Creek relatives visited the party. After getting drunk the Indians paraded up and down Savannah's streets, singing and whooping.[30]

Mathews and Francis returned to Savannah again in December 1741 and spent most of the winter there. In February 1742, while Francis was returning to Mount Venture in the garrison boat carrying sixty gallons of illegal trading rum, officials at Frederica seized the barrels and staved them. When Mary Mathews heard about the incident she became enraged and uttered vengeful threats of retaliation by her Creek friends. In May, Jacob and some of his rangers were again in Savannah, causing trouble for the local officials.[31]

Although complaints of the above incidents had reached Oglethorpe he did not discipline Mathews; nevertheless, he was undoubtedly trying to think of a way to bring the ranger captain into line. Mathews was offensive to Savannah's officials and the Mount Venture garrison had been dangerously under-manned for more than half of its existence. But whatever Oglethorpe attempted in the way of discipline would have to be very, very tactful. He had commissioned Mathews to com-mand the garrison because of his wife's influence with the powerful Lower Creek nation, and he probably would have accepted Mathews's shortcomings rather than risk alienating those Indians. His problem was solved in June 1742 when Mathews, never a healthy man, became very ill and retired to his cowpen near Savannah where he died soon afterward. Lieutenant Francis inherited the command of the Mount Ven-ture Rangers.[32]

Before the invasion of Florida, Oglethorpe had intended to form the scout-boat crews into a company of boatmen, but he was unable to begin organization of the company until the fall of 1740. In October he commissioned Mark Carr, a Scottish gentleman, as the company's captain. Previously, in 1739, Carr had established a plantation called Hermitage on the north bank of the Turtle River on present Hermitage Island, four and one-half miles northwest of the modern town of Brunswick. Oglethorpe made service in the scout boats more appealing by naming the new unit the Marine Company of Boatman, issuing a distinctive uniform, and requiring an enlistment of only one year. The company was authorized a captain, a lieuten-ant, two sergeants, two corporals, a drummer, and one hundred privates. However, veteran scouts were unwilling to reenlist in his company and Captain Carr was forced to travel to Virgin-ia and Maryland where he spent more than six months recruit-ing his marines.[33]

During Carr's absence Oglethorpe assigned a corporal-guard of regulars to protect his Hermitage plantation from Indian raids. Unfortunately, their presence was not much of a deter-rent. Before dawn on 18 March 1741 a large party of Yemassee conducted a surprise attack on the plantation during which four men were killed and several were wounded before they could escape. Surprisingly, the women and children, left to the mercy of the Yemassee, were treated very well. The war party merely locked them in the cellar of the main house while they burned the other buildings and conducted a systematic pillage. They loaded their plunder into a large canoe belonging to the plantation and started down the Inland Passage toward Florida. When Oglethorpe received word of the raid he reacted quickly by dispatching scout boats in pursuit. The war party was heavily burdened and had to travel very carefully in order to bypass Forts Saint Andrews, Prince William, and Amelia undiscovered. The scout boats managed to catch the slow-moving Indians and, in the resulting clash, recaptured the canoe and a horse that it was transporting.[34]

During the latter part of May 1741 Captain Carr and his new company, composed of Virginians, Marylanders, and South Carolinians, arrived at Saint Simons Island in two sloops. They were clothed in uniforms, the appearance of which is unknown, but it is likely that the only items they were issued were coats, the remainder of the clothing being their own. If the coats followed the style of British regular marine regiments they would have been red like the Forty-second Regiment's except for a slightly different style and another color in the cuffs and lapels.[35]

Captain Carr rebuilt Hermitage, also called Carr's Fort, and surrounded the buildings with four blockhouses for protection. He also established a second plantation across the Turtle River on Blyth Island, a more protected location. Carr's company included two scout boats, the *Speedwell,* having twelve oars, a three-pounder cannon, and four swivel guns, and the *Old Scout Boat* (the *Georgia?*), having ten oars and three swivel guns. The latter craft was coxswained by William Germain, who probably held the rank of sergeant. The swift shallow-draft boats, like most scout boats, were large dugout canoes shaped from giant cypress trees, well designed for patrolling the Inland Passage and for the clandestine delivery of Indian war parties into Florida. After Kenneth Baillie, the cornet of the Highland Rangers, escaped from his prison in Spain he returned to Georgia via England. In June 1742 Ogelthorpe commissioned him

a lieutenant in Captain Carr's Marine Company, for he refused
to continue his service under Captain Mackay in the Highland
Rangers.[36]

Ogelthorpe had intended to organize all the scout-boat crews
into one marine company. However, because of personnel
problems, two companies and a separate crew emerged. Captain Carr could not enlist more than forty men, only enough
to man the two scout boats and garrison his fortified plantation.
The veteran scouts refused to enlist in the Marine Company
because of the low pay; therefore, in order to provide crews
for the remaining boats, Oglethorpe was forced to reenlist the
veterans at a higher wage and organize them into a separate
unit.[37]

Noble Jones, the Marine Company's forty-year-old senior
lieutenant, commanded two of these veteran crews stationed
near Savannah. The scout boat *Savannah,* coxswained by Jones,
had ten oars and a swivel gun, and the *Skidaway,* coxswained
by Thomas Upton, had six oars and a swivel gun. Jones had
come to Georgia with the first shipload of colonists and was
one of the few original settlers still alive. He had been a scout-boat commander since August 1740 upon his return from Florida where he had served as a lieutenant in the South Carolina
Regiment. Although Jones was technically one of Captain Carr's
officers, he was not under his direct orders and his two boat
crews were, in fact, listed separately as the Northern Company
of Marines. They were stationed near Jones' Fort on his plantation called Wormsloe at Skidaway Narrows on the Isle of Hope
opposite Burntpot Island. The fort was a redoubt consisting
of a stockade surrounding a blockhouse with a protruding
upper floor.[38]

To further complicate the disposition of the marines, the
crew of a scout boat stationed on Saint Simons Island, the
Frederica, coxswained by Daniel Demetre, having ten oars and
a swivel gun, seems to have been independent of both marine
companies. Besides the marines' boats there was Oglethorpe's
boat the *Cutter,* two other boats belonging to the regiment,
two supply piraguas, and the *Darien* and *Saint Andrews* scout
boats manned by Highlanders.[39]

One of Oglethorpe's greatest needs was for ships to protect
the Georgia seacoast from Spanish privateers. Most of the Brit-

ish men-of-war in the area were, of necessity, concentrated at Charles Town where enemy privateers found richer pickings. During 1740 and 1741 Oglethorpe formed his own provincial navy, consisting of the schooner *Walker* and the sloops *Faulcon* and *Saint Phillip*. Each of the small vessels, purchased in Charles Town and manned mostly by South Carolina seamen, was heavily armed with cannons and swivel guns. Soldiers from the Forty-second Regiment sailed aboard the vessels as marines and manned the oars when added speed was necessary. The *Walker*, which was also called a half-galley, could carry ninety soldiers and was rowed with thirty oars.[40]

Not all of Oglethorpe's activities during the period 1740 to 1742 were defensive. He accompanied his provincial navy on at least two raids against Spanish shipping. In addition, British privateer ships cruised along the Florida coast looking for lesser-armed Spanish supply ships to plunder. Unfortunately, Governor Montiano of Florida was also issuing letters of marque to privateers from Cuba, Mexico, and Florida who seem to have been more successful than their British counterparts.[41]

Oglethorpe's most effective offensive weapon was his Indian allies who conducted a number of raids into Florida. Unfortunately for the British, few warriors were available. However, Lower Creek journeyed to Frederica to accompany the raids after Chigelley, their principal headman, was angered during a conference with the French at Fort Toulouse in May 1740. The Upper Creek also moved closer to the English at that conference when one of their micos, Wolf of Muccolossus (Muklasa), courageously protected an English trader from the threats of pro-French Creek and Choctaw. In June 1741 Chigelley visited Frederica and promised Oglethorpe additional aid. Nevertheless, the Creek could spare only a few warriors for operations in Florida because they were on the verge of a war with the Choctaw and had actually been at war with the Cherokee since the fall of 1740.[42]

Captain Thomas Jones, the half-Indian ranger, lead most of the Indian raids. He probably had to recruit a new party of Indians after each raid, for it was the Indians' habit to return to their towns where they displayed their trophies and boasted of their prowess in battle. Each new Indian recruit received a new trade musket, a hatchet, and a blanket, and was provided with corn for provisions. The Indian trade must have suffered because the warriors were hunting for humans instead of deer. Spaniards probably never felt entirely safe outside the walls of Saint Augustine without a military escort. In November 1741 Jones and a mixed party of Creek, Yamacraw, and Uchee returned to Frederica with two Spanish soldiers as prisoners, one of whom was the lieutenant of the troop of dragoons stationed in Saint Augustine. The Indians were always very proud of their prisoners and usually turned them over to their women who tortured them to death. In order to prevent that from happening Oglethorpe ransomed the prisoners with horses from the colony's precious herds, the only item the Indians would accept in trade.[43]

During the early months of 1742 Oglethorpe began another drive to increase the size of his ranger force, for at the end of 1741 the two troops and five frontier garrisons had totaled only one hundred men. Because of their mobility the rangers were ideally suited for patrolling the beaches of Saint Simons and Cumberland Islands and the trails leading into the colony. More important, Oglethorpe would desperately need additional horsemen when the Spaniards landed an invasion force. The rangers, acting as dragoons, could move rapidly from one point to another on horseback and then dismount and fight as infantry.

In March 1742 Oglethorpe commissioned twenty-one-year-old John Milledge as quartermaster of the English Rangers and placed him in command of Fort Argyle. He was instructed to augment the garrison to twenty rangers, but only a handful of additional men were recruited. Milledge had been aboard the first ship that had landed in Savannah and by the summer of 1734 both his father and mother had died leaving twelve-year-old John as the head of the family, which consisted of a younger brother and two younger sisters. Milledge matured quickly and became an excellent provider. Oglethorpe liked the boy and it was probably his influence that made Milledge a minor leader in the Savannah militia in 1740. Milledge served as Fort Argyle's commander during the subsequent five years and proved to be an exceptionally good officer.[44]

Fort Argyle's outworks had been completely reconstructed

by 1741. The earthen wall and the moat, with a palisade planted in the bottom, were not repaired. The new wall was a stockade, eleven feet high and constructed with upright logs; it was higher, tighter, and more substantial than a palisade. Fireplaces and chimneys of brick were built in the barracks and houses. The rangers patrolled and carried messages between Savannah and Darien on horseback, and they also patrolled the Ogeechee River and carried supplies in their garrison boat, the *Fort Argyle*.[45]

Thomas Jones, who had been leading the Indian war parties, recruited a group of South Carolinians and organized them into a troop of rangers. Jones was commissioned captain of the troop, which included a quartermaster, whose name is unknown, and twelve rangers. They arrived at Frederica about late January 1742. Captain Jones and half of his troop were stationed on Saint Simons Island while his quartermaster and the other half of the troop were posted at Fort Prince William on Cumberland Island.[46]

Oglethorpe had attempted to organize a unit of rangers at Savannah and another at Ebenezer in October 1740. There may have been enough men to serve as rangers, especially at Ebenezer, but there were not enough horses for sale either in Georgia or South Carolina. A few horses were purchased in the spring of 1741, but they went to the existing ranger units as replacement mounts. Although the unit destined for Savannah seems not to have been raised, a party of six rangers under the command of Thomas Bichler was established at Ebenezer about March 1742 after a number of horses were purchased in Virginia. Several of Ebenezer's Salzburger settlers also served in the English Rangers at Fort Argyle and at Mount Venture.[47]

In May 1742 about a dozen Virginia horsemen under the leadership of John Williams arrived in Georgia as volunteer rangers. Captain William's troop of rangers was stationed either on Saint Simons Island or at Bachelor's Redoubt northwest of Frederica.[48] Georgia's provincial military forces had taken on an international flavor with soldiers speaking Gaelic, German, and several dialects of English.

Oglethorpe had little time to do more. During the latter part of May a patrol of Lieutenant Scroggs's English Rangers from Bachelor's Redoubt collided with a scouting party of Ye-massee Indians. That same week a British man-of-war had a brief encounter with a small fleet of Spanish vessels carrying troops and supplies from Cuba to Saint Augustine. Oglethorpe hurriedly sent an officer by boat to Charles Town asking the South Carolina Assembly and the British navy to assist him in repelling the imminent invasion. A few days later Captain Mackay and a detachment of his Highland Rangers rode over-land to South Carolina with a second request for help. Ogle-thorpe knew that the government of South Carolina was reluctant to come to his relief, and even if they did decide to help their reaction would be too slow. During the middle of June, Oglethorpe was pleasantly surprised by the arrival of a ship from England carrying Captain Horton's new grenadier company. They disembarked on Jekyll Island and made camp on the north end near Horton's house.[49]

On 21 June, Spanish ships and boats exchanged cannon fire with Fort Prince William on the southern tip of Cumberland Island. The long-dreaded invasion had begun.[50]

XII

The Spanish Invasion of Georgia
May–July 1742

Spanish arms had been victorious throughout the Americas. Oglethorpe's failure in Florida was insignificant compared with the two catastrophic defeats that British invasion forces under Vice-Admiral Vernon suffered at Cartagena in present Colombia and at Santiago, Cuba.[1] In the fall of 1741 King Philip V of Spain felt confident enough to assume the offensive. On 20 October he sent orders to the governor of Cuba to organize quickly a gigantic raiding expedition whose mission was to devastate Georgia and the southern portion of South Carolina by "sacking and burning all the towns, posts, plantations and settlements."[2] Following the accomplishment of its mission the expedition was to withdraw quickly leaving a wasted countryside to terrify and demoralize the British.[3]

Juan Francisco de Güemes, governor of Cuba, began immediate preparations to raise three thousand soldiers and a strong fleet for an attack on Beaufort, South Carolina, sometime between April and June 1742. Following Beaufort's destruction, plans called for Spanish Negroes, speaking various African dialects, to filter through the remainder of South Carolina, inciting the black slaves to revolt, while the remainder of the expedition was to drive south, laying waste the Georgia settlements.[4]

In early May 1742 Güemes appointed Governor Montiano of Florida as the commanding general of the expedition. Güemes had been able to gather only six hundred regulars and seven hundred militia in Cuba and he expected Montiano to furnish another four hundred regulars and one hundred militia from

Florida. By now Güemes had changed the expedition's initial target from Beaufort, South Carolina, to Saint Simons Island, Georgia, an objective that was tactically more sound. Following the defeat of General Oglethorpe's Forty-second Regiment, from whom little resistance was expected, the expedition was to move north along the coast, destroying the Georgia settlements. Güemes ordered that the campaign was to be conducted with the minimum loss of Spanish lives, and more than once he emphasized that after devastating the British settlements Montiano must immediately withdraw to Cuba and Florida since British counterattacks were inevitable.[5]

After several delays a third of the fleet, ten vessels, sailed from Cuba for Saint Augustine on 21 May. A week later, near the Florida coast, they met the *Flamborough,* a British man-of-war that was conducting a reconnaissance for Oglethorpe. In the running battle that followed two Spanish galleys and a sloop ran aground. A boatload of British seamen attempted to plunder the sloop but were captured by Spanish soldiers from the beached galleys. The *Flamborough* ran to Charles Town for repairs and the Spanish vessels continued on to Saint Augustine.[6]

The main element of the fleet left Cuba on 26 May and was soon buffeted and dispersed by a storm that prevented their assembly at Saint Augustine until 4 June. Governor Montiano and his officers then spent a week finalizing plans for the attack on Saint Simons Island. They had excellent information concerning the southern portion of the island and the sound, but they knew practically nothing about the town and fort of Frederica or the routes leading to it. The army intended landing on the open beach on the southeastern side of the island and then attacking westward, severing communications between Frederica and Fort Saint Simons. Following the initial attack the fleet would sail into Saint Simons Sound and assist the landing force in destroying the garrison of Fort Saint Simons. The remainder of the campaign would be planned and conducted as events warranted.[7]

The Spanish army totaled about 1,950 officers and men. Regulars included two battalions of infantry, a regiment of dragoons, a small detachment of artillery gunners, all of whom were from Cuba, and six companies of pickets (provisional companies) from Saint Augustine. The dragoons were dismounted, but they carried their bridles and saddles, expecting to ride captured British horses. Militia included two battalions and six independent companies. Two companies were composed of Negroes, several of whom were escaped South Carolina slaves. A company of scouts and sixty Indians served as a reconnaissance force.[8]

By 10 June the expedition was ready to sail. The Saint Augustine contingent was to embark the following day and join the Cubans outside the harbor, but thunderstorms, winds, and a high sea prevented them from leaving the harbor for several days. Finally, at seven o'clock on the morning of 20 June the expedition of fifty-two men-of-war, schooners, sloops, galleys, half-galleys, piraguas, and other small boats set sail toward Georgia with a fair wind and high hopes.[9]

Numerous delays had caused the expedition to start very near the hurricane season. The following day, about half way to Saint Simons, a strong west-northwest wind caused the sea to run very high, forcing the smaller craft to separate from the fleet and seek shelter near the shore. Later that day about fifteen of the separated craft (four half-galleys, two schooners, and several piraguas) rendezvoused and attempted to run into Cumberland Sound to escape the wind. In the attempt they collided with the cannons of Fort Prince William and the schooner *Walker* that was anchored there. After exchanging cannon balls with the British for about an hour the Spanish boats sailed to the north end of Cumberland Island and anchored in the entrance of Saint Andrews Sound out of the range of Fort Saint Andrews's cannons.[10]

The next day, 22 June, a scout boat arrived at Frederica and reported the clash. General Oglethorpe immediately mounted a horse and rode to Fort Saint Simons. Seamen hanging onto the rigging of the merchant frigate *Success* anchored near the fort could see the Spanish boats in the mouth of Saint Andrews Sound ten miles to the south. Oglethorpe ordered his and Mackay's companies to march from Frederica to Fort Saint Simons, and he began preparations to move a large portion of the Forty-second Regiment to reinforce the forts on Cumberland Island where he expected a major Spanish attack.[11]

Oglethorpe would be more than courageous during the ensuing month; his actions would appear suicidal. He was only slightly depressed by the lack of support from the South Carolinians who had been heaping scorn upon him, but he was extremely dejected by what he considered his abandonment by the British government. With fewer than a thousand men, no men-of-war, and only a small amount of artillery, defeat must have appeared certain, but he was determined to inflict as much havoc as possible among the invading army.[12] Although a large portion of the Forty-second Regiment would prove unreliable, enough regulars and provincials would be inspired by his reckless courage to fight ferociously.

Two days later Oglethorpe completed preparations for the reinforcement of Cumberland Island and ordered Captain Horton to move his grenadier company and a party of Indians from Jekyll Island to Fort Saint Andrews. Shortly afterward Oglethorpe embarked portions of two companies of regulars into three scout boats and started down the Inland Passage, having ordered Major Heron to follow with a larger detachment of the regiment. Although Horton and his grenadiers seem to have reached Cumberland Island without incident, Oglethorpe and his little convoy, following shortly afterward, were not as fortunate. From the southern end of Jekyll Island south to Fort Saint Andrews is a distance of six and one-half miles across Saint Andrews Sound, a row of more than an hour. The Spanish vessels, anchored less than four miles to the southeast, immediately sighted the scout boats making their run across the sound. The crews of the Cuban half-galleys, the same boats that had plagued Oglethorpe in 1740, weighed anchor and began rowing and sailing to cut the scout boats off. Oglethorpe's marines pulled desperately on their oars but the scout boats were weighted down with soldiers and small field cannons. The Spanish half-galleys had the wind to their backs and were riding the tide, and within a short time the opposing craft were within range of one another. Lieutenant William Tolson of the Forty-second Regiment was the ranking officer in the last scout boat of the column. More than a hundred yards ahead of him Oglethorpe's small boat and a large Spanish half-galley belched white smoke and erupted with blasts from swivel guns. Certain that the first two scout boats would be destroyed, Tolson lost his nerve and ordered the coxswain to steer for the safety of Satilla River off the starboard side.

Although he was later placed under arrest for cowardice it must be pointed out that his craft, being last, was in the dangerous position of having to face all four of the half-galleys that were fast approaching. His evasion may have saved a scout boat and a large detachment of regulars. Oglethorpe's *Cutter* and the other scout boat fortunately slipped past the lead half-galley and pulled out of range before the Spanish craft could come about and give chase.[13]

When Oglethorpe arrived at Fort Saint Andrews he ordered the garrison of regulars to spike the cannons, gather their equipment, and withdraw to Fort Prince William. One fort was easier to defend than two; however, there is no indication of why Oglethorpe picked Fort Prince William, which was further removed from the headquarters at Frederica, unless Fort Saint Andrews was in worse condition and was tactically more difficult to defend. The abandonment was so hurried and incomplete that some of the cannons were left unspiked, several scores of hand grenades remained intact, and over fifty of the rangers' horses were left inside of a corral instead of being turned loose on the island.[14]

The battle in Saint Andrews Sound had been observed from ships' rigging at Fort Saint Simons, but the great distance and the gunpowder smoke obscured the results. The soldiers' fears that Oglethorpe and most of his men had perished were seemingly confirmed when Lieutenant Tolson returned the following morning. The shock was great, but Major Heron began taking immediate steps to increase his defenses. He and his officers wisely decided not to follow Oglethorpe's orders to reinforce Cumberland Island; it was no time to divide the remaining forces. He sent a request to Savannah for all the volunteers who could be recruited. An order was dispatched to Darien for the Highland Independent Company of Foot to assemble as many men as possible and move to Saint Simons Island. He wrote the South Carolina government two letters telling them of his plight.[15]

The next day, at Fort Prince William, Oglethorpe watched the Spanish boats fleeing past Cumberland Island toward Saint Augustine. They had been unable to make contact with the main fleet and probably believed they were in danger of being attacked by British ships. Thinking the danger to Fort Prince

William was past, Oglethorpe boarded the *Walker* and returned to Saint Simons Island with Captain George Dunbar's company, which had been serving as marines aboard the schooner. His arrival at Fort Saint Simons boosted the Georgians' morale tremendously; however, if they believed the danger to be past they were soon disappointed. On 28 June the main Spanish fleet of thirty-six ships and boats appeared on the horizon.[16]

The following afternoon the Spaniards anchored about ten to twelve miles northeast of Fort Saint Simons. Oglethorpe sent his schooner and a sloop out to reconnoiter the fleet, but they did not leave the protective range of the shore batteries. About sunset one of his large scout boats approached the fleet, but it turned back before coming into range. These demonstrations had some effect, for during the night two Spanish launches encountered one another in the darkness and nervously exchanged some swivel-gun fire before recognizing each other.[17]

When the winds stopped blowing on 1 July, Montiano decided to initiate a landing on the southeastern beaches of Saint Simons Island. The Spanish soldiers loaded into the small ships' boats, but while they were maneuvering into formation a sudden squall scattered them, forcing the landing's cancellation. It was apparent to Montiano that a landing on the open beach was too dangerous. The ships could not approach the shore to support the landing because of the risk of being driven aground by a sudden wind, and the small boats were in danger of capsizing in the high surf. The half-galleys and piraguas could have executed the landing, but most of them were still missing after being separated by the storm. However, the fleet could not sit in the open sea; any day a hurricane could appear. A more urgent problem was the lack of drinking water. After being at sea for more than a week all the smaller boats were out of water and were drawing daily rations of only a pint per man from the flagship and its supply ship. Montiano and his officers resolved to force their way boldly into Saint Simons Sound past the fort and conduct a landing on the southwestern end of the island in the calm of the harbor. High winds forced them to remain in the open sea for two more days until 4 July when Montiano took the fleet to within about five or six miles of the entrance of Saint Simons Sound where they anchored to wait out the night.[18]

Oglethorpe had used his time well. After arming volunteers, impressed men, and indentured servants he assigned them to the provincial companies, all of which were short of men. Another troop of rangers was organized by recruiting a few Frederica settlers and commandeering their horses and saddles from private owners. Practically nothing is known about this troop, but it may have been commanded by Captain Richard Kent who had been at Frederica for about two weeks with a few of his Augusta Rangers. Quartermaster Thomas Hunt's detachment of the Troop of English Rangers and half of Captain Thomas Jones's troop of rangers had been patrolling the beaches for several days. Lieutenant Robert Scroggs's detachment of English Rangers and Captain John Williams's troop of rangers were ferried over from the mainland. Captain Hugh Mackay, Jr., and his detachment of the Troop of Highland Rangers returned from Charles Town and the remainder of his troop, under Quartermaster Hugh Morrison, probably arrived from Darien along with Lieutenant Charles Mackay's Highland Independent Company of Foot. Captain Mark Carr's Marine Company of Boatmen came from his fort at the Hermitage. Oglethorpe gathered as many Indians as possible by giving lavish presents and promising more. Mary Mathews sent down a few of her Lower Creek kinsmen who were at Mount Venture, Squirrel King and his Chickasaw arrived from their town near Augusta, and Toonahowi (deceased Tomochichi's nephew) and a few Yamacraw had apparently been at Frederica for some time. In addition to the guard schooner *Walker* and the guard sloop *Faulcon* there were Captain William Thompson's heavily armed merchant frigate *Success* and eight privately owned sloops that had recently arrived with supplies. Oglethorpe commandeered all these vessels and impressed their civilian crews into his army. Of the Forty-second Regiment of Foot, only three companies and detachments of others, about three hundred men, were at Fort Saint Simons. The remainder of the regiment. about two hundred men belonging to Captain Horton's grenadier company and parts of three foot companies, remained at Fort Prince William. Oglethorpe's total fighting

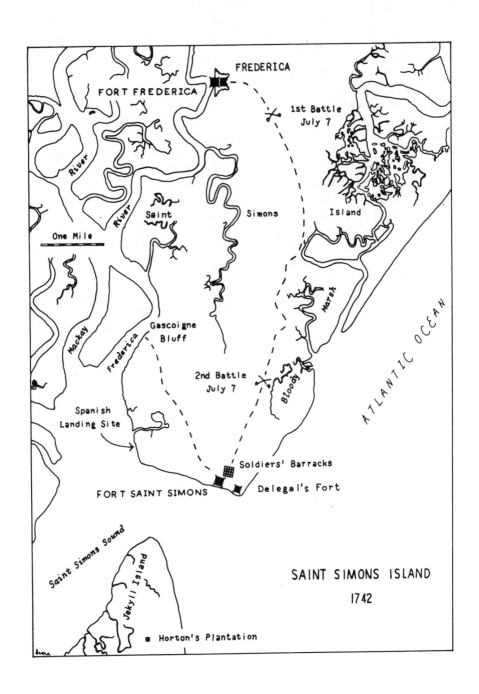

FREDERICA

FORT FREDERICA

1st Battle
July 7

River

Saint

Simons

Island

One Mile

Mackay

Frederica

Gascoigne
Bluff

Marsh

2nd Battle
July 7

Bloody

ATLANTIC OCEAN

Spanish
Landing Site

Soldiers' Barracks

Delegal's Fort

FORT SAINT SIMONS

Saint Simons Sound

Jekyll Island

SAINT SIMONS ISLAND

1742

● Horton's Plantation

force on Saint Simons Island was approximately five hundred men. On 4 July he spoke to each unit, urging them to stand by their liberties and their country, despite all odds.[19]

At seven o'clock on the morning of 5 July 1742 Governor Montiano signaled his fleet to begin the attack. After sailing to within about four miles of Fort Saint Simons they dropped anchor to await the afternoon tide. In the intervening time a galley and two half-galleys rowed into the entrance of Saint Simons Sound and spent several hours reconnoitering the channel while under fire from the British cannons. At three o'clock in the afternoon they rowed back to the fleet and reported the channel's course. The galley and two half-galleys then returned to the entrance of the sound where they spaced themselves along the channel and bravely anchored within range of the British cannons, serving as buoys for the fleet's entrance. The tide was coming in and a fresh breeze was blowing over a calm sea toward land.[20]

The British cannon crews, composed of regular soldiers, were standing by with loaded cannons and burning ropes. The nondescript flotilla of small British vessels was anchored near the shore to the west of Fort Saint Simons in a position to throw broadsides at the Spaniards as they passed.

About three-thirty or four o'clock in the afternoon the Spaniards weighed anchor and began running the gauntlet of British cannons with Montiano's flagship in the lead. The resulting exchange of fire was heavy, but the leading ships managed to enter the sound without much difficulty. A Spanish cannon ball struck one of the British heavy cannons, wrecking its carriage and causing casualities among its crew. The heavily armed Spanish ships in the lead turned on the British ships and boats that were anchored to the west of Fort Saint Simons. The sloop *Faulcon,* the smallest vessel in Georgia's navy, sank to the bottom of the sound with part of its hull shot away. A Spanish man-of-war attempted to come alongside and board the frigate *Success,* but was repulsed by the ship's cannons and musket fire from Captain Carr's marines and a detachment of regulars on board. Another Spanish ship attempted the same maneuver with the schooner *Walker,* but it was also driven off. The British gunners finally found the proper range and began scoring hits on the small Spanish vessels in the rear of the column. The last vessel had the misfortune to run aground where it served as a stationary target for British gunners until the tide lifted it free an hour later. By five-thirty the entire fleet was anchored in the north end of Saint Simons Sound near the mouth of Frederica River, safely beyond the range of the British batteries. The Spaniards reported only five men killed.[21]

Montiano did not take the time to gloat over his easy victory. The landing site he had chosen, a dry marsh just below Kings Creek and a mile and a half northwest of Fort Saint Simons, was nearly unoccupied except for small numbers of rangers and Indians who had arrived to observe the fleet. Montiano feared that if he waited until morning to conduct the landing Oglethorpe would occupy the area with soldiers and cannons during the night. At six o'clock in the evening Montiano's ship raised a red signal flag, ordering an immediate assault landing.[22]

The subsequent landing was executed with near perfection. The initial phase was under the command of Lieutenant Colonel Antonio Salgado, the same officer who had defeated the British at Fort Mosa two years before. His five hundred men disembarked from the ships in longboats and began rowing toward the landing site in the wake of the galley, two half-galleys, and a packet boat that swept the beach with cannon and swivel-gun fire, scattering the Georgia rangers and Indians. The supporting fires continued until seven o'clock when the first company of fifty men charged ashore and hurriedly established outposts in the woods beyond the marsh. Salgado and the remainder of his assault element landed immediately afterward.[23]

The second body of soldiers, mostly grenadiers, were not able to land until ten o'clock that night because of the outgoing tide and an unfavorable wind. By the time Governor Montiano and his staff stepped ashore an hour later about a thousand men had landed. Despite the darkness the entire army was ashore by morning. The landing was not entirely unopposed; a party of Indians made the first of their hit-and-run attacks during the night and carried off five men as prisoners for Oglethorpe's interrogation. Although the prisoners told Oglethorpe that Montiano had about five thousand men, the Spanish army on Saint Simons Island could not have included many more than fifteen hundred, for a large number of soldiers were on board the thirteen boats that remained separated from the fleet.[24]

While the Spaniards were landing, Oglethorpe was hurriedly evacuating the southern end of Saint Simons Island, preparing to retreat to Frederica before their route of escape was severed. His soldiers worked throughout the evening spiking cannons and throwing food and equipment into the sound. About midnight, when the wind shifted and began blowing to sea, he ordered the frigate *Success,* the schooner *Walker,* and a large South Carolina commercial sloop to fight their way out of the sound and make a run for Charles Town. They weighed anchor and sailed quietly past the Spanish galley that was intended to prevent their escape. Since the other boats were either too badly damaged, too lightly armed, or too undermanned to attempt a breakout, they were set on fire. Fortunately, most of the scout boats had previously been sent to Frederica. After the major work had been accomplished the regiment assembled and marched north along the trail to Frederica. Not long after midnight the British flag was lowered from Fort Saint Simons and the remainder of the British followed with Oglethorpe and the rangers bringing up the rear, carrying the numerous wounded and stragglers on their horses.[25]

On the Georgia mainland the settlers panicked. Women and children fled from Darien to Fort Argyle and beyond, while those from Savannah hastily sought refuge in Abercorn and other outlying settlements in an attempt to somehow evade the rape and pillage that they believed was imminent. Fear was only slightly less prevalent in South Carolina, for the real prize for any enemy fleet would have been the sacking of Charles Town. The assembly quickly called the militia to duty, began repairing the town's fortifications, authorized rangers to patrol the frontier, and ordered provincial vessels outfitted to accompany British men-of-war in an attack on the Spanish fleet. All quarrels with Georgia were temporarily forgotten.[26]

XIII

Oglethorpe's Revenge
July–September 1742

At daylight on 6 July 1742 Yemassee Indians were rummaging excitedly among Fort Saint Simons's spoils. Since Oglethorpe had abandoned the area during the darkness of the previous night, the destruction of useful items had been incomplete and a large quantity of weapons, equipment, livestock, and food remained intact. Three wounded seamen had been unfortunately overlooked and left behind to the Spaniards' mercy. The Indians immediately killed and scalped one of the men who threatened them with his sword, but they ignored the other two for the weapons and equipment. These two men were later captured by Spanish soldiers and were given decent treatment. At four o'clock in the morning, after a few Indians reported to Montiano that Fort Saint Simons was vacant, two companies of grenadiers were sent southeast along the beach to verify the information. The entire Spanish army followed two hours later.[1]

The Spaniards spent the remainder of 6 July posting guards, making camp, and inventorying the spoils at Fort Saint Simons. To the staff's dismay the soldiers inadvertently burned several buildings containing a large quantity of food and some cattle and goats that had been penned up. That night Oglethorpe's Indian allies struck again, killing a dragoon and a Yemassee Indian.[2]

Montiano was in a hurry to finish Oglethorpe off, but he did not know which of several trails led to the British headquarters at Frederica, six miles to the north. At six o'clock on Wednesday morning, 7 July, he dispatched Captain Nicholas

Hernández with twenty-five men of his scout company and forty Yemassee Indians to discover the Frederica trail. At the same time Captain Sebastian Sánchez set out with a company of fifty regulars to reconnoiter the road, present Kings Way, leading to Gascoigne Bluff where Montiano intended to disembark his field artillery.[3]

Captain Sánchez and his company almost immediately took a wrong branch of the road to the bluff and, after walking in a half circle to the right, they stumbled on the trail to Frederica where they met Captain Hernández's company. The two captains joined forces and continued the reconnaissance toward Frederica with Sánchez in command. For four and one-half miles the narrow trail skirted the savannah marshlands on the eastern side of the island, turning northwest through higher, wooded ground toward Frederica during the remaining three and a quarter miles. The Spaniards made good progress. Before nine o'clock they were within a mile and a half of Frederica.[4]

William Small, one of Georgia's most experienced rangers, and four other rangers of Captain Thomas Jones's troop of South Carolinians were patrolling the trail. About a mile and a half from Frederica the rangers suddenly reined to a stop, face-to-face with the lead element of the Spanish force. The Spaniards and Indians dived for cover while the rangers wheeled their horses around, exchanging shots. A lead ball from one of the Spaniards' muskets went through Small's leg and deep into his horse. Horse and rider floundered in the trail while the Indians swarmed over them with their hatchets.[5]

The four surviving rangers raced to Frederica where they fearfully reported that the Spaniards were almost at the town gate. Oglethorpe mistakenly assumed that the Spanish reconnoitering party was the advance party for Montiano's entire army. He ordered Captain Raymond Demere's company of the Forty-second Regiment, which was on standby as the reserve guard, to prepare to march. But there was no time to wait for Demere's company to assemble; Oglethorpe intended to attack the Spaniards on the narrow trail before they could reach the cleared area near the town and place their units in formation. The Highland Company, mustering between thirty and forty men, was the only infantry unit in formation prepared to march. Oglethorpe commandeered a horse and began leading the Highlanders out of the town gate and down the trail at a run. He was quickly joined by Captain Thomas Jones with his rangers, Toonahowi and a party of Yamacraw and Creek, Lieutenant Scroggs and a detachment of English Rangers, and Captain William Gray of South Carolina with a party of Squirrel King's Chickasaw from near Augusta. Running a long distance during a July day in Georgia is exhausting, especially if you are carrying about twenty-five pounds of weapons and equipment; nevertheless, six Highlanders and most of the Indians managed to keep up with the galloping rangers.[6]

About a mile southeast of Frederica, as the disordered body of provincials and Indians rounded a slight bend in the wood-enclosed trail, they saw the Spaniards' lead element on the other side of a small open savannah to their front. Captain Sánchez was moving his reconnoitering party toward a nearby creek bed that he intended to use as a defensive position. Without hesitating, Oglethorpe spurred his horse toward them. For the Chickasaw, Yamacraw, Creek, and Highlanders, all warlike by tradition, the charge represented life at its best. If the rangers felt the rising temperature of fear they had little time to reflect upon it; they swept the lead element aside and collided with the main body of Spanish regulars, scouts, and Indians. Oglethorpe and his followers never relinquished the momentum they gained from their surprising charge. Two Spaniards threw down their weapons and surrendered to Oglethorpe who was at the head of his men. Toonahowi, wounded in his right arm, drew a pistol with his left hand and killed a Spanish officer who was threatening him. Lieutentant Scroggs plunged his horse into the milling Spaniards and forced the surrender of their commander, Captain Sánchez. Captain Hernández was captured shortly afterward. The Spaniards' resistance disintegrated and they began stumbling wildly into the woods and back along the trail. Oglethorpe and the rangers pursued a party of fleeing Spaniards about three and a half miles before calling a halt to wait for Mackay's Highlanders and Demere's regulars to catch up. The Creek, Chickasaw, some Highlanders, and a few rangers remained near the battle site, running down the terrified survivors. The Spaniards suffered thirty-six men killed, captured, or missing, and most of the remainder were temporarily lost in the woods and thickets. The British lost one man, a Highlander, from heat exhaustion.[7]

Oglethorpe, expecting that Montiano would soon send units to counterattack, decided to position the soldiers to block the trail against any Spanish advance while he returned to Frederica to assemble the remainder of his army for a "showdown" battle with Montiano. The position Oglethorpe selected to block the trail was between four and a half and five miles south-southeast of Frederica on the western edge of present Bloody Marsh. He placed Captain Demere and his company of about sixty regulars, who had just arrived from Frederica, on the left (east) side of the trail and the Highland Company and the rangers, about forty-five to fifty men, on the right (west) side. A branch of Bloody Marsh, an open savannah perhaps a hundred yards wide, lay perpendicular to their front (south). The trail crossed this spongy marsh on a narrow causeway of brush and logs and led into the dense woods between the British positions. While Oglethorpe returned to Frederica the regulars and provincials prepared their blocking position by building several small piles of fallen logs and limbs in the tree line as protection from Spanish musket balls.[8]

Meanwhile, a few Spaniards of the defeated reconnoitering party arrived at Fort Saint Simons about noon and reported the clash. Montiano reacted quickly by ordering Captain Antonio Barba to take three companies of grenadiers, probably between 150 and 200 men, and march to the battle site in order to protect the withdrawal of the members of the reconnoitering party, most of whom were scattered in the dense woods. The relief force set out and began picking up stragglers from the reconnoitering party as they marched north. Clouds had been gathering and now a light steady rain began to fall.[9]

About three o'clock in the afternoon Captain Barba's grenadiers began crossing a narrow causeway spanning a marsh. A few survivors of the defunct reconnoitering party, who were acting as guides, noticed some piles of brush and logs situated in the woods on the far side of the marsh which they could not remember having seen before. Barba called a halt and sent a few men forward to investigate. When they drew near the far side of the marsh the brush and trees on both sides of the trail suddenly erupted with the blasts and smoke from dozens of muskets. Several Spaniards were cut down while running to the rear. Barba formed his three companies inside the cover of the trees on the south side of the marsh and began placing a disciplined fire on the British positions. A steady drizzle of rain held the smoke close to the ground, obscuring the scene. The Spaniards were shouting and their drummers were loudly beating Barba's commands. Demere's regulars became excited and a few turned and fled. They were soon followed by more. Finally, three whole platoons broke and ran along with Captain Demere and another officer.[10]

At Frederica, Oglethorpe was forming the regiment, Carr's Marine Company, and the other troops of rangers when he heard the distant firing. After ordering the units to follow, he spurred his horse toward the battle. About two miles north of the marsh he met Captain Demere and the three fugitive platoons who informed him that the entire force had been routed; however, Oglethorpe could still hear firing and ordered them to return with him to the marsh. An officer, whose identity is unknown, disobeyed and continued toward Frederica.[11]

Half of the British force had held courageously. To the left of the trail Lieutenant Patrick Sutherland and Sergeant John Stewart of Demere's company had somehow managed to hold a platoon of about fifteen men in place. To the right Lieutenant Charles Mackay's Highland Company and the rangers seem not to have ever considered leaving the battle. For about an hour Sutherland's and Mackay's outnumbered soldiers continued firing steadily across the marsh at the Spanish grenadiers.[12]

The Spaniards were unaware that almost half of the British force had fled. About four o'clock, after firing all their ammunition, Captain Barba formed the three companies into marching order and began an orderly retreat to Fort Saint Simons. They reported an officer and six men killed, probably in the first few seconds of the fight, and two wounded men had been captured.[13]

The Spaniards had just completed their withdrawal when Oglethorpe arrived. His elation is easy to imagine, for if the entire British force had been routed the effect on the morale of both regulars and provincials could have been disastrous. Instead, the brave stand by the soldiers under Sutherland and Mackay made the Spaniards seem less ominous and gave

Oglethorpe's army new-found courage. Captain Demere's abashed regulars arrived soon after in company with Captain Carr's marines and another platoon of the regiment. Before evening about half of the Forty-second Regiment, the troops of rangers, and most of the Indians had assembled at the marsh. Oglethorpe and his army cautiously advanced to within about a mile and a half of Fort Saint Simons where they spent the night sleeping on the trail. At dawn Oglethorpe dispatched Indian scouts who soon returned and reported that the Spaniards had withdrawn into their fortifications. Oglethorpe saw little hope of enticing Montiano into a battle in the open so he marched the army back to Frederica, arriving there about noon. Captain Horton's grenadier company, two foot companies, and the Fort Saint Andrews garrison arrived at about the same time from Fort Prince William after crossing Saint Simons Sound in full view of the Spaniards. Oglethorpe's force on Saint Simons Island, which now numbered between seven hundred and eight hundred men, worked frantically to improve Frederica's defenses.[14]

Montiano and his soldiers were as stunned as Oglethorpe and his army had been after their defeat at Fort Mosa two years before. The two battles on the Frederica trail had not been catastrophes; the Spaniards had suffered losses of perhaps 10 percent of the units involved. Nevertheless, the effect on morale was tremendous. Two well-armed parties had entered the dark narrow trail and had been thrown back, both within the space of five hours. During the first battle a Spanish force had been almost trampled by a nondescript group composed of a few horsemen, a half-dozen white men in skirts, and numerous painted Indians. The second battle, the "Grenadier Fight," had been fought with a British force that was completely hidden in the woods.[15]

Although later accounts of the day's activities credit the second battle, now called the Battle of Bloody Marsh, as having the greater impact, the first battle actually inflicted the greater loss and shock to the Spaniards. The second battle was significant, however, for the fact that the British soldiers had won an engagement without Oglethorpe's personal leadership, and it is perhaps for this reason that he commented so favorably on its outcome.[16] British estimates of Spanish losses for both battles ranged between 150 and 200, probably about four times their actual number. It has always been and will always be the custom of soldiers to overestimate grossly their enemy's casualties.

Oglethorpe's rangers and Indian allies began a deadly watch over the Spanish camp, ambushing stragglers and small parties. During 7 and 8 July they killed eight men. The Spanish-allied Yemassee Indians were afraid to patrol too deeply in the woods because of the British-allied Indians. In addition, they had enriched themselves with plunder and were ready to return to Saint Augustine and celebrate. The Spaniards were soon forced to fortify their outposts as protection against the Indian raids.[17]

Spanish morale began to plummet. The sight of the ragged half-starved survivors from the defeated reconnoitering party which continued to arrive at Fort Saint Simons was extremely disconcerting (two days after the battle Captain Hernández arrived in camp, having escaped his captors). The hurricane season could begin any day, making travel on the open sea extremely dangerous. They were sure that the British vessels that had escaped four days ago had spread the news of the invasion and a relief fleet of the British navy could be expected shortly. Ever in the backs of their minds was the stern warning of the governor of Cuba that the safe withdrawal of the army and fleet must be assured.[18]

On 9 July, Montiano held a council of war with his discouraged officers. Since an attack up the only trail to Frederica was impractical, they decided to reconnoiter the river leading to Frederica in order to determine the feasibility of moving the soldiers and artillery by boat to the vicinity of the British headquarters. On the morning of 10 or 11 July a naval lieutenant took the galley and two half-galleys on a reconnaissance up the Frederica River. When they arrived in sight of Fort Frederica they were greeted by cannon balls roaring over their heads and mortar bombs exploding in the river beside them. The Spaniards came about and rowed downriver with Oglethorpe and a number of scout boats in pursuit. They had not had time to conduct an adequate reconnaissance.[19]

About this time Samuel Cloake, a seaman from the man-of-war

Flamborough, whom the Spaniards had captured during the sea battle off Florida in May, escaped from a Spanish ship and made his way to Frederica. He reported that the Spaniards were "down-hearted," they were terrified of the British allied Indians, and the Cuba and Florida contingents were bickering with one another. Oglethorpe seems to have been previously unaware of the great impact the two British victories of 7 July were having on Spanish morale, but he need only to have reflected on the mood of his own army following the defeat at Fort Mosa two years earlier in order to assess the Spaniards' present mood.[20]

Oglethorpe wisely decided to conduct a night raid against a portion of the Spanish camp in order to terrify them further. On the evening of 12 July he marched south with a five-hundred-man raiding force consisting of half of the Forty-second Regiment, the Highland Company, Captain Carr's Marine Company, and two troops of rangers. Just before two o'clock the next morning they quietly halted about a mile and a half north of Fort Saint Simons while a scouting party was sent forward to reconnoiter the Spanish camp. During the halt a Frenchman, apparently a civilian seaman who had recently been impressed into Carr's Marine Company, pulled the trigger on his musket, shattering the night's silence with the resulting shot. Whether the discharge was accidental or intended is unknown, but in either case he knew he would receive severe punishment for alerting the Spaniards. He ran into the woods, arriving at the Spanish camp an hour later. Oglethorpe realized that an attempted raid against the alerted camp could be disastrous; therefore, after the British drummers taunted the Spaniards by beating the "Grenadiers' March" for half an hour, the raiding force returned to Frederica.[21]

That same morning Oglethorpe cunningly sent a letter via a freed Spanish prisoner to the Frenchman. The letter alluded to a mythical conspiracy between them and instructed the Frenchman to understate the British strength. In addition, he was instructed to offer to pilot the Spanish boats up the Frederica River into a British ambush. As planned, the letter was immediately waylaid and given to Montiano. Thus, even though the Frenchman gave the Spaniards accurate information, they were suspicious of him. Nevertheless, his statement that help was expected shortly from the British colonies to the north reminded them that this was a real danger.[22]

A great fear began to take shape in Montiano's mind. A coordinated attack by Oglethorpe's army and a British fleet might destroy his invasion force and make the safe withdrawal of the Spanish ships and men impossible. About twelve-thirty in the afternoon his apprehension was greatly increased when five British ships from South Carolina appeared to the north. Both Montiano and his officers fearfully assumed that these vessels were the advance guard for a larger fleet. After a brief conference with his principal officers Montiano ordered an immediate retreat. The larger ships of the fleet were to leave by the open sea while the army under Montiano was to take the boats down the Inland Passage to Saint Augustine, destroying Forts Saint Andrews and Prince William on the way. The Spaniards were in a great hurry to leave Georgia; by late afternoon they had finished razing Fort Saint Simons and most of the army had been ferried across the sound to Jekyll Island. At sunset the ships sailed out of Saint Simons Sound and the boats started down Jekyll River.[23]

By the morning of 15 July they had ferried the army from the southern end of Jekyll Island to Fort Saint Andrews on Cumberland Island. They burned the abandoned fort and exterminated the herd of horses penned there. Early on 17 July, Montiano divided his force; the schooners, sloops, and other boats sailed to Florida by the open sea while he took four half-galleys and a number of piraguas, which had just rejoined him after being separated since 21 July, down Cumberland River toward Fort Prince William.[24]

Sixty men of Major Heron's company and a detachment of rangers, all under the immediate command of Lieutenant Alexander Stewart, were garrisoning Fort Prince William. They were entirely ignorant of what had taken place on Saint Simons Island, but they probably feared the worst. Therefore, on 16 July, Oglethorpe landed a messenger on the northern tip of Cumberland Island in plain sight of the Spaniards. He ran the length of the island to Fort Prince William and informed Stewart of the Spaniards' defeat and ordered him to resist the Spaniards' attacks until Oglethorpe arrived with reinforcements.[25] Oglethorpe's message probably gave the garrison the necessary courage to prevent their destruction.

When Montiano approached the southern end of Cumberland Island on the morning of 18 July he attempted to land two hundred men with orders to attack Fort Prince William's flimsy defenses. Eight rangers, seven from Jones's troop and one from the English troop, rode out of Fort Prince William's stockade and began firing at the boats from behind a sand dune. Misjudging the defenders' strength, Montiano canceled the landing. The half-galleys continued to the vicinity of Fort Prince William and began trading cannon balls with Lieutenant Stewart's garrison. After an hour of bombardment, during which some damage was inflicted on the fort's stockade, Montiano led his boats out of the sound into the open sea and sailed for Florida.[26]

That same day Oglethorpe loaded his provincial rangers and marines into a flotilla of scout boats and moved south on the Inland Passage toward Fort Prince William. Lieutenant Noble Jones had probably arrived shortly before from Savannah with his Marine Company, adding his little craft to the scout-boat flotilla. On 20 July, Oglethorpe stopped briefly at Fort Prince William and then continued on to Florida to determine the location of Montiano's army. The Georgians landed briefly on the south bank of the Saint Johns River where they burned several palmetto huts in an old Spanish camp and carried off two large cedar crosses for souvenirs. By 22 July they had returned to Frederica.[27]

A relief fleet from Charles Town, consisting of 4 British naval ships and 8 armed provincial vessels, having a total of 1,092 men and 144 large cannons, arrived off Saint Simons Island on 26 July. However, on 30 July, Captain Charles Hardy took his ship, the *Rye*, and all the other vessels, except two South Carolina provincial galleys, back to Charles Town because of unfavorable winds and the likelihood of a Spanish attack against South Carolina. Captain Hardy returned to Georgia on 14 August after being berated by the South Carolina Council for his lack of action, and within ten days a fleet had assembled consisting of six British men-of-war, six armed vessels from South Carolina and Georgia, and Georgia's marine scout boats. Oglethorpe was understandably bitter about the lack of previous support from the Royal Navy and South Carolina; nevertheless, he intended to take advantage of the fleet's presence by conducting a punitive counterattack against Saint Augustine.[28]

To Governor Montiano's dismay Oglethorpe's fleet appeared off Saint Augustine Harbor on 27 August. Two days later, British ships' boats, Georgia scout boats, and South Carolina galleys began riding the incoming tide toward the entrance to the harbor under the covering fire of the men-of-war. Their objective was to destroy the hated six Cuban half-galleys, lying just inside the harbor, and the lookout on Anastasia Island. The Cuban half-galleys' gunners had not lost their skill. One man was killed in the scout boat in which Oglethorpe was a passenger, two were wounded, and the boat's boom was shot away by a nine-pounder ball. When Major Heron tried to land his element on Anastasia Island the high surf capsized a number of boats. At nightfall the attacking boats withdrew to the protection of the men-of-war.[29]

The following day the British anchored to the south near Matanzas Inlet. Oglethorpe decided to destroy a large stone blockhouse that the Spaniards were building on an island just inside the inlet (present Fort Matanzas National Monument). On 30 August he personally took two scout boats and sounded the entrance to the inlet, discovering that the surf was too high to conduct a landing. It appears that one of the blockhouse cannons made a skillful hit on one of the scout boats, and its crew was barely able to row to a man-of-war before it sank. The surf continued high and the following day the appearance of an even stronger wind forced Oglethorpe to abandon the counterattack and sail for home.[30]

Oglethorpe and his men returned to Frederica on 4 September 1742, exhausted after ten weeks of campaigning but flushed with pride and self-confidence. Oglethorpe had finally retaliated for the defeat and personal shame he had suffered in Florida during 1740. With considerable gratification he wrote, "We have had some Satisfaction for the Blood at Moosa."[31]

Oglethorpe was unquestionably a true hero, one of those rare men who, with forethought, commit acts of great personal danger. It could be said that his bravery was deliberately designed to serve as an example for his regular and provincial soldiers whose courage was doubtful, that his love for Britain inspired him, or that a psychological depression caused by a feeling that defeat was certain compelled him to suicidal actions. All three factors and others effected him to some extent; however, if one analyzes his previous record it becomes evident that he was always in the vanguard of every skirmish within his vicinity, regardless of the possible compelling circumstances. Quite frankly, Oglethorpe loved to fight. He had not engaged in a bloodletting tavern brawl since he was twenty-six years old—he was a gentleman—but close combat with an enemy was acceptable behavior. Whether questionable or admirable, his fondness for the excitement of battle was chiefly responsible for the Spaniards' defeat. Granted, Frederica's location, surrounded by thick forests and marshes, was tactically excellent, and it is also true that nature's wind and sea had favored British arms. However, if Oglethorpe and his soldiers had cowered behind their earthen walls the Spaniards would probably have put them to the sword, and by September most of the settlements north to Beaufort, South Carolina, would likely have been in flames. Based upon their previous and subsequent combat records, there is little reason to believe that either the regulars or the provincials would have taken offensive action without Oglethorpe's leadership.

XIV

Raid and Counterraid

1742–1743

General Oglethorpe believed the Spaniards would soon return and attempt a conquest of Georgia and South Carolina,[1] a conviction that was reinforced by an incident at Mount Venture near the Altamaha River in early November 1742.

Lieutenant William Francis had continued to command the Mount Venture garrison of rangers following the death of Captain Jacob Mathews. In October 1742 the unit became a detachment of the Troop of English Rangers, and Francis became lieutenant of the troop, assuming the position formerly held by Robert Scroggs who was promoted to Captain. Without Captain Mathews's bad influence Francis apparently developed into a fair officer. However, in early November 1742 he made the mistake of going to Frederica with fourteen of his men, leaving only four rangers and an Indian servant to guard the trading fort containing his German wife and new baby.[2]

In the early morning hours of 7 November a war party of Yemassee Indians quietly surrounded the trading fort and attacked it at dawn. After exchanging musket fire with the rangers for two hours the Indians succeeded in setting the main house on fire. The rangers had no doubt of the eventual outcome; the nearest friendly soldiers were at Fort Argyle, fifty miles to the east. After being promised that they would not be killed, the rangers laid down their arms and walked out of the stockade. The Yemassee generously left Mrs. Francis and her child unharmed at Mount Venture and set out on the southward trail toward Saint Augustine with their prisoners. Within a short time, however, the warriors' attitude underwent a drastic change from generosity to savagery. The cause is unknown, but some incident apparently provoked them into an intense rage. The war party halted and two rangers, Mark McNeal and George Bigwall, were suddenly killed. Several Indians then ran back to Mount Venture where they caught Mrs. Francis and her baby and tomahawked them to death. When their violent emotions subsided they continued toward Saint Augustine.[3]

Nottoway, a Florida Indian who had been captured during his youth and sold into slavery (probably to Mary Mathews) pretended friendship with his Yemassee captors. On the fifth day of his captivity, when they allowed him to go hunting by himself, he escaped and brought news of the disaster to Oglethorpe. Solomon Shad and Joseph Upjber, the other prisoners, were delivered to Saint Augustine where they were placed on display.[4]

Nottoway reported that his captors had bragged about the great numbers of Spaniards who were gathering at Saint Augustine for another invasion of Georgia. Oglethorpe began a new campaign to raise additional forces. The ranger troops and garrisons were ordered to increase their strength to a total of 173 men. In February 1743 Captain John Williams returned overland from a recruiting mission in Virginia and North Carolina with thirty volunteer horsemen. Initially there were more, but during the trip eight of the new rangers changed their minds and deserted. Oglethorpe's most ambitious recruiting project was the organization of a second battalion for the Forty-second Regiment of Foot. Brevet Lieutenant Colonel Alexander Heron was dispatched to the Virginia-Maryland border where he enlisted 211 men, uniformed them in red coats, and brought them to Georgia where they served from December 1742 to October 1743.[5]

The Spaniards had set a precedent when they perpetrated the raid on Mount Venture by giving their Indian allies the necessary courage to conduct additional raids against Georgia's settlements. During the first week of February 1743 another Yemassee war party penetrated Georgia's frontier defenses and crossed the Altamaha River. Fortunately, they were detected and a large party of rangers and Indian trackers set out in pursuit, forcing them to retreat before causing any damage.[6]

While the Yemassee Indians were increasing their attacks against Georgia the British-allied Indians had become reluctant to conduct raids into Florida. Spanish dragoons stationed in Saint Augustine had repulsed every Indian war party that Oglethorpe had lately dispatched. However, the British suddenly received an unforseen bonus as a result of renewed raids of the Yemassee; the Creek appeared to be on the verge of abandoning their twenty-five year tradition of neutrality. During the latter part of 1742 the Lower Creek had apparently been leaning toward the Spaniards, but after the Yemassee destruction of Mary Mathews's Mount Venture trading post, Chigelley, the Lower Creek principal mico, dispatched a large war party to Oglethorpe's assistance in order to avenge his kinswoman.[7]

Oglethorpe decided that the only way to discourage the Spaniards and to encourage his Indian allies would be to conduct a major punitive raid into Florida. During the latter part of February 1743 he assembled and inspected a detachment of about two hundred regulars from the Forty-second Regiment, which included a portion of Captain William Horton's granadier company, part of a foot company (Captain George Dunbar's) under acting company commander Lieutenant James Wall, detachments of other foot companies, and some of the Virginia recruits. Captain Robert Scroggs with part of his English Rangers and Captain John Williams's troop of rangers loaded their horses aboard the schooner *Walker* and two civilian schooners that had been hired to transport the raiding force. On Sunday, 27 February, the regulars and rangers sailed from Frederica down the Inland Passage under the command of Captain Horton. While the schooners were struggling to negotiate the water passage around Cumberland Island, they were passed by several scout boats and piraguas carrying General Oglethorpe and his escort, Captain Mark Carr with a detachment of his Marine Company of Boatmen, Lieutenant Charles Mackay and part of his Highland Independent Company of Foot, the Virginia recruits of the Forty-second Regiment, and seventy Lower Creek warriors.[8]

On 3 and 4 March the granadiers and rangers disembarked temporarily on Amelia Island while the remainder of the raiding force landed on Cumberland Island at Fort Prince William on the opposite side of Cumberland Sound. The fort had recently been rebuilt by adding a high thick wall of sand retained by logs. Two large cannons were mounted on movable platforms inside a triangular ravelin in front of the fort.[9]

About noon on 4 March, Oglethorpe embarked all the provincial soldiers and Virginia recruits in the scout boats and set out to reconnoiter and secure a landing site on the south bank of the Saint Johns River. Two days later, after establishing a camp near present Mayport, Florida, he ordered the soldiers of the Forty-second Regiment to join him. They arrived at the camp on 9 March and received a briefing on the mission and a ration of beer.[10]

Meanwhile, the Creek warriors had moved out of the Saint Johns River camp with the purpose of taking a few prisoners. After quietly approaching Saint Augustine they prepared an ambush on the western bank of the Diego River between Fort San Marcos and abandoned Fort Mosa. A Spanish piragua loaded with about forty pioneers (engineer soldiers) had the misfortune to sail quite close to the river bank where the Creek were concealed. When the piragua drew abreast of the ambush site the Indians fired a point-blank volley of musket fire into the closely packed soldiers. At least one of the Spaniards maintained a measure of self-control and immediately returned fire, killing one Indian. The remainder of the terrified soldiers responded naturally by pushing and shoving their way to the opposite side of the boat, causing the long narrow piragua to turn over. The Creek dragged five of the Spaniards from the river and immediately killed, mutilated, and scalped them. With one of their number dead the Creek were giving no quarter. Other soldiers probably drowned in the river. Before the warriors could kill more Spaniards the gunners in Fort San Marcos began firing cannon balls in their direction, forcing them to retreat.[11]

During their return to the Saint Johns River camp the Creek brazenly identified their route by setting fire to large areas of forest and savannah. The ambush had taken Governor Montiano and his people by surprise and they probably watched despondently as the gray smoke from the numerous fires rose skyward, giving the impression that the whole countryside was burning.[12]

On the afternoon of 11 March the cocky Creek warriors

approached the British camp singing, whooping, and firing their muskets and pistols. General Oglethorpe was majestically seated on a buffalo robe surrounded by his officers, prepared to offer a reception designed to please the pompous Creek. The warriors displayed five scalps, a severed hand, and a few severed arms. Oglethorpe later reported that they had killed about forty Spaniards, a traditional exaggeration. He shook the hand of each warrior and thanked him in the Muskogee language. Afterwards he wined and dined the micos, hoping to persuade them to accompany his soldiers on a march to Saint Augustine in an attempt to entice the Spaniards into an ambush; however, the Indians wanted to return home with their trophies. Three days later most of them left for Frederica. Only Toonahowi, the loyal Yamacraw, and three others remained.[13]

Despite the need for additional Indian scouts Oglethorpe was determined to march to Saint Augustine and try to provoke Governor Montiano into attacking him. At three o'clock on the afternoon of 14 March he assembled a raiding force that probably numbered between two and three hundred regulars and provincials and began marching south along the sea beach, leaving a small party of regulars to guard the boats. Oglethorpe and the rangers rode ahead as the advance party, the other provincials and regulars comprised the main body, and the Virginia recruits marched in the rear.[14]

After less than an hour of marching, the column was halted on the beach and each man received a pint of beer, which had been delivered by a boat, to lighten his step. The relationship between Oglethorpe and the soldiers of his regiment was more harmonious than it had ever been because of their victory over the Spaniards during the previous summer. Ogelthorpe had completely regained his confidence and the soldiers were responding positively to his excellent leadership. He also enjoyed increased rapport with his officers and he conducted frequent training seminars during which he gave them instructions in various military subjects. He kept the regiment busy and well trained, believing that idle and poorly trained soldiers perform badly in battle and can easily become disloyal to their officers. Oglethorpe shared his own personal provisions with his officers and he continued to be generous with rations of

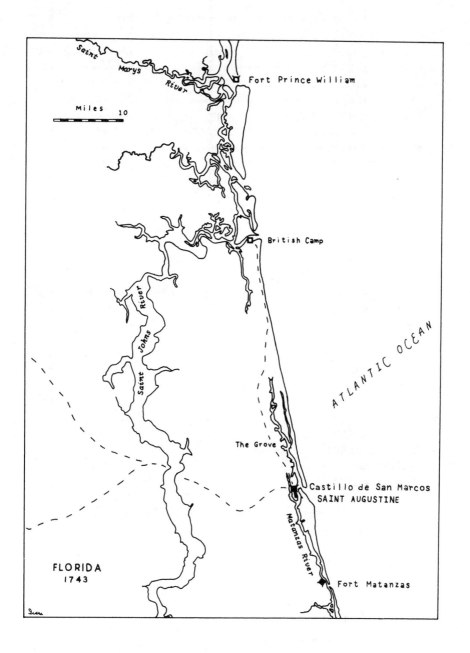

Fort Prince William

Miles 10

British Camp

ATLANTIC OCEAN

Saint Marys River

Saint Johns River

The Grove

Castillo de San Marcos
SAINT AUGUSTINE

Matanzas River

FLORIDA
1743

Fort Matanzas

beer. He had long required his officers to follow a practice that would not have gone unnoticed among the soldiers; while on campaign officers were required to live much like their men, marching on foot and carrying their own knapsacks of provisions and canteens of water. In Oglethorpe's army the few available horses were for mounting rangers and carrying the sick. Oglethorpe made a point of serving as an example to his men. When the soldiers complained about the brackish water and the souring beef he drank and ate nothing else, pretending satisfaction. Later, when some Indians rudely appropriated his cabin aboard the schooner *Walker* he pretended not to notice and slept on the open deck to quiet his soldiers' grumblings about the Indians' disrespect. However, despite his polished leadership, he was quick to punish offenses with the severe measures traditional for that age. After two thirsty soldiers broke ranks and ran to a stream of water he had them tied neck to heels as punishment for their lack of discipline. Perhaps because of such severe measures, a few regulars continued to desert to the Spaniards.[15]

On the morning of 15 March the raiding force left the beach and marched along the road to the deserted ruins of Fort Diego. The entire countryside north and west of Saint Augustine had remained unpopulated by the Spaniards since 1740 because of the danger of British and Indian raids. Marching in north Florida was no easier than it had been three years before. Sand got into shoes and wore blisters, at night the heavy dew caused the blowing sand to stick to skin and clothing, and hot days created a terrible thirst that could not be relieved by the brackish water. Several of the Virginia recruits became exhausted and were sent back to the camp on the Saint Johns River. Others, who collapsed, were allowed to ride the rangers' horses for a time.[16]

At noon on 16 March the raiding force stopped at the Grove to allow the soldiers' to quench their terrible thirst and to rest during the heat of the day. At five o'clock they continued on, reaching a point about three miles north of Saint Augustine by eight o'clock in the evening. They moved off the road and lay down to sleep. About three o'clock the following morning one of the sentries could not be found and it was assumed that he had deserted. Since Oglethorpe feared that he might lead a Spanish force to their location, everyone was roused from their sleep and marched northward for about four hours. He halted the raiding force at daybreak and placed them in ambush positions around a marsh on their back trail hoping to surprise the Spanish force that was expected to follow. After waiting a short while Oglethorpe became impatient and led half a dozen rangers boldly toward Saint Augustine to entice the Spaniards into his ambush. When the Spanish outguards sighted him they retreated into the town and, although he rode contemptuously near the town's walls, Governor Montiano would not order his dragoons to give chase. After a while Oglethorpe grew discouraged and returned to his concealed soldiers who were suffering from thirst and insect bites.[17]

Despite the physical discomforts Oglethorpe planned to keep his raiding force hidden for at least three days, during which time he hoped to lure the Spaniards into the ambush. However, that night another soldier of the Forty-second Regiment, a private named Eels, deserted to the Spaniards with information regarding the raiding force's strength and disposition. Oglethorpe ordered an immediate withdrawal to their camp on the Saint Johns River. After a brutal forced march with Oglethorpe and the rangers guarding the rear, carrying a few exhausted soldiers on their horses, the raiding force arrived at their camp on the afternoon of 18 March and prepared to depart for home.[18]

During the following day the rangers were transported across the Saint Johns River and began their long ride home, while Lieutenant Charles Mackay and his Highland Company were sent on a reconnaissance up the river in their scout boat *Darien.* Twenty fresh Creek Indian warriors, who had arrived on the previous day, set out toward Saint Augustine in an attempt to secure a few scalps; however, they returned after four days, having been defeated by a force of Yemassee during a small skirmish at the Grove. Seventy additional warriors—Cherokee, Upper Creek, and Lower Creek—arrived on 20 March. Five days later fifty of those Indians marched toward Saint Augustine with the hope of avenging the first war party's defeat, but neither the Yemassee nor the Spaniards would offer them battle.[19]

A naval patrol consisting of the British man-of-war *Rye,* South

Carolina's *Charles Town Galley,* and Georgia's frigate *Success* anchored near the camp on 21 May. Oglethorpe, discouraged for not having inflicted any damage on the Spaniards, proposed to Captain Charles Hardy, commander of the *Rye,* that he assist in landing a raiding force on Anastasia Island near Saint Augustine. The Spaniards kept all their cattle on the island and Oglethorpe intended to destroy them in order to deprive Saint Augustine of part of its food supply. But Captain Hardy was not eager for action and refused to participate.[20]

Determined to raid the island even if he had to use his own small vessels, Oglethorpe embarked over eighty men, half of whom were Indians, in the schooner *Walker,* commanded by Captain Celeb Davis, and a couple of scout boats. Captain William Thompson's frigate *Success,* now on full-time duty as part of Georgia's provincial navy, served as escort. Captain Carr and his marines remained at the mouth of the Saint Johns River to wait for the return of the second war party of Indians while the remainder of the regular and provincial soldiers boarded the other schooners and small boats and returned to Georgia.[21]

When the *Walker* arrived off Anastasia Island during the afternoon of 28 March, Oglethorpe boarded his personal boat the *Cutter* and approached the beach to determine if a landing were possible. It was unfortunate that the surf was too high to permit a safe landing because only three Spanish scouts were on the beach to oppose them. Disappointed, Oglethorpe returned to the *Walker.* On 29 and 30 March he attempted a landing further down the island near recently completed Fort Matanzas (present Fort Matanzas National Monument). The sea was again too rough and a landing proved impossible. The Indians on board were in poor spirits and wanted to disembark. Oglethorpe gave up his plan to destroy the Spaniards' cattle and began the return trip to Georgia, reaching Frederica on the last day of March.[22]

Oglethorpe's raid was generally well conducted and timely. It reinforced Governor Montiano's belief that the British were preparing a second invasion of Florida and forced him on the defensive. Montiano's timidity and Oglethorpe's propaganda speeches convinced Georgia's Indian allies that the Spaniards had lost their courage and gave the Indians the impetus to conduct successful raids into Florida during the ensuing two years. Oglethorpe was not quite ready to believe his own propaganda that Montiano had permanently assumed a defensive posture, but he obviously suspected that this was the Spaniard's new strategy.[23]

General Oglethorpe had wanted to return to England as early as August 1740 to attend to personal business, but the requirement for his presence in Georgia had been too great. By the summer of 1743 it became imperative that he travel to London. Since the beginning of the war he had continually pressed the British government for additional soldiers and money for the defense of Georgia, but, except for the grenadier company and a small amount of money for provincial soldiers, they had ignored him. Consequently, he had expended more than £60,000 of his personal funds for Georgia's defense, thereby crippling his estate.[24] Only by personally appearing before the British House of Commons, of which he was a member, would the government likely pay more attention to Georgia's military requirements and reimburse his depleted fortune.

Lieutenant Colonel William Cook had returned to London during the summer of 1742, but time and distance did not cool his hate for General Oglethorpe. He began voicing accusations against his commanding officer and in early 1743 he officially preferred nineteen charges, the most vicious of which was that the general had made his soldiers pay for food that was to have been issued gratis. In February the War Office ordered General Oglethorpe to return to England to answer Cook's charges at a court-martial.[25]

On 23 July 1743 Oglethorpe sailed for England. He would never see Georgia again.[26]

XV

In the King's Pay
1743–1747

Upon arriving in London during September 1743 General Oglethorpe was given the respect reserved for a hero. Any doubts regarding his ability as a general had been dispelled by his defeat of the Spaniards. During March 1744 he made a successful plea to the British House of Commons for restitution of the personal fortune that he had expended for Georgia's defense. In April the Treasury Office reimbursed him £66, 109.13.10.[1]

A hearing, rather than a court-martial, was held on 7 and 8 June 1744 for the investigation of Lieutenant Colonel Cook's charges of maltreatment and fraud against General Oglethorpe. Before the end of the second day the board, composed of several prominent generals, dismissed the charges. Less than two weeks later Cook's commission was withdrawn for alleging "19 false groundless and malicious articles against his Colonel."[2]

Most of the senior officers of the Forty-second Regiment of Foot had also returned to England. Some were on personal business and others served as witnesses at Oglethorpe's hearing. Upon Cook's dismissal from the army Alexander Heron was promoted to lieutenant colonel and Hugh Mackay, Sr., was promoted to major, but both officers tarried in England.[3]

Meanwhile, the war between England and Spain had expanded to the continent of Europe. Prussia attacked Austria, France sided with Prussia in order to seize the Austrian Netherlands (modern Belgium), and England allied with Austria against France, the traditional enemy. Thus began the War of Austrian Succession, known as King George's War in North America.

In Georgia the declaration of war with France was announced during the summer of 1744. French Louisiana was now an official enemy.[4]

Command of the Georgia military establishment was temporarily inherited by Captain William Horton, commander of the Forty-second Regiment's grenadier company. During the summer of 1745 he was promoted to major in the place of Hugh Mackay, Sr., who retired.[5] Horton lacked administrative ability; his records and letters were sparse and incomplete. Nevertheless, he did maintain Georgia's defenses intact for four years despite the enormous responsibility, Oglethorpe's growing disinterest, and a minimum of support from the British government.

By the spring of 1744 Horton had become apprehensive concerning the future existence of the Georgia provincial military units. He was also alarmed about his personal liability for their maintenance, for he had been subsisting those units by issuing them unauthorized bills of exchange. As a result, Oglethorpe began a campaign to promote the British government's assuming the expense and responsibility for the provincials. In September 1744 a royal warrant was issued, placing the units in the king's pay retroactive to September 1743, the date upon which Oglethorpe's personal payments had ceased. Under the royal warrant the provincial establishment was authorized 140 rangers, 115 Highlanders, 108 marines, and 180 seamen. Even though the units were placed in crown pay their status was Georgia provincial rather than British regular, and their officers held provincial rather than royal commissions.[6]

The ranger establishment authorized Georgia to maintain two large troops, each of which was to have included one captain, two lieutenants, one cornet, four quartermasters, two French-horn players, and sixty private rangers. The large number of officers was necessary because each of the small forts that served as a ranger station was commanded by an officer. Technically, all of the small troops (English, Highland, Williams's and Jones's) and separate garrisons (Augusta, Mount Pleasant, and Ebenezer) were to have been integrated into the two new troops. However, the new ranger establishment was completely ignored. Each of the several troops and garrisons continued as a separate unit. The only recognition of the royal warrant's requirements was an attempt to fit the ranger officers into the ranks authorized, an administrative detail that was necessary for fiscal accounting purposes.[7]

Lieutenant William Francis retained his rank in the new establishment, and he apparently assumed acting command of the Troop of English Rangers. Captain Robert Scroggs, the troop's former commander probably died shortly after March 1743, the date his existence was last recorded in period documents. Mount Venture, where Francis's detachment had been stationed, was not rebuilt after its destruction in November 1742. In 1746 Mary Bosomworth (the widow of John Musgrove and Jacob Mathews, who had recently married the Reverend Thomas Bosomworth) built another trading fort west-northwest of Mount Venture on the north side of the "Forks" (the junction of the Oconee, Okmulgee, and Altamaha Rivers), but there is no evidence that the new post received a garrison. Lieutenant Francis and his party of English Rangers may have been the detachment that occupied Scroggs former station, Bachelor's Redoubt at White Post, located northwest of Frederica. Another detachment of English Rangers remained at Frederica on Saint Simons Island under Quartermaster Thomas Hunt. A few of Hunt's men and a detachment of regulars manned a lookout called South Point, located on the ruins of Fort Saint Simons. When a ship appeared off Saint Simons Sound a ranger from South Point rode to Frederica with the news. Quartermaster John Milledge continued to command the English Rangers stationed at Fort Argyle. That outpost resumed its former importance after the destruction of Mount Venture which made Savannah vulnerable to hostile approach from the southwest.[8]

Captain Hugh Mackay, Jr., commander of the Troop of Highland Rangers, died in December 1742, following a two-month illness. Quartermaster Hugh Morrison, the troop's only remaining officer at that time, assumed temporary command. General Oglethorpe had probably been searching for ways to reward Lieutenant Charles Mackay of the Highland Company for the heroism he had displayed during the Spanish invasion of 1742. After Captain John Mackintosh returned from Spanish captivity in late 1743 to resume command of the Highland Company, Charles Mackay was transferred to the Troop of

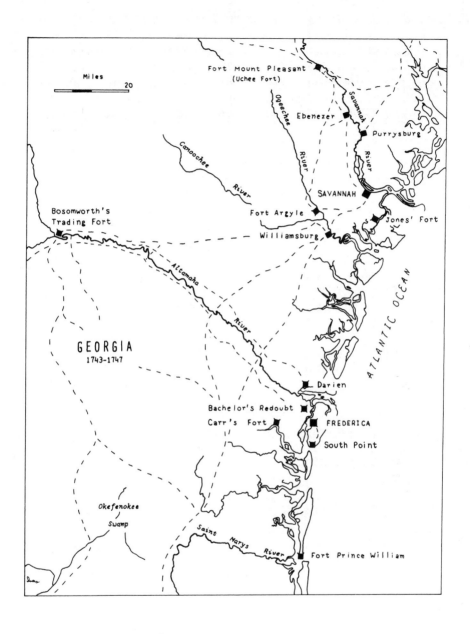

Miles
20

Fort Mount Pleasant
(Uchee Fort)

Ebenezer

Purrysburg

Ogeechee River

Canoochee River

Savannah River

SAVANNAH

Bosomworth's
Trading Fort

Fort Argyle

Jones' Fort

Williamsburg

ATLANTIC OCEAN

Altamaha River

GEORGIA
1743-1747

Darien

Bachelor's Redoubt

Carr's Fort

FREDERICA

South Point

Okefenokee
Swamp

Saint Marys River

Fort Prince William

Highland Rangers as its new commander. Evidence suggests
that he became one of the only two ranger captains authorized
by the royal warrant of 1744. Perhaps the detachment of rangers
that was stationed on the ruins of Fort Saint Andrews on
Cumberland Island was the Highland Rangers under Captain
Mackay. The greater part of the troop was posted in Darien,
for during April 1746 Hugh Morrison, now promoted to cornet,
was stationed there with twenty rangers. He was assisted by
Quartermaster James McQueen who had returned from Spanish
captivity with Captain Mackintosh.[9]

In 1743 the Highland Rangers were still carrying Scottish
weapons and they had begun wearing items of traditional
Highland clothing. A typical Highland Ranger probably wore
a flat blue bonnet, a tartan jacket, buckskin knee breeches
with stockings and shoes (or brogues), and during cold weather
he might have worn a tartan shoulder plaid. Tartan cloth of
unknown patterns was available from the trustees' store in
Savannah.[10]

It is probable that General Oglethorpe attempted to clothe
all the Georgia rangers in a common uniform after his return
to England, for during 1745 he raised a cornet and six ranger
recruits in England who reportedly wore cocked hats with a
green cockade pinned to the side and a blue coat faced with
red.[11] However, without Oglethorpe's commanding presence
in Georgia it is doubtful that many of the rangers were induced
to wear a standard uniform.

Captain Richard Kent, commander of the Augusta garrison,
was the senior ranger officer. His garrison, one of the largest
bodies of rangers, was authorized thirty men, but it probably
seldom included more than twenty. He maintained sergeants
in the garrison even though the royal warrant did not authorized
noncommissioned officers for the rangers. Kent assumed responsibility for Okfuskee Fort in the Upper Creek nation in
December 1742. Ambrose Morrison, who was both an Augusta
tavern keeper and a sergeant in the garrison, and two other
Augusta Rangers were stationed there until at least June 1743
and perhaps much longer. A prominent South Carolina trader
built another fort near Okfuskee during 1744 as a refuge for
the traders, but it was never garrisoned.[12]

South Carolina still maintained a garrison at Fort Moore

under the command of Captain Daniel Pepper, but most of
the Indian traders had moved their operations across the
Savannah River to Augusta, apparently to escape prosecution
for debts in South Carolina. Nevertheless, the Charles Town
merchants still controlled the Indian trade and the government
of South Carolina maintained the greatest influence in Indian
affairs.[13]

A small detachment of rangers commanded by William
Atcheson Finlay was stationed among the Lower Creek. Finlay,
an Indian trader, had lived in the Creek nations as Oglethorpe's
constable since December 1741. When the rangers were placed
in the king's pay Finlay received a commission as quartermaster.
He seems to have been stationed at the Uchee, or Yuchi, town
on the western bank of the Chattahoochee River, at the Lower
Trading Path's crossing site, eleven and a half miles south
of present Columbus, Georgia. Finlay provided Major Horton
with excellent information of French political activity in the
Creek towns. However, he apparently exercised no control over
the unruly Indian traders; even though England and France
were at war the Georgia and South Carolina traders continued
to provide supplies and equipment to the nearby French
garrison of Fort Toulouse.[14]

Captain Thomas Jones continued to command a small troop
of rangers that probably still included a quartermaster and
about a dozen men. Beginning in September 1744, when the
maintenance of the provincial units was assumed by the British
government, only two ranger captains were authorized. Jones
received a commission as lieutenant; however, the embarrass-
ment of the demotion was softened by dubbing him a "captain
lieutenant," a rank that was simply addressed as "captain." His
small troop may have conducted infrequent patrols on Jekyll,
Amelia, Talbot, and Fort George Islands. Major Horton also
employed Jones to organize the Indian war parties that rendezvoused at Frederica for raiding forays into Florida. Jones
developed a drinking problem that interfered with that duty,
and during his periods of drunkeness he stirred up trouble
among the Indians by enticing them to demand increasingly
greater rewards for their services. Since Jones respected Mary
Bosomworth, a fellow part-Indian, Horton asked here to come
to Frederica in late 1744 and assist him in dealing with the

Georgia Provincial Soldiers, 1739–1747
Highland Ranger, Seaman, and Creek Indian Warrior

(Drawing by Bill Drath)

Georgia Provincial Soldiers, 1739–1747
Marine, Ranger, and Highlander

(*Drawing by Bill Drath*)

ranger officer.[15] She apparently resolved Jones's problem.

John Williams was also demoted to lieutenant when the rangers were placed in the king's pay; however, like Thomas Jones, he was tactfully designated a captain lieutenant. Before leaving Georgia, Oglethorpe had contracted with Williams to recruit additional men from Virginia for his troop of rangers. The members of the troop were to receive land grants near the Ogeechee River below Fort Argyle from where they could assist Fort Argyle's garrison in guarding the major southwestern approaches to Savannah, whose security had seriously diminished since the destruction of Mount Venture. In September 1743 Williams rowed up the Ogeechee River and chose the land on which to station his troop. During the reconnaissance he severely frightened the inhabitants of Savannah when his troop and Fort Argyle's garrison exchanged salutes of gunfire. A week later Williams was granted six thousand acres on the western side of the Ogeechee River, two-thirds of which lay to the south of Sterling Creek and one-third to the north. In August 1744 he moved his rangers and their families to that site, spending the remainder of the summer and fall building homes and clearing land. Their settlement, which they soon named Williamsburg, seems to have been located above Sterling Creek, either at present Richmond Hill or on the site of abandoned Sterling's Fort, one and three-quarter miles to the southeast. In the summer of 1746 several more families from North Carolina and probably Virginia joined the settlement.[16]

Captain John Barnard, commander of the Mount Pleasant garrison of rangers, received a commission as quartermaster in the new ranger establishment. Nevertheless, he continued to be courteously addressed as "captain." A lasting friendship had developed between Barnard and Captain Kent of Augusta as a result of Kent's stops at Mount Pleasant while traveling on the Savannah River.[17]

Thomas Bichler, commander of Ebenezer's handful of German-speaking rangers, was also commissioned a quartermaster. He and his men were under the exclusive direction of Reverend John Bolzius, Ebenezer's capable leader. In March 1744 Bichler was made Ebenezer's constable, giving him both military and police authority in the community. Bolzius had trouble, however, in persuading Bichler to fulfill his duties as constable because additional pay was not forthcoming.[18]

Oglethorpe compared the Georgia rangers to regular British dragoons. The ranger troops "not only carry advices through these vast Forests & swim Rivers, but in Action, by taking an Enemy in Flank and Rear, do great Service. . . . They also are of great Service in watching the Sea Coasts, since they can swiftly move from one Place to another, and engage to advantage Men with wet arms & Accoutrements, before they can be able to form themselves after landing."[19] The small garrisons of rangers "upon the passes of the River[s] and the Roads to the Indian Countrey . . . having horses patroll about the Countrey, and thereby give alarms of Indian Enemies, intercept Spies &ca."[20]

In April 1746 the Georgia rangers apparently included 15 officers and 122 men. However, a comparison between the reported strength and the actual strength would undoubtedly have disclosed irregularities. An enterprising officer could increase his own wages or better the lot of his men by employing some of the common frauds of that period. The simplest artifice was to enlist a fictitious person and collect his pay. Additional deceptions included enlisting young sons of soldiers and continuing dead men and deserters on muster rolls. A very humane ruse was the continuation of disabled veterans on the active rolls in order to guarantee them a means of subsistence. Oglethorpe would not have allowed most of the above practices during his tenure in Georgia; he had been paying the provincials out of his own pocket. Once the crown assumed their payment, however, the officers of the Georgia rangers and other provincials could have been expected to practice a certain amount of fraud.[21]

In late 1743, as the result of a prisoner exchange, Captain John Mackintosh returned to Georgia from his long captivity in Spain and resumed command of the Highland Independent Company of Foot. Under the royal warrant of September 1744 the company continued to be authorized a captain, two lieutenants, an ensign, a surgeon, four sergeants, four corporals, two drummers, and one hundred men. However, the old problem remained—Georgia did not have enough Highlanders to fill the company even though recruits were occasionally sent from

England. In 1743 thirty mutineers from the Highland Regiment of Foot were transferred from Britain to Georgia and were probably assigned to the Highland Company. In 1746 the Highland Company was reportedly at half strength, having three officers, four noncommissioned officers, no drummers, and fifty-two privates.[22]

The Highlanders apparently did not feel the need for drums, and, strangely, the available records do not mention their having bagpipes. However, that instrument was so highly revered by Highland soldiers that its presence in Georgia is likely. The bagpipe was a psychological stimulant; when the piper played traditional clan music the Highlanders' nationalistic spirit was aroused and they felt more courageous.[23]

Members of the Highland Company were issued a uniform consisting of traditional Highland clothing, although its exact description is unknown. However, during the same period the Highland companies in Scotland wore a blue bonnet, a red jacket and waistcoat, a belted plaid (a little kilt, the modern kilt, was worn during hot weather and for undress), stockings, and shoes or brogues. The belted plaid and little kilt were made of a dark blue, green, and black cloth in a pattern commonly called the government (modern Black Watch) tartan. Since Georgia's Highland Company was modeled after the independent companies in Scotland, its soldiers were possibly clothed in the same manner. The government tartan may not have been utilized, but custom and the account of an eyewitness suggests that Captain Mackintosh clothed his entire company in a common tartan pattern in order to create uniformity. Their weapons were Scottish pistols, dirks, broadswords, targets (shields), Brown Bess muskets, and bayonets.[24]

Captain Mark Carr continued to command the Marine Company of Boatmen. During March 1744 Spanish-allied Indians made another predatory raid on his principal plantation, Hermitage (also called Carr's Fort), and captured five marines who were cutting trees at some distance from the well-fortified house and outbuildings. The war party of forty-three Yemassee shoved their prisoners into dugouts and began paddling toward Florida. The alarm was spread and the next day, after Carr's marines and a party of Yamacraw under Toonahowi assembled, a pursuit was initiated. After several hours of rowing down the Inland Passage they caught the Yemassee on the northern side of the Saint Johns River where a bitter skirmish followed. During the fight at least five Yemassee were killed, one was taken prisoner, and the five marines were rescued from their captors. A marine sergeant was severely wounded and Toonahowi, probably Britain's most courageous and loyal ally on the southern frontier, was killed.[25]

In early 1746 Captain Carr's Marine Company included Lieutenant Kenneth Baillie, eight noncommissioned officers, two drummers, and sixty privates. Carr maintained half of the company at Hermitage while Baillie and the other half occupied the eastern side of Blyth Island, three or four miles to the south-southeast, where they cleared and farmed a new plantation.[26]

Noble Jones was promoted to captain lieutenant of the marines in March 1743. Under the royal warrant of 1744, which placed the Georgia marines in the king's pay, Jones held the position of Captain Carr's executive officer, but in truth he remained in command of a separate unit, the Northern Company of Marines, which continued to be stationed near his fort on Wormsloe plantation near Savannah. In 1746 the Northern Marines included Captain Jones, four noncommissioned officers, a drummer, and fifty-one men.[27]

The combined marine companies were not to exceed a total of 108 officers and men, according to the royal warrant, but in 1746 they were reportedly overstrength with 129 men, much to the British government's irritation.[28] Oglethorpe described the Georgia marines as "a hardy kind of Men thoroughly acquainted with all the Water Passages and row by Night and Day. They can live by fishing and shooting and are not easily to be prevailed with to Serve unless by Hope of large Gain, they Generally carry the Indians on all Expeditions. They are as contented in Woods as in Houses. They are excellent scouts."[29] Marines were issued a uniform, perhaps a coat and hat, and they were probably armed like the regular soldiers with swords, muskets, and bayonets.[30]

The Georgia provincial navy continued to maintain the frigate *Success,* carrying twenty-two cannons; the schooner *Walker* with fourteen cannons; the sloop *Saint Phillip,* having ten cannons; and the supply piragua *Bathesda.* The armed vessels occasionally patrolled the Georgia coast in an attempt to protect British merchant craft from French and Spanish privateers, but they, like the British navy's ships, were spread too thin to offer much protection. During 1744 and 1745 almost every British ship traveling between Georgia and England was captured. Nearly as discouraging to Georgians was the knowledge that the Spanish enemy in Saint Augustine was being supplied by sloops and schooners belonging to a few Charles Town merchants. When accused of aiding the enemy the merchants argued that the trade was legal.[31]

By 1744 soldiering employed more men than any other occupation in Georgia. William Stephens, who seldom wrote any flattery concerning the military, observed that "a labouring man no sooner sets his foot [in Georgia] but he can find good pay with little work, by entering in som Branch or other of the Military Service."[32]

Life in Georgia's provincial military units was idle, primitive, and lonely. All units (rangers, Highlanders, and marines) were to patrol the approaches into Georgia by horse or boat and give early warning of an enemy's approach. However, it would have been very difficult to induce the officers and their soldiers to conduct skillful patrols month after month, year after year. Although patrolling was dangerous, that aspect would have quickly dulled after conducting numerous patrols without enemy contact. Patrolling was distasteful to officers and men alike principally because of the discomforts of rain, cold, and heat; the hard work of pulling on a scout boat oar or sitting in a saddle for hours at a time; and the absence of any immediate tangible results. Adequate patrolling was probably performed only during periods of alarm immediately following Yemassee raids,[33] and it is doubtful that any serious patrolling was conducted after the year 1745 when armed conflict on the Anglo-Spanish border practically ceased.

Every garrison and detachment of the companies of Georgia provincials was apparently divided into three sections, or parties. Work details, training, and patrolling were probably performed by each section as a unit. A section probably lived in its own barracks hut, farmed a common garden plot, and served as a "mess" for preparing and eating meals. Each section assumed responsibility for mounting guard in its fort every third day.

Usually, a soldier manned his guard post for two-hour periods during daylight and stood one-hour shifts during darkness. Those guards who were not on post were, nevertheless, required to remain on the alert, dressed and with weapons ready. An officer was supposed to check the guard posts and the barracks at irregular hours twice during each night. Training and drill as conducted by regular British units would have been virtually unknown, for there was no need for parade formations or disciplined fire by platoons in ranks. The provincials were employed principally for patrolling which demanded skill in skirmishing, ambushing, and raiding. However, there is no indication that they practiced those skills either, and training was probably restricted to competitive shooting at a mark with muskets. Noncommissioned officers (sergeants and corporals) were responsible for the maintenance of weapons by requiring the soldiers to sand off rust with emory paper and apply a protective coating of olive oil.[34]

After 1745, when the danger from Spanish raids had subsided, the Georgia provincial soldiers devoted more and more time to personal occupations. Practically all of the officers had crude plantations on which they profitably engaged in farming and cattle raising, hiring some of their own soldiers as laborers. Officers of garrisons near the Indian nations engaged in the Indian trade. Some of the soldiers had small plots of land where, with minimum exertion, they raised enough corn and black cattle to supplement their incomes. In most cases they were squatters, farming ungranted land.[35]

The Georgia provincials were apparently very lazy. This was probably, in part, because of a lack of incentive; a private's opportunities for a promotion or a commission were almost nonexistent, and the long periods between skirmishes with the enemy caused a degree of indifference. Another contributing factor was their frequent poor health, which discouraged hard work and sapped their strength. The warm months between May and October was the time for dying; typhoid, malaria, and numerous other fevers killed the newcomers and weakened the veterans. Intestinal parasites, dysentery, and the lack of a well-balanced diet probably kept most of the soldiers underweight.[36]

The small wooden frontier forts offered extremely primitive

living conditions. The crude huts were hot in summer, cold in winter, leaked when it rained, and were a constant fire hazard. The soldiers were plagued by flies during the day and mosquitos at night; the only relief came from building a fire upwind and sitting in the smoke. Rats and mice ran rampant in the living quarters and supply buildings. There was no escape from the filth and smells that resulted from packing people and horses inside a small enclosure with minimum sanitary facilities. These men and their families had never acquired the habit of bathing and therefore would have been inured from infancy to the smell of unwashed bodies. Personal possessions, including furniture, were meager. Beds consisted of a homemade frame, laced cord for springs, a straw mattress, a pillow, and a blanket. They seldom owned more than one suit of clothes, patched and stiff with dirt. Rains turned the interiors of the forts into a mire where men and horses floundered in ankle deep mud; forts having poor drainage soon became shallow ponds. In the coastal forts, which were built on sandy soil, the dry periods were even more uncomfortable because fine sand blowing from nearby dunes covered everything and easily found its way between clothing and skin.[37]

Deer, turkey, and other wild game were available in the nearby woods and fish were plentiful in the rivers. Luxuries such as butter, cheese, chocolate, and bread could be purchased in Savannah, but they were expensive. The staple food was corn raised in small cleared fields near the forts. Holes were dug a step apart and half a dozen kernels were planted in each. Between the rows of corn "hills" Indian beans or peas were planted with corn stalks serving as bean-poles. Corn was roasted when green, and after ripening it was hulled for hominy or ground into corn meal for the preparation of mush, johnnycake, or corn pone.[38]

The soldiers possessed humble backgrounds in the lower stratum of society where illiteracy was the norm. Their vulgar manners and speech were the result of both their backgrounds and the circumstances of their frontier environment. Consciously or unconsciously they violated most of the courtesies and politeness as practiced by the "better sort." Conversation was vulgar, loud, and blunt. Humor was probably centered around human misfortune and based partly on the "practical joke." When psychological tensions could not be released against the Spaniards it was vented against fellow soldiers through frequently flaring tempers and fights. Drunkenness from rum punch and long hours of sleep would have served as the popular mental escape from garrison life and desertion was a last resort. The isolated forts were seldom visited by a minister, but the soldiers were not inclined to practice their Christianity anyway. However, the Georgia soldiers really had no need for a refined culture because life on the frontier was too raw, too impoverished to sustain false modesty.[39] Nevertheless, the soldiers and their families knew friendship and felt compassion. While William Harvey, a ranger, lay on his deathbed he willed his meager belongings to a fellow ranger and his wife "who have taken care of me during this sickness."[40]

One of the most discouraging aspects associated with living in an isolated garrison was the lack of women. A few soldiers had wives, but the remainder suffered a near-womanless existence. Lucky was the soldier who was allowed the opportunity of spending a few days in Savannah or Frederica where, if he was adept with the opposite sex, he might receive the favors of a loose-moraled indentured servant girl. If not, he could resort to a whore. The rangers in those forts near the Indian nations were the most fortunate of all the garrisons, for the women of the southern nations were considered very pretty, and many rangers, like the traders, kept Indian wives, some temporarily, some permanently. This practice was advantageous to the colony as well as to the rangers; the Indian women made good wives and bore the rangers' children, and the rangers increased their potential for rapport with the Indian warriors by learning and practicing some of their languages and customs.[41] It is interesting but sometimes appalling to realize how quickly young soldiers will "go native" when they begin cohabitating with local women.

Recreation in the forts was homemade. The rangers undoubtedly raced their horses while the marines probably held scout-boat races, and, like soldiers everywhere, they would have gambled their pay on the results. Other popular sports on the southern frontier included bullbaiting, which involved dogs fighting a chained bull, and a type of football that was probably similar to modern soccer. Saint George's Day (23 April), the king's birthday (30 October), Oglethorpe's birthday (21 December), and several other holidays were celebrated with dancing, games, and heavy drinking. One of the soldiers' favorite diversions was the entertainment of visitors. Visits between garrisons were not uncommon and strong friendships developed as a result.[42] The soldiers' principal day-to-day method of relaxation and recreation was probably sitting at twilight with clay pipe and rum punch, telling stories and reliving encounters wth the Spaniards.

Thus, during the 1743–47 period over four hundred provincial soldiers were maintained in Georgia at British expense. Georgia and South Carolina were fortunate that neither Spain nor France chose to attack, for the provincial units were of doubtful efficiency by 1746. They were practically never utilized for offensive operations and they seldom conducted patrols.

The provincials would probably have regained the good efficiency that they had possessed during 1742–43 if Oglethorpe had returned to Georgia and reassumed personal command. But in September 1744 he married Elizabeth Sambrooke in a union designed to provide a prominent husband to one party and financial security to the other. Within a few months he became involved in England's struggle to put down the Jacobite Rebellion, the Scottish attempt to place Prince Charles, heir of the deposed Stuarts, on the throne of Britain. Oglethorpe was commissioned a major general in March 1745. During the fall of that year he was in northern England with a volunteer regiment of horsemen and a few Georgia rangers, the latter having been recruited for duty in Georgia but temporarily diverted to help fight the Scottish rebels.[43]

When the rebels began their retreat toward the Scottish border in early December 1745 Oglethorpe was ordered to lead his horsemen in an encircling movement to cut them off. He pushed his soldiers over one hundred miles of unimproved roads that were covered with ice and snow in less than three days. They apparently arrived in a position from where they could block the rebels' escape; however, that night Oglethorpe withdrew to a distance of five miles and did not begin his movement toward the enemy until about eleven o'clock the following morning. By then Prince Charles and his rebels had escaped. Criticism of his failure to halt the enemy's retreat began almost immediately. He and his horsemen were not allowed to accompany the army as it pursued Prince Charles and finally defeated him at the Battle of Culloden.[44]

When Oglethorpe returned to London in February 1746 he found that the animosity aroused by his failure had grown in intensity. Two accusations were being voiced. First, it was suggested that he had not possessed the necessary courage to meet the Scots in battle. Second, it was rumored that he was in sympathy with the Jacobites, some of whom had been his active correspondents. Adding to the suspicion was the fact that the Oglethorpe family had previously exhibited Jacobite leanings. But he certainly did not lack courage, and his principal biographer was convinced that he had no political affiliation with the Jacobites. Oglethorpe's reasons for not setting out in pursuit until eleven o'clock on that morning in question were that his soldiers were exhausted, they had to forage for food, and they were outnumbered four to one. There seems to be little reason to doubt the honesty of his statement. Whether or not his reasons were justified is unclear.[45]

The ill will expressed against Oglethorpe deflated his enormous pride and established a drastic turnabout from his hero's reception three years previously. He became quarrelsome, even lashing out at his friends. In April 1746 a London newspaper reported that he was preparing to leave for Georgia during the following month. He may have intended to hide in North America in order to escape the London criticism, but he stayed in England, perhaps at the insistence of the War Office, and during August he was served with notice that he was to be court-martialed. He prepared his defense well and numerous witnesses appeared on his behalf. A formal court-martial composed of a board of general officers acquitted him of all charges in October 1746.[46]

Officially, Oglethorpe's name was cleared, but his reputation seemed even more tarnished following his court-martial. During more than twenty years of public life his vanity and arrogance had soured many men against him while his success and obvious expertise in leadership had made many others envious. Now they gleefully turned upon him. He isolated himself from the public eye, both socially and professionally. A few faithful friends and admirers continued to support him; he was promoted to lieutenant general in September 1747, and he was reelected to Parliament during the same year. However, the War Office refused to give him a major command in the European fighting, as he requested, and Parliament refused to appoint him to important committees.[47]

While Oglethorpe sulked in seclusion he virtually ignored his command in Georgia. Concurrently, the British government began searching for methods to reduce its burdensome military expenses, for although King George's War did not end until late 1748, serious peace movements were underway by the fall of 1746. In November the War Office determined, after an extensive study, that the Georgia rangers, Highlanders, most of the marines, and the navy were no longer necessary for the southern frontier's defense. They felt that the Forty-second Regiment, a handful of scout boats, and the Indian allies would be adequate. The War Office's decision was strategically sound because the Anglo-Spanish border was very quiet. There was further justification based on administrative grounds. Major William Horton, temporarily in command of the forces in Georgia, had not provided the War Office with muster rolls for the provincial units since they had been placed in the king's pay; therefore, the government had no way of knowing how many men were actually employed in that service. In fact, the actual existence of the provincial units was suspect. Even the required monthly reports of the Forty-second Regiment had been sporadic. It may be conjectured that General Oglethorpe's fall from grace within the military profession contributed to the War Office's decision. The fact that he took little interest in the provincials' welfare after 1745 obviously resulted in their misuse and an absence of administrative reporting. In early December 1746 the secretary at war recommended that the Georgia provincials not be continued in the king's pay. Three weeks later King George II ordered the units to disband.[48]

For one reason or another Major Horton did not receive the disbandment order and the provincials remained on duty until finally, in early June 1747, Lieutenant Colonel Alexander Heron returned from England and assumed command of the military establishment in Georgia. Two weeks later, on 24 June, he officially disbanded the rangers, Highlanders, and seamen. Only four scout boats and their crews, whose designation was changed from marines to boatmen, were retained on duty. About four hundred unemployed veterans, perhaps more than one-quarter of the Georgia labor force, were suddenly and unexpectedly released upon the already distressed economy. Georgia's principal industry ceased to exist. Many of the veterans who had originally abandoned their land grants to join the provincial army now applied for charity.[49]

XVI

The End of an Era
1747–1749

The disbanding of the rangers, marines, and Highlanders caused a chill to settle upon both the Georgians and South Carolinians.[1] King George's War still continued and although the Spaniards were held in contempt following their humiliation in Georgia during 1742, their continued ability to raid isolated British settlements and plantations was well recognized. More frightening was the possibility of an overland attack from Mobile by French regular soldiers and their Choctaw Indian allies. Viewed from the present the French had no such ability during King George's War; however, to the period observer in Frederica or Charles Town the potentialities of his ancient enemy were blocked only by the Creek and Chickasaw Indian nations that lay between Louisiana and the British colonies. Although the Chickasaw hated the French, they were few in number, and the Creek seemed to waiver between both European factions, causing constant uncertainty as to their future course of action. Since frontier defense could not depend upon unpredictable Indian allies, Georgia and South Carolina were forced to reshuffle their small contingents of regular and remaining provincial soldiers to fill the gaps left by the disbanded Georgia provincials who had been in the king's pay. Unfortunately, the mutual distrust and jealousy that had arisen because of competition over the Indian trade and their defeat in Florida during 1740 had divided the two British colonies, resulting in uncoordinated and wasteful defense efforts.

After General Oglethorpe's departure in 1743 the Forty-second Regiment of Foot idled in its garrison at Frederica under the acting command of Major William Horton. Horton was plagued with the usual problems of a commander in a small frontier garrison where the local town's economy was primarily dependent upon the soldiers. Ideally, the civilian population was to have been governed by President William Stephens and the assistants who resided in Savannah and were represented in Frederica by bailiffs (magistrates who conducted court), a court reporter, constables (law enforcement and court officials), and tything-men (law enforcement officials) who were to enforce the laws of England. Oglethorpe had cunningly combined military and civilian rule in Frederica by having two of his officers appointed as bailiffs; however, both men were now absent in England. The third bailiff, John Calwell, a civilian, made a feeble attempt to exercise jurisdiction over civil and criminal matters, but the real law at Frederica was Major Horton's military rule. John Terry, the recorder, was obstinate and outspoken concerning Major Horton's usurpation of civilian power. His courageous but futile attempts to assert civilian jurisdiction led to severe harassment by regimental officers including threats of bodily harm and finally a charge of rape. Although a Savannah jury found him innocent, he was ruined financially and spiritually by the charge. In the end Major Horton won. With General Oglethorpe's support in London, the trustees commissioned him conservator of the peace at Frederica, a position that allowed him to hold court with jurisdiction over misdemeanors and minor civil actions such as small debts.[2]

Lieutenant Colonel Alexander Heron returned to Frederica from England in June 1747 and assumed acting command of the Forty-second Regiment. After disbanding the rangers, marines, and Highlanders according to orders from the secretary at war, he allowed the Georgia frontier to remain devoid of military protection for a year. Except for a detachment stationed at Fort Prince William on the south end of Cumberland Island, he retained all seven companies at Fort Frederica on Saint Simons Island, making no attempt to rebuild forts Saint Simons and Saint Andrews that had been destroyed by the Spaniards in 1742. He believed that the entire regiment would be required to defend Frederica in the event of a Spanish or French invasion and, judging by the regiment's generally poor past performance, he was probably correct. However, the remainder of the colony was left unprotected. Some Georgians apparently registered complaints with the trustees, for in August 1748 Heron received Oglethorpe's orders to garrison the frontier forts with the regular soldiers.[3]

Oglethorpe's own company, under the command of Captain Lieutenant George Cadogan, was transferred to Fort Augusta, and Richard Kent, former commander of the rangers who had been garrisoned there, was commissioned as one of his lieutenants. A corporal and seven men were placed at Ebenezer where the Salzburgers built them a new house. Captain George Dunbar's company was stationed at Darien as a garrison for that settlement's fort, and John Mackintosh, former commander of the disbanded Highland Independent Company of Foot, was given a lieutenant's commission and assumed acting command during Dunbar's absence in England. A detachment from that company was to have occupied Fort Argyle, but it is likely that the old ranger fortification continued to decay without a garrison. Heron maintained communications with the two detached companies by a post rider, Peter Grant, who regularly rode the forest paths between Frederica and Augusta.[4]

The remaining five companies continued to garrison Fort Frederica under the following company commanders: Lieutenant Colonel Heron, Major Horton (until his death in late 1748 at which time Lieutenant Archibald Don apparently assumed acting command), Captain Raymond Demere, Captain Patrick Sutherland (who returned from England in August 1748), and Captain James Mackay who commanded the grenadiers.[5]

Lieutenant Colonel Heron was apparently more active in military affairs than his predecessor, Major Horton. He began building brick and tabby barracks at Frederica to replace the one hundred miserable clapboard huts called the "Soldiers Camp," which had been destroyed by fire in February 1747. Fort Prince William was rebuilt and a new battery was added. He even conducted a minor raid into Florida near the Saint Johns River in July 1748.[6]

Heron, like Major Horton before him, had poor rapport with the civil officials of Georgia. He carried on the business of a merchant in addition to his military duties, buying ships' cargoes and retailing the wares, and he was accused of establishing a monopoly and inflating his prices. Another controversy arose concerning the disposition of cargoes of captured Spanish and French vessels that privateer Captain Celeb Davis brought into port. Disposition of captured property was made by British vice-admiralty courts, the nearest being located in Charles Town, and in order to retain the cargoes in Frederica, Heron established a provisional court of admiralty whose illegality was well known.[7]

The red-coated soldiers of the Forty-second Regiment were apparently typical of regular soldiers in all periods of history. They tended to be irresponsible and lazy, drank too much rum, complained constantly, used profanity, believed that most women were "fair game," and functioned well as soldiers only when led by officers who trained them hard and treated them fairly. In the Forty-second Regiment the officers caused as much or more trouble than the privates. Their penchant for dueling has been previously discussed, but they were just as notorious in their relationships with women. There were, of course, prostitutes in Frederica; a Mrs. Campbell, a soldier's wife, was known for operating a "Lewd house," but the town's wives, daughters, and servant girls were nevertheless reportedly unsafe from the criminal intentions of some of the officers and soldiers. Lieutenant Probart Howarth was apparently the most reckless of the officers in his affairs with women. John Terry reported that he had attempted to rape his servant girl while she was returning from church. During 1744 Terry recounted another incident in which Howarth allegedly horse-whipped and raped Margaret Fletcher, the wife of a soldier, in her own house in the presence of three other officers, and she reportedly escaped their assaults only by jumping out of her window. Howarth avoided prosecution by giving his victim a settlement of £10 to silence her charges. However, even those private soldiers who were brought to trial for rape were probably seldom convicted because a court-martial was reluctant to convict men when many of the "rapes" were thought to have been mutually arranged liaisons that had been rudely interrupted.[8]

One of the regiment's most unfortunate incidents involved Lieutenant George Sterling. Although the background of the affair is not clear beyond the fact that he was reportedly insane, the severe treatment he suffered and the hate expressed toward him hint that he was a suspected homosexual. In late 1743 several officers entered his house, overturned his possessions, and broke his sword. When Sterling attempted to present a complaint to the civilian magistrate another officer interrupted the proceeding. Shortly afterward Major Horton transferred him to Fort Prince William where he remained for two years until his health failed and he was returned to Frederica and placed under the surgeon's care. In the summer of 1747 he received Lieutenant Colonel Heron's permission to take leave in England, and while aboard a boat bound for Port Royal, where he was to board a ship, he committed suicide by cutting his throat.[9]

Recruits were occasionally sent from England, but the regiment no doubt remained understrength. The soldiers continued necessary guard duty and the normal fatigue details associated with living in garrison. However, platoon drill and training with musket and bayonet received far less emphasis than during previous years because a large part of the soldiers' time was spent performing personal occupations. A number of soldiers farmed land at New Hampton on the north end of Saint Simons Island, at least one soldier served as an apprentice silversmith, another worked as a barber, and others hired themselves out as workers on the island's wharf and plantations. Most of the officers obtained nearby land grants that were farmed by their indentured servants, their soldiers, and reportedly by a few contraband Negro slaves. Major Horton had rebuilt his plantation on Jekyell Island which the Spaniards had destroyed, and in late 1746 it consisted of a large house, a barn full of barley, a twenty-ton stack of hay, a garden, eight acres of indigo, and eight horses.[10]

In the eyes of the British government, the Forty-second Regiment was hardly necessary considering the more pressing need for regiments in Europe where France was being engaged in the War of Austrian Succession and in Scotland where the Jacobite Rebellion had just been suppressed. Consequently, the flow of supplies to Frederica was severely restricted until, by late 1748, there was not even enough ammunition to supply the companies. Heron's relationship with President Stephens and the assistants in Savannah had deteriorated to such an extent that he felt he could "expect but little from such a

Sett of needy wretches."[11] In February 1749 he was forced to seek help and cooperation from South Carolina, a step that should have been taken long before. Appearing before Governor James Glen and his council in Charles Town, Heron asked for Indian presents, gun powder and musket balls, and advice concerning the maintenance of Georgia's military boats. The council refused to provide him with Indian presents, advising him to stop dispensing presents as a form of charity to every Indian family who beached a canoe at Frederica and to restrict Indian visits to invitations only. Ammunition for the regiment was loaned from the Charles Town magazine. And the council advised Heron to sell his old boats and vessels and buy new scout boats.[12]

Upon the disbanding of the Georgia provincial forces only a few boatmen had been retained to man four scout boats, all of which were so old that a full-time carpenter was hired to maintain them. Daniel Demetre, a former sergeant of the marines, was master of the boatmen and under him were three coxwains who commanded the other three boats. According to the South Carolina Council's advise, the schooner *Walker* (sometimes called a half-galley), the scout boat *Frederica,* and the piragua *Bathesda* were sold in the spring of 1749. The money from their sale was used to purchase two new scout boats, the sixteen-oared *Hanover,* and the ten-oared *Prince George* (Demetre's boat), and to repair at least one of the old scout boats. Three crews were retained on duty.[13]

South Carolina had always maintained a provincial army and navy despite the existence of regular and provincial forces in Georgia. Small garrisons were maintained at Fort Johnson to guard Charles Town Harbor and at Fort Moore across the Savannah River from Georgia's garrison at Fort Augusta. Rangers patrolled the frontier during 1744, 1746, and 1748, and two scout boats continually reconnoitered the Inland Passage from their stations at Port Royal and maintained communications with Frederica, Georgia. The most useful of South Carolina's provincial units were two large heavily armed rowing craft, the *Charles Town Galley* and the *Beaufort Galley;* both of these were probably similar in size and armament to the Cuban half-galleys that the Spaniards in Saint Augustine utilized so successfully. Beginning with their introduction in

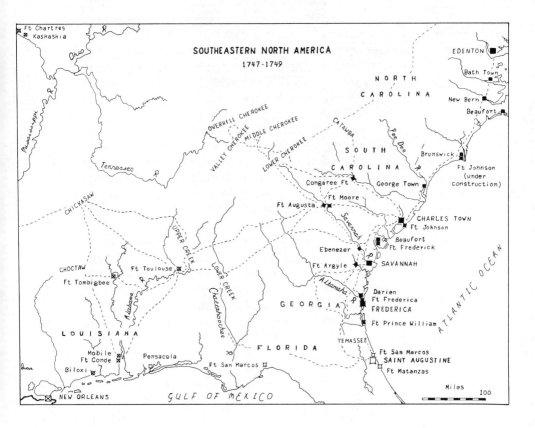

SOUTHEASTERN NORTH AMERICA
1747-1749

1742 they regularly accompanied British men-of-war on cruises along the Florida coast because of their capability of running into the shallow coastal creeks and rivers while chasing Indian canoes or Spanish launches. Unfortunately, the *Charles Town Galley* was destroyed by high winds in early 1744 and the *Beaufort Galley* was deactivated in late 1747 because of public resentment over the high cost of its maintenance.[14]

The provincial forces were a great fiscal burden to South Carolina whose citizens had long suffered under heavy taxes collected for military purposes. In 1742 the assembly petitioned the king for three companies of regular infantry to be stationed in the colony under the direction of Governor Glen. After two years of lobbying by South Carolina agents in London, the units were approved and the following men were commissioned captains and designated as commanders: Alexander Vanderdussen, former commander of the South Carolina Regiment during the 1740 invasion of Florida; Pascall Nelson, a former lieutenant in an independent company stationed in New York; and Robert Hodgson, formerly of the Forty-ninth Regiment. The three units were designated Independent Companies of Foot, having no regimental designation; however, Vanderdussen was given a brevet commission as lieutenant colonel, suggesting that, in the event of an invasion, the three companies possessed the capability of being employed as a battalion under his command. Their uniforms were similar, although probably less elaborate than those of Oglethorpe's Forty-second Regiment: red breeches, waist-coat, and coat with green cuffs and lapels.[15]

The officers, noncommissioned officers, and 60 men arrived in Charles Town in January 1746; the remaining 240 privates were recruited in America. Most of the soldiers were stationed in barracks that were constructed near Charles Town, but in early 1747 a detachment from Captain Nelson's company garrisoned Fort Moore and another from Captain Hodgson's company occupied Fort Frederick near Beaufort. During the following year another detachment was stationed at a new Congaree Fort built on the site of modern Cayce, South Carolina.[16]

The separate military forces of Georgia and South Carolina would have had difficulty in repelling a major invasion from Louisiana or Florida because of their lack of coordination, but, fortunately for the British, the French and Spaniards were restrained from military adventures by the Chickasaw and Creek Indians.

By far the best ally of the British was the Chickasaw nation, located between the Mississippi and Tennessee Rivers in the modern states of Tennessee, Mississippi, and Alabama, with one town near Fort Moore in South Carolina and another near the Upper Creek nation. Even though their fighting strength numbered only about 450 they were the most successful warriors in southern North America, having been consistently victorious over the French and their Choctaw allies during a near continuous war that had begun in 1720. The Chickasaw women were also reportedly ferocious in defense of their towns, employing weapons like their men. In 1736 the French invaded the Chickasaw nation from both Louisiana and Illinois, but the Chickasaw, using superb tactics, destroyed the Illinois portion of the army and then severely defeated Governor Jean Bienville's force from Louisiana when he tried to capture the town of Akia. Governor Bienville again invaded the Chickasaw nation in late 1739 and early 1740, but he withdrew without ever engaging his enemy in battle. During the 1740s the Chickasaw continually raided French settlements, ambushed roads, and made movement on the Mississipppi River extremely hazardous.[17]

Because of the influence of Mary Bosomworth with the Lower Creek, a few Creek warriors joined bands of Yamacraw and Chickasaw (from near Fort Moore) in their raids into Florida during the 1743-45 period. In early September 1744 Daniel Demetre transported a party of warriors to Florida in two scout boats. The Indians landed on the south bank of the Saint Johns River and quietly moved toward Saint Augustine on foot. Near the town they discovered and began following the tracks of a large patrol of Spanish dragoons leading back toward the Saint Johns River. They soon caught up with a small party that was riding far to the patrol's rear, killing an officer and two men and capturing two others. At the same time Demetre's marines began firing at the main body of dragoons who were riding along the bank of the river. The Indians were hurrying toward the river to assist the marines when they saw the dragoons retreating along the river bank in their direction. After forming a hasty ambush behind a row of sand dunes, they opened fire when the dragoons came between them and the river. After quickly reloading their muskets they conducted a screaming charge from the tops of the dunes into the milling horsemen, and before the Spaniards could escape their trumpeter was lost, eight dragoons killed, and one was captured. Not one Indian was hurt. During the following spring another party of Indians conducted an equally successful raid, capturing eleven Spaniards. At that time four parties of Indians, a total of 115 warriors, were operating out of Frederica. Each warrior was provided with a trade musket, a blanket, and food for himself and his family who generally accompanied him to Frederica.[18]

By 1746, however, an anti-British attitude was spreading

among both the Upper and Lower Creek. That turn of events was part of the Creek Indians' traditional neutrality in diplomatic affairs; their policy was to maintain an independence by never subjugating themselves to any European or Indian nation. But, in reality, this manifestation of nationalism was not realistic.[19] A Georgia schoolmaster correctly appraised their dependence upon Britain by observing that a war with the Creek was "contrary to all Reason, for tho they might Abuse or Kill some of the Traders amongst them for their Villany and folly, yet 'tis by no means their Interest to be at odds with the English whilst none other Nations can at this time furnish 'em with the Necessaries they want."[20] In accordance with the schoolmaster's expectations, the Upper Creek quickly suppressed their anti-British talk when a new war with their old enemy, the Cherokee, prompted the need for British gunpowder. Lieutenant Colonel Heron was able to dampen the recently increased Spanish and French sentiment among the Lower Creek with the help of Mary Bosomworth, whose cousin Malatchi had replaced old Chigelley as the principal mico in 1747. The Creek flirtation with the Spaniards ended in August 1748 when a mico named One Eyed King led a war party into Florida and killed the principal Yemassee mico and seven of his men. Shortly afterward a Yemassee war party retaliated by raiding an encampment and killing fifteen Creek.[21]

Those deadly bloodlettings between two Indian nations, operating as agents of their European allies, were nearly the last skirmishes of King George's War on the southern frontier. In October 1748, after seven months of bargaining, the warring European powers agreed to peace at Aix-la-Chapelle in modern Germany. The British government began almost immediately to cut the size of its army, and orders were drafted in November to reduce the number of regular soldiers stationed in Georgia and South Carolina. The Forty-second Regiment and the three Independent Companies in South Carolina were ordered disbanded; however, in order to provide the frontier with a measure of protection from Indians and from possible future Spanish and French intrigues, three new Independent Companies of Foot were ordered organized for duty in Georgia and South Carolina. In December the secretary at war wrote General Oglethorpe, informing him that his commission as commander-in-chief of South Carolina and Georgia had terminated.[22]

Captain George Dunbar, returning to Georgia from England in April 1749, probably carried the Forty-second Regiment's deactivation orders. During May the company commanders rendezvoused with their men at Frederica; Dunbar's company returned from Darien and Oglethorpe's company was transported by water from their distant station at Fort Augusta. Of between 500 and 600 soldiers, 151 volunteered to settle in Georgia, a few enlisted in the three new Independent Companies, and the remainder prepared to return to England. On 29 May 1749 the regiment held its final formation at Frederica. The soldiers received their back pay and promptly became drunk on rum sold by the company sutlers.[23]

The year 1733 began a military era on the southern frontier, and the year 1749 brought that era to a close. The War of Jenkins's Ear–King George's War was over, Georgia's career as a military buffer colony was ended, and the drums of the British regulars and the Georgia provincials were silent. Naïve visions of fortified frontier villages populated with free yeomen farmers, carrying a hoe in one hand and a musket in the other, evaporated forever in July 1749 when the Georgia trustees legalized the use of Negro slave labor.[24] No longer were settlements strategically located for defense; of all the towns and forts settled during the military era, only Savannah, Augusta, and Darien survived. The military no longer served as Georgia's principal industry. Regimental and provincial officers no longer exercised excessive influence in civil affairs. Military command of the southern frontier was transferred from the commander of the forces in Georgia to the governor of South Carolina, and Georgia became a military backwater; only a few regulars and a single crew of boatmen were maintained on duty.[25]

The sixteen years between 1733 and 1749 were also James Edward Oglethorpe's personal era. During most of that period he was the dominent personality, both politically and militarily, on the southern frontier. By utilizing various degrees of diplomacy and armed force, he worked to carry out Britain's imperialistic policy, much of which he had formulated. He made numerous mistakes, but the life of a man of action will naturally include failures. He was a man of distinction and, although he was vain and pompous and had other faults, one should be envious of his extraordinary leadership ability, his great courage, and his compassion for his fellow human beings.

In 1749, at the age of fifty-three, Oglethorpe abandoned the social and professional seclusion that he had entered in 1746 as a result of public criticism concerning his actions during the Jacobite Rebellion, and he began devoting his energies to Parliamentary work. Over one-third of his life still lay ahead of him, and he would enjoy additional successes and suffer new failures. However, he severed all contact with Georgia, attending his last trustees' board meeting on 16 March 1749. He had lost interest in American adventures.[26]

Oglethorpe's involvement with Georgia spanned only about one-sixth of his eighty-nine years, but long-ago hardships, companions, and triumphs on the southern frontier furnished some of his fondest memories in his old age.[27] The pipes and drums of London military parades undoubtedly stirred the old warrior's passions and welled up a sad longing for glories briefly grasped before life's inevitable current carried him out of reach.

Notes

AO: Exchequer and Audit Office Papers, British Public Record Office

BPRO: British Public Record Office, London

CGHS: *Collections of the Georgia Historical Society*

CO: Colonial Office Papers, British Public Record Office

CRG: *Colonial Records of Georgia*

CRG: Colonial Records of Georgia (manuscript)

CSP, AWI: *Calendar of State Papers, Colonial Series, America and the West Indies*

Ga-Ar: Georgia Archives, Atlanta

GHQ: *The Georgia Historical Quarterly*

SC-Ar: South Carolina Archives, Columbia

SCCHJ: *South Carolina Commons House Journals*

SCCHJ: South Carolina Commons House Journals (manuscript)

SCCJ: *South Carolina Council Journals*

SCCJ: South Carolina Council Journals (manuscript)

SCHGM: *The South Carolina Historical and Genealogical Magazine*

SCHM: *The South Carolina Historical Magazine*

SCUHJ: South Carolina Upper House Journals

T: Treasury Office Papers, British Public Record Office

WO: War Office Papers, British Public Record Office

Chapter I

1. Verner W. Crane, *The Southern Frontier, 1670–1732* (Ann Arbor, 1959), pp. 5, 1–10, 24, 25.

2. Ibid., pp. 3–46, 87, 88, 162; Oliver P. Chitwood, *A History of Colonial America* (New York, 1961), pp. 47, 49-139, 182, 183, 186, 187.

3. Ibid., pp. 41–43, 45–47, 182, 183, 188–90; Crane, *Southern Frontier*, pp. 4, 10, 11, 28, 31–33, 71–81.

4. Ibid., pp. 158–61.

5. Frank J. Klingberg, *An Appraisal of the Negro in Colonial South Carolina* (Washington, 1941), pp. ix, x, 1, 47.

6. For information concerning the southeastern Indians see John R. Swanton, *The Indians of the Southeastern United States* (Washington, 1946).

7. Crane, *Southern Frontier*, pp. 94, 95, 164, 167.

8. Ibid., pp. 167–83; Chapman J. Milling, *Red Carolinians* (Columbia, 1969), pp. 135–50.

9. Thomas Cooper and David J. McCord, eds., *The Statutes at Large of South Carolina*, 10 vols. (Columbia, 1836–41), 3:23, 24, 39; 7:66, 67; South Carolina Commons House Journal (hereafter cited as SCCHJ [manuscript] or *SCCHJ*, [published]), 13 Dec. 1716, South Carolina Archives, Columbia (hereafter cited as SC-Ar), Transcript Green Copy No. 5, 203. For the locations of the forts see the following maps: John Barnwell, [Southeastern North America], ca. 1722, [Sketch Map of the Rivers Santee, Wateree, Saludee, &c., with the road to the Cuttauboes], ca. 1736, and Mapp of Beaufort in South Carolina, 1721. See William P. Cumming, ed., *The Southeast in Early Maps* (Chapel Hill, 1958), for information concerning most period maps. No rangers were on duty between late 1718 and 1723, and Congaree Fort was abandoned in 1722.

10. Crane, *Southern Frontier*, pp. 81–86, 88–107, 228–37, 256.

11. Ibid., pp. 246–51; J. H. Easterby, ed., *SCCHJ*, 1 July 1741, p. 82; Copper, *Statutes*, 3:335.

12. Robert L. Meriwether, *The Expansion of South Carolina, 1729–1765* (Kingsport, 1940), pp. 17–20, 32–109; Crane, *Southern Frontier*, pp. 292–95.

13. Meriwether, *Expansion*, pp. 6, 185, 188; Eugene M. Sirmans, *Colonial South Carolina: A Political History, 1663–1763* (Chapel Hill, 1966), pp. 158–70, 185, 186.

14. Ibid., pp. 207, 208; Crane, *Southern Frontier*, pp. 303–25.

Chapter II

1. South Carolina Council Journal (hereafter cited as SCCJ), 26 Jan. 1733; British Public Record Office (hereafter cited as BPRO); Colonial Office Papers (hereafter cited as CO) 5/434, p. 11.

2. Sarah B. G. Temple and Kenneth Coleman, *Georgia Journeys* (Athens, 1961), pp. 7–9; Phinizy Spalding, "South Carolina and Georgia: The Early Days," *The South Carolina Historical Magazine* (hereafter cited as *SCHM*) 69 (Apr. 1968):84–89; Clarence L. VerSteeg, ed., *A True and Historical Narrative of the Colony of Georgia by Patrick Tailfer and Others with Comments by the Earl of Egmont* (Athens, 1960), p. 149. South Carolina normally designated her ranger units according to the

section of the frontier that they protected. Cooper, *Statutes*, 3:24.

3. SCCJ, 26 Jan. 1733, CO 5/434, p. 11.

4. James McPherson's Plat, Plat Book, SC–Ar, 1:271, 272; Robert E. Peeples, "A Miles Genealogy," *SCHM* 66 (Oct. 1965): 230.

5. SCCJ, 26 Jan. 1733, CO 5/434, p. 11; William De Brahm, *A Map of South Carolina and a Part of Georgia* (London, 1757). Purrysburg was established about the middle of December 1732. *South Carolina Gazette* (Charles Town, 1732–75), 20 Dec. 1732; John R. Swanton, *Early History of the Creek Indians and Their Neighbors* (Washington, 1922), pp. 108, 109; Temple and Coleman, *Georgia Journeys*, pp. 11, 17.

6. Ibid., pp. 9–14; E. Merton Coulter, ed., *The Journal of Peter Gordon, 1732–1735* (Athens, 1963), p. 39.

7. The best descriptions of the South Carolinians' working clothing of the period may be found in the advertisements for runaway indentured servants in the *South Carolina Gazette* during the years 1732–40. Also see Meriwether, *Expansion*, pp. 174, 175; McCord, *Statutes*, 9:61, 62; Harold L. Peterson, *Arms and Armor in Colonial America, 1526–1783* (New York, 1956), pp. 161, 162, 164–68, 184, 208, 227, 231, 234–37.

8. South Carolina Upper House Journal (hereafter cited as SCUHJ), 6–8 Oct., 1,6 Dec. 1726, CO 5/429, pp. 5, 8–10, 12, 13, 33, 71, 85, 86; ibid., 6 Mar. 1728, SC-Ar, Council Journal No. 4, pp. 154, 168; A. J. Salley, ed., *SCCHJ*, 22 Feb. 1727, p. 139; Cooper, *Statutes*, 3:316, 335, 359; period descriptions place Saltcatchers Fort (also called Rangers Fort) about three-quarters of a mile east of the present village of Yemassee. "A New Voyage to Georgia," *Collections of the Georgia Historical Society* (hereafter cited as *CGHS*) 9 vols. in 13 parts (Savannah, 1840–1916), 2:51; McCord, *Statutes*, 9:86, De Brahm, *A Map of South Carolina and a Part of Georgia*; Public Treasurer, SC-Ar, Ledger A, p. 86; Easterby, *SCCHJ*, 23 Jan. 1738, pp. 409–11.

9. *South Carolina Gazette*, 7 July 1733; T. F. Lotter, *A Map of the County of Savannah* (London, 1740).

10. *South Carolina Gazette*, 7 July 1733.

11. Amos A. Ettinger, *James Edward Oglethorpe, Imperial Idealist* (Oxford, 1936), pp. 47, 58, 67, 68, 79, 81, 82, 88, 89, 97–99, 109, 111–28, 266, 269, 274–76, 326, and the photograph of the period painting of Oglethorpe.

12. A. S. Salley and Mable L. Webber, eds., *Death Notices in the South Carolina Gazette, 1732–1775* (Columbia, 1954), p. 16. Following his service in Georgia, McPherson commanded a South Carolina troop called the Southern Rangers during 1744, 1746, and 1751. Easterby, *SCCHJ*, 29 June, 3, 4 July 1744, pp. 217, 222, 224, 420; 17 Feb. 1747, pp. 191, 192; McPherson's Commission, 7 July 1744, Miscellaneous Records, SC-Ar, FF, 1743–1746, pp. 92, 93; W. L. McDowell, ed., *Documents Relating to Indian Affairs, 1750–1754* (Columbia, 1958), p. 22.

13. Lotter, *A Map of the County of Savannah; South Carolina Gazette*, 7 July 1733.

14. James Oglethorpe to the Trustees, 17 Sept. 1733, Egmont Papers, Phillipps Collection, University of Georgia Libraries, 14200, p. 113; James Oglethorpe, State of the Colony of Georgia in America, Mar. 1735, ibid., p. 513; John Barnwell, A Plan of King George's Fort, 1722; John Muller, *A Treatise Concerning the Elementary Part of Fortification* (London, 1746), pp. 196–208; Lotter, *A Map of the County of Savannah*.

15. Joseph W. Barnwell, ed., "Fort King George—Journal of Col. John Barnwell," *South Carolina Historical and Genealogical Magazine* (hereafter cited as *SCHGM*) 27 (Oct. 1926): 198; Edwin Tunis, *Colonial Living* (Cleveland, 1957), pp. 31, 32.

16. Oglethorpe to the Trustees, 17 Sept. 1733, Egmont Papers, 14200, p. 113; Oglethorpe, State of the Colony, ibid., p. 513; Lotter, *A Map of the County of Savannah.*

17. Ibid.; Thomas Wright, A Map of Georgia and Florida, 1763.

18. Barnwell, "Fort King George," pp. 197, 198; George F. Jones, ed., *Detailed Reports on the Salzburger Emigrants Who Settled in America . . . Edited by Samuel Urlsperger,* 2 vols. (Athens, 1968), 1:60.

19. Oglethorpe, State of the Colony, Egmont Papers, 14200, p. 513; James Wright to the Board of Trade, 15 Nov. 1766, Allen D. Chandler and Lucian L. Knight, eds., *The Colonial Records of the State of Georgia,* 25 vols. (Atlanta, 1904–16); vols. 20 and 27–39 in typescript at the Georgia Archives, Atlanta (hereafter cited as *CRG* [published] or CRG [manuscript]), 28, pt. 2:429. For period fortification construction methods see Albert C. Manucy, *The Fort at Frederica* (Tallahassee, 1962), pp. 9, 28–42; Muller, *Treatise,* pp. 196–208. During 1966 the author assisted Vietnamese militiamen in building forts similar to Fort Argyle.

20. See note 19.

21. See note 19.

22. Oglethorpe, State of the Colony, Egmont Papers, 14200, p. 513; Tunis, *Colonial Living,* pp. 29–32; Temple and Coleman, *Georgia Journeys,* pp. 13, 44, 129.

23. See note 19.

24. Latrines were seldom mentioned in descriptions of Georgia forts. John D. Combes, while serving as assistant director of the Institute of Archeology and Anthropology, The University of South Carolina, found no latrines during his complete excavation of Fort Prince George (1753–68) in northern South Carolina during 1966–68.

25. Oglethorpe to the Trustees, 17 Sept. 1733, Egmont Papers, 14200, p. 113.

26. Oglethorpe, State of the Colony, ibid., p. 517; Andrew Grant (and others) to the Trustees, 15 Mar., 1735, CRG, 20:196; Temple and Coleman, *Georgia Journeys,* pp. 83, 84.

27. Ibid., pp. xv, 24–26, 59; An Act to prevent the Importation and Use of Rum and Brandies in the Province of Georgia, 3 Apr. 1735, *CRG,* 1:44–49; Common Council, 21 Nov. 1733, ibid., 2:47; Thomas Cristie to the Trustees, 6 Dec. 1735, CRG 20:328, 329; John C. Miller, *The First Frontier: Life in Colonial America* (New York, 1966), pp. 183–87; Jones, *Detailed Reports on the Salzburger Emigrants,* 2:77.

28. Easterby, *SCCHJ,* 15 Dec. 1736, p. 156; Temple and Coleman, *Georgia Journeys,* p. 180; Oglethorpe, State of the Colony, Egmont Papers, 14200, p. 516.

29. Swanton, *Indians of the Southeastern United States,* p. 92; Crane, *Southern Frontier,* p. 187; Cooper, *Statutes,* 3:24, 88–90, 180.

30. SCCHJ, 19, 31 Jan., 16 Feb., 15 May 1723; 15 June 1724, SC-Ar, Transcript Green Copy, Commons House Journals No. 6, 1722–24, pp. 136, 157, 207, 245, 362; Cooper, *Statutes,* 3:180, 181, 244; John Barnwell, [Map of Southeastern North America]; De Brahm, *A Map of South Carolina and a Part of Georgia;* Andrew Allen Plat, Plat Book, SC-Ar; 1:196; William Bellinger to Francis Nicholson, 31

Aug. 1723, Original Papers, Letters, etc. from the Governors, BPRO, CO 5/359; Salley, *SCCHJ*, 4, 9 June 1724, pp. 8, 18, 21; SCCHJ, 27 Apr. 1716, SC-Ar, Transcript Green Copy No. 5, 1716–21, p. 88.

31. Thomas Broughton to Thomas Causton, 28 Apr. 1735, CRG, 20:283; most Georgia fortifications that were built in 1733 and 1734 were in very bad repair by 1737. John Wesley, Account of the condition of the forts and settlements in Georgia, Sept. 1737, Egmont Papers, 14203, pp. 90, 91.

32. Public Treasurer, SC-Ar, Ledger A, pp. 4, 18, 29, 74, 75; William Stephens, A State of the Province of Georgia, 10 Nov. 1740, *CRG*, 4:665, 666; Swanton, *History of the Creek Indians*, p. 309; SCUHJ, 20 July 1731, SC-Ar, Council Journal No. 5, pt. 1, p. 117; Cooper, *Statutes*, 3:181, 182; Salley, *SCCHJ*, 14 Apr. 1725; 30 Apr. 1726, pp. 90, 103, 104; 9 Mar. 1727, p. 166.

33. McCord, *Statutes*, 9:61, 62, 65; Salley, *SCCHJ*, 9 Apr. 1725, p. 82.

34. Cooper, *Statutes*, 3:181; see note 8, this chapter.

35. SCCJ, 16 Aug., 6 Sept. 1732, CO 5/434, pp. 1–2a; William Stephens's Journal, 13 Feb. 1740, *CRG*, 4:511.

36. SCCJ, 26 Jan., 1733, CO 5/434, p. 11.

37. *South Carolina Gazette*, 30 Mar. 1734; Broughton to Causton, 28 Apr. 1735, CRG, 20:283; SCCHJ, 9, 29, Mar. 1734, CO 5/433, 147; SCUHJ, 28 Mar. 1734, CO 5/435, p. 23.

38. Ibid., 28 Mar. 1734; 26 Mar. 1735, pp. 23, 45; ibid., 4 Apr. 1734, CO 5/433, p. 165; Robert Parker, Jr., to the Trustees, 1 Feb. 1735, CRG, 20:235.

39. Ibid., SCUHJ, 26 Mar., 28 Apr. 1735, CO 5/435, pp. 45, 65, 66; Broughton to Causton, 28 Apr. 1735, CRG, 20:283; Oglethorpe, State of the Colony, Egmont Papers, 14200, p. 516.

40. Ibid., pp. 513, 514, 516, 517; Temple and Coleman, *Georgia Journeys*, pp. 2, 3, 100, 117; Wesley, Account of Forts, Egmont Papers, 14203, pp. 89–91; VerSteeg, *Colony of Georgia*, pp. 145–50. Sterling's Fort was located on the western bank of the Ogeechee River about a half mile north of the conflux of Sterling Creek and the Ogeechee. John H. Goff, "Short Studies of Georgia Place Names, No. 110, Sterling Creek," *Georgia Mineral Newsletter* 17 (1964–65):67; Furze and Yonge to the Council of Trade and Plantations, 8 Mar. 1735, Cecil Headlam and others, eds., *Calendar of State Papers, Colonial Series, America and the West Indies* (hereafter cited as *CSP, AWI*) 35 vols., in progress (London, 1860–), 1734–35, p. 388.

41. Ibid.; Oglethorpe, State of the Colony, Egmont Papers, 14200, pp. 513–17; Meriwether, *Expansion*, p. 27n.

Chapter III

1. Swanton, *History of the Creek Indians*, plate 2, p. 442; Swanton, *Indians of the Southeastern United States*, map 11, pp. 153, 154, 289, 352, 373, 693–95; SCCHJ, 9 Mar. 1734, SC-Ar, Commons House Journal No. 8, 7 Feb.–31 May 1734, p. 154; Crane, *Southern Frontier*, pp. 110, 112, 115, 116, 260, 261; William Bull to the Council of Trade and Plantations, 25 May 1738, *CSP, AWI*, 1738, p. 100; Easterby, *SCCHJ*, 15 Dec. 1736, p. 90.

2. Temple and Coleman, *Georgia Journeys*, pp. 17, 19; Edward Kimber, *A Relation or Journal of a late Expedition to the Gates of St. Augustine in Florida* (London,

1744), p. 31; Newton D. Mereness, ed., "A Ranger's Report of Travels with General Oglethorpe, 1739–1742," in *Travels in the American Colonies* (New York, 1916), pp. 220, 221; Oglethorpe to Harman Verelst, 7 Dec. 1741, CRG, 35:400.

3. Crane, *Southern Frontier,* pp. 115, 225–27.

4. *South Carolina Gazette,* 9 Mar. 1734; Oglethorpe to the Trustees, 2 Apr. 1734, Egmont Papers, 14200, p. 170.

5. *South Carolina Gazette,* 9 Mar. 1734; SCCHJ, 8 Mar. 1734, SC-Ar, Commons House Journal No. 8, 7 Feb.–31 May 1734, pp. 57, 58, 60, 61; Common Council, 18 Apr. 1743, *CRG,* 2:413; Crane, *Southern Frontier,* pp. 169, 191, 230; Oglethorpe to the Trustees, 2 Apr. 1734, Egmont Papers, 14200, pp. 170, 171; Cooper, *Statutes,* 3:400.

6. Captain Patrick Mackay's Commission, 13 Mar. 1734, Miscellaneous Records, EE, 1741–43, SC-Ar, p. 48; Common Council, 16 July 1735, *CRG,* 2:112; William Harden, "James Mackay of Strothy Hall, Comrade in Arms of George Washington," *The Georgia Historical Quarterly* (hereafter cited as GHQ) 1 (June, 1917):81; William Mackenzie to I. K. Tefft, 1 Feb. 1844, William Mackenzie Papers, Georgia Historical Society Library, Savannah; VerSteeg, *Colony of Georgia,* p. 146; *South Carolina Gazette,* 16, 23, 30 Mar. 1734.

7. Instructions for Mr. Patrick Mackay Agent to the Creeks, 27 Apr. 1734, Miscellaneous Records, EE, 1741–43, SC-Ar, pp. 53–57.

8. Deposition of Jeremiah Nott, 4 July 1735, Easterby, *SCCHJ,* 15 Dec. 1736, p. 118.

9. Mackay to Causton, 8 July 1734, Egmont Papers, 14200, p. 212; Oglethorpe to Lieutenant Governor Thomas Broughton, 16 Feb. 1736, Easterby, *SCCHJ,* 15 Dec. 1736, p. 126; ibid., 5 June 1736, pp. 126, 127; ibid., 1 July 1736, pp. 127, 128; Crane, *Southern Frontier,* pp. 162–86.

10. Governor Robert Johnson to Oglethorpe, 20 Jan. 1735, CRG, 20:178, 179; Sirmans, *Colonial South Carolina,* pp. 187, 188.

11. *South Carolina Gazette,* 11 May 1734; Mackay's Commission, Miscellaneous Records, EE, p. 48; Instructions for Mackay, ibid., pp. 55, 56; Capt. Patrick Mackay for the Independ't Company, 20 Mar. 1734; 4 Oct. 1735, ibid., pp. 51, 52; Mackay to Oglethorpe, 20 Nov. 1734, CRG, 20:61; ibid, 29 Mar. 1735, p. 545; Robert McPherson, ed., *Journal of the Earl of Egmont, 1732–1738* (Athens, 1962), 24 Sept. 7, 10 Oct. 1735, pp. 109, 112–14; Common Council, 23 May 1745, *CRG,* 2:454; Robert Parker, Jr., to the Trustees, 1 Feb. 1735, CRG, 20:235; Temple and Coleman, *Georgia Journeys,* p. 271; Francis Moore, "A Voyage to Georgia begun in the year 1735," *CGHS* 1 (1840):102, 123; Oglethorpe to the Trustees, 16 Mar. 1736, *CRG,* 21:104; Nott's Deposition, Easterby, *SCCHJ,* 15 Dec. 1736, p. 117.

12. Mackay for the Independ't Company, 20 May 1734, Miscellaneous Records, EE, pp. 50, 52; Mackay to the Trustees, 10 Aug. 1734, CRG, 20:9, 10; Common Council, 23 May 1745, *CRG,* 2:453.

13. Mackay to the Trustees, 20 Nov. 1734, CRG, 20:55, 56; Nott's Deposition, Easterby, *SCCHJ,* 15 Dec. 1736, p. 118. Tobias Fitch was later removed from his office as Indian commissioner. Johnson to Oglethorpe, 28 Jan. 1735, *CRG,* 20:178, 179.

14. Ibid.; Mackay to Oglethorpe, 20 Nov. 1734, ibid., pp. 58, 61; ibid., 29 Mar. 1735, p. 540.

15. Mackay to the Trustees, 10 Aug. 1734, ibid., pp. 9, 10; Mackay to Oglethorpe,

20 Nov. 1734, ibid., p. 58; Mackay for the Independ't Company, 4 June–22 Aug. 1734, Miscellaneous Records, EE, pp. 50, 51.

16. Mackay to Oglethorpe, 20 Nov. 1734, ibid., 20:58; Crane, *Southern Frontier,* p. 127.

17. Mackay to Oglethorpe, 20 Nov. 1734, CRG, 20:59; Mackay to the Trustees, 10 Aug. 1734, ibid, p. 10; Parker to the Trustees, 1 Feb. 1735, ibid., pp. 235, 236.

18. Mackay to Oglethorpe, 20 Nov. 1734, ibid., pp. 60, 61; Common Council, 23 May 1745, *CRG,* 2:453; Parker to the Trustees, 1 Feb. 1735, CRG, 20:237.

19. Mackay to Oglethorpe, 20 Nov. 1734, ibid pp. 60, 61; Adrain Loyer to Oglethorpe, 15 Jan. 1735, ibid., p. 127; Trustees to the Bailiffs and Recorder, 29 May 1735, ibid., 29:115.

20. Mackay to Oglethorpe, 20 Nov. 1734, ibid, 20:60, 61; Instructions for Mackay, Miscellaneous Records, EE, p. 56; Common Council, 23 May 1745, *CRG,* 2:453; Samuel Eveleigh to Oglethorpe, 19 Oct. 1734, Egmont Papers, 14201, p. 271; Mackay to the Trustees, 20 Nov. 1734, CRG, 20:55-57. The countryside around the Uchee town was later called Mount Pleasant. Stephens's Journal, 3 Oct. 1740, *CRG,* 4:660. For the location of Mount Pleasant see De Brahm, *A Map of South Carolina and a Part of Georgia.*

21. Mackay to Oglethorpe, 20 Nov. 1734, CRG, 20:61. The exact date Mackay left the Uchee town is unclear; Common Council, 23 May 1745, *CRG,* 2:452, 453, 455.

22. Thomas Eyre to Robert Eyre, 4 Dec. 1740, Egmont Papers, 14205, p. 172; Mereness, "Ranger's Report," pp. 219, 220; Eyre to Eyre, 4 Dec. 1740, Egmont Papers, 14205, p. 173.

23. Mackay to Oglethorpe, 29 Mar. 1735, CRG, 20:545.

24. *South Carolina Gazette,* 6 July 1734; Mereness, "Ranger's Report," p. 219; Moore, "Voyage to Georgia," pp. 49, 51.

25. Mereness, "Ranger's Report," p. 219; Eyre to Eyre, 4 Dec. 1740, Egmont Papers, 14205, p. 173; The Deposition of John Cadownhead, 4 July 1735, Easterby, *SCCHJ,* 15 Dec. 1736, p. 115. For the location of Coweta and the other Creek towns see Swanton, *History of the Creek Indians,* plates 1 and 2.

26. Swanton, *Indians of the Southeasterm United States,* pp. 289, 352, 373, 386–93.

27. Ibid., pp. 386–91, 682–84; Eyre to Eyre, 4 Dec. 1740, Egmont Papers, 14205, p. 173; Mereness, "Ranger's Report," p. 220.

28. Mackay to the Trustees, 23 Mar. 1735, CRG, 20:539.

29. Mackay to Causton, 27 Mar. 1735, ibid., p. 323; Mackay to Oglethorpe, 29 Mar. 1735, Ibid., pp. 543, 544; Swanton, *History of the Creek Indians,* pp. 265, 266, 289, 304; Causton to the Trustees, 20 June 1735, Egmont Papers, 14201, pp. 36–39; John J. TePaske, *The Governorship of Spanish Florida, 1700–1763* (Durham, 1964), p. 134.

30. Swanton, *Indians of the Southeastern United States,* pp. 457, 464, 564, 690–97, 731, 732. An excellent summary of Creek customs and culture is contained in David H. Corkran, *The Creek Frontier, 1540-1783* (Norman, 1967), pp. 3–40.

31. Mackay to the Trustees, 23 Mar. 1735, CRG, 20:535, 536. Tustegoes seems to have been Tusilgis Tco'ko, a branch town of Kasihta. The Deposition of Thos. Johns, 4 July 1735, Easterby, *SCCHJ,* 15 Dec. 1736, p. 119; ibid., 2 Dec. 1736, p. 138; Swanton, *History of the Creek Indians,* p. 225.

32. Mackay to Causton, 27 Mar. 1735, CRG, 20:322.

33. Mackay to Oglethorpe, 29 Mar. 1735, ibid., p. 544; Mackay to the Trustees, 23 Mar. 1735, ibid., pp. 536–39; John Fenwick to Oglethorpe, 3 Apr. 1735, Egmont Papers, 14200, pp. 531, 532; Diron Dartaguette to the Governor of South Carolina, 20 June 1735, *CRG,* 21:8, 9; John R. Swanton, *Indian Tribes of the Lower Mississippi Valley and Adjacent Coast of the Gulf of Mexico* (Washington, 1911), pp. 217–35.

34. Nott's Deposition, Easterby, *SCCHJ,* 15 Dec. 1736, pp. 117, 118; The Deposition of William Williams, 4 July 1735, ibid., p. 113; Swanton, *History of the Creek Indians,* pp. 244, 245; Mackay to the Trustees, 20 Nov. 1734, CRG, 20:55.

35. Williams's Deposition, Easterby, *SCCHJ,* 15 Dec. 1736, pp. 113, 114.

36. Ibid., p. 114.

37. Moore, "Voyage to Georgia," p. 182; Causton to the Trustees, 14 Dec. 1736, *CRG,* 21:289; Coll. Oglethorpe's State of Georgia, 11 Oct. 1739, Egmont Papers, 14204, p. 133; Mackay to Broughton, 12 July 1735, Easterby, *SCCHJ,* 15 Dec. 1736, p. 122; John H. Goff, "The Path to Okfuskee Upper Trading Route in Georgia to the Creek Indians," *GHQ* 39 (Mar. 1955):5, places Okfuskee Fort on the eastern bank of the Tallapoosa.

38. Mackay to Broughton, 12 July 1735, Easterby, *SCCHJ,* 15 Dec. 1736, p. 122; MacKay to Causton, 27 Mar. 1735, CRG, 20:324; Crane, *Southern Frontier,* pp. 124, 125, 152.

39. Depositions by William Williams, John Cadownhead, Wm. McMullins, Jeremiah Nott, Thos. Johns, and George Coussins, 4 July 1735, Easterby, *SCCHJ,* 15 Dec. 1736, pp. 114, 116, 118–20; Mackay to Broughton, 12 July 1735, ibid., pp. 121–23; Mackay to Thomas Jones [Johns], 28 May 1735, *CRG,* 21:10, 11. As early as November 1734 at least six of the Cherokee traders had decided to ignore the 1734 South Carolina trading act, which imposed the expensive fees, and to operate from Georgia. Eveleigh to Oglethorpe, 20 Nov. 1734, Egmont Papers, 14200, p. 296; Cooper, *Statutes,* 3:400, 401.

40. An Act for maintaining the Peace with the Indians in the Province of Georgia, 3 Apr. 1735, *CRG,* 1:31–44; Common Council, 18 Apr. 1743, ibid., 2:414; Moore, "Voyage to Georgia," p. 102.

41. Williams's and Edwards's Depositions, Easterby, *SCCHJ,* 15 Dec. 1736, pp. 114, 120, 121.

42. Public Treasurer Ledger, SC-Ar, A, p. 2; Common Council, 23 May 1745, *CRG,* 2:455; Causton to the Trustees, 14 Dec. 1736, ibid., 21:289; Fenwick to Oglethorpe, 3 Apr. 1735, Egmont Papers, 14200, p. 531.

43. Mackay to Causton, 27 Mar. 1735, CRG, 20:322; Causton to the Trustees, 20 June 1735, Egmont Papers, 14201, p. 41.

44. Francisco del Moral Sánchez to the Governor of South Carolina, 27 Apr. 13 May, 10 July 1735, *CRG,* 21:5–7, 9, 10; Eveleigh to William Jeffreys, 4 July 1735, Egmont Papers, 14201, p. 71; Dobree to Verelst, 8 July 1735, ibid., p. 117; Sirmans, *Colonial South Carolina,* pp. 188, 189; Broughton to Mackay, 4 July 1735, CRG, 20:434.

45. Common Council, 23 May 1745, *CRG,* 2:471; Gauston to the Trustees, 20 June 1735, Egmont Papers, 14201, pp. 42–44; Broughton to the Georgia

Magistrates, 29 July 1735, ibid., p. 160; Mackay to Oglethorpe, 20 Nov. 1734, CRG, 20:60.

46. Mackay for the Independ't Company, 11 July 1735, Miscellaneous Records, EE, p. 52; Causton to the Trustees, 20 June 1735, Egmont Papers, 14201, pp. 40, 43; Dobree to Verelst, 8 July 1735, ibid., p. 118; Causton to the Trustees, ibid., p. 149.

47. Mackay to Broughton, 12 July 1735, Easterby, *SCCHJ*, 15 Dec. 1736, pp. 121–23; Broughton to Mackay, 4 July 1735, CRG, 20:434–36; Georgia Magistrates to Broughton, 21 July, Egmont Papers, 14201, pp. 133–35; Broughton to the Georgia Magistrates, 29 July 1735, ibid., pp. 157–60.

48. Ibid., pp. 158, 160; Common Council, 18 Apr. 1743, *CRG*, 2:413; Eveleigh to Jeffreys, 4 July 1735, Egmont Papers, 14201, p. 71; Causton to the Trustees, 25 July 1735, ibid., p. 153; ibid., 15 Oct. 1735, p. 206; Moore, "Voyage to Georgia," p. 94; Causton to the Trustees, 20 Nov. 1735, *CRG*, 21:58.

49. Benjamin Martyn to Broughton, 5 Jan. 1736, Easterby, *SCCHJ*, 15 Dec. 1736, p. 125; Trustees to Mackay, 10 Oct. 1735, CRG, 29:205, 206; Trustees to Broughton, 2 Jan. 1735, ibid., 206–9.

50. Moore, "Voyage to Georgia," pp. 94, 101, 102, 123; Causton to the Trustees, 14 Dec. 1736, *CRG*, 21:289. The effective date of the discharge was 27 April 1735, Common Council, 23 May 1745, ibid., 2:456.

Chapter IV

1. Crane, *Southern Frontier*, pp. 235–46; SCCJ, 15 Mar. 1728, Council Journal Number 4, SC-Ar, p. 173; ibid., 25 May 1733, Council Journal Number 5, SC-Ar, pp. 451, 452; Salley, *SCCHJ*, 5 Mar. 1734, p. 89.

2. Meriwether, *Expansion*, p. 20. Samuel Eveleigh, a prominent South Carolina merchant, had strongly recommended to Oglethorpe that he quickly garrison the Altamaha River. Eveleigh to Oglethorpe, 5 Aug. 1734, Egmont Papers, 14200, pp. 231, 232; McPherson, *Egmont's Journal*, 5 Mar., 25 June, 9 July, 24 Sept. 1735, pp. 78, 97–99, 108.

3. Harden, "James Mackay," p. 81; W. R. Williams, ed., "British-American Officers, 1720–1763," *SCHGM* 33 (July 1932):189; McPherson, *Egmont's Journal*, 12 Nov. 1735, p. 117; Moore, "Voyage to Georgia," pp. 90, 108, 109; Oglethorpe to the Trustees, 13 Feb. 1736, *CGHS*, 3:10, 11; Mackay to the Trustees, 23 Sept. 1735, *CRG*, 21:22; George Dunbar to the Trustees, 21 Oct. 1735, ibid., p. 25; Causton to the Trustees, 20 Jan. 1736, ibid., p. 71; Oglethorpe to the Trustees, 27 Feb. 1736, ibid., pp. 75, 76.

4. Ettinger, *Oglethorpe*, p. 156; McPherson, *Egmont's Journal*, 29 Oct. 1735, 19 May 1736, pp. 115, 152; Moore, "Voyage to Georgia," pp. 80, 84, 90–94, 101; George F. Jones, ed., "Von Reck's Second Report from Georgia," *The William and Mary Quarterly* 22 (Apr. 1965):320, 321.

5. Moore, "Voyage to Georgia," pp. 101, 102; Oglethorpe to the Trustees, 13 Feb. 1736, *CRG*, 22:453; Annual Expenses of the Northern and Southern Divisions, 12 Aug. 1737, CRG, 29:430, 431, 433, 435; Extract of letters from Georgia, 7 Mar., 12 Apr. 1736, Egmont Papers, 14201, pp. 313, 314, 389, 390.

6. Moore, "Voyage to Georgia," pp. 103, 104.

7. Larry E. Ivers, "Scouting the Inland Passage, 1685–1737," *SCHM* 73 (July 1972), 117–29.

8. Moore, "Voyage to Georgia," pp. 104, 106, 107; McPherson, *Egmont's Journal,* 11 Feb. 1736, pp. 132, 133.

9. Moore, "Voyage to Georgia," pp. 108, 109; Manucy, *Fort at Frederica,* pp. 5–7.

10. Moore, "Voyage to Georgia," pp. 106, 109–12; Oglethorpe to the Trustees, 27 Feb. 1736, *CRG,* 21:76.

11. Moore, "Voyage to Georgia," pp. 112, 113. For the construction and appearance of a piragua see Ivers, "Scouting," pp. 120, 123.

12. Moore, "Voyage to Georgia," pp. 112–14; Manucy, *Fort at Frederica,* pp. 7–11.

13. Oglethorpe to the Trustees, 16 Mar. 1736, *CRG,* 21:104; Moore, "Voyage to Georgia," p. 115.

14. Ibid, pp. 120–23; Easterby, *SCCHJ,* 23 Jan. 1738, p. 411; Forts Committee, Georgia Department of Archives and History, "Fort St. Andrews, Fort Prince William," *Georgia Magazine* 11 (Aug.–Sep., 1967):22, 23; De Brahm, *A Map of South Carolina and a Part of Georgia;* Thomas Wright, A Map of Georgia and Florida, 1763; John McKinnon, [Map of Cumberland Island], 1802.

15. Samuel Augspourger's Oath, 13 Feb. 1739, CRG, 39:479. Plan dun petit Fort pour L'Isle de St. Andre, ca. 1765, *CGHS,* 7, pt. 3, shows the outline of Fort Saint Andrews's original "Star-work"; Moore, "Voyage to Georgia," pp. 126, 127, 136; Benjamin Martyn, An Account Showing the Progress of the Colony of Georgia, 1741, *CRG,* 3:389; Eveleigh to Oglethorpe, 14 Apr. 1736, Egmont Papers, 14201, p. 398; VerSteeg, *Colony of Georgia,* p. 144.

16. Trevor R. Reese, *Colonial Georgia: A Study in British Imperial Policy in the Eighteenth Century* (Athens, 1963), p. 55; Moore, "Voyage to Georgia," pp. 104, 105, 124.

17. Ibid., pp. 124–26.

18. Ibid., pp. 128, 129; Oglethorpe to the Trustees, 29 Dec. 1739, *CRG,* 22, pt. 2, p. 288; Common Council, 2 July 1735, ibid., 2:109; Reese, *Colonial Georgia,* p. 56. Samuel Eveleigh had hinted to Oglethorpe that he ought to build and garrison a fort on the north bank of the Saint Johns River in order to lay claim to the country between that point and the Altamaha River. Eveleigh to Oglethorpe, 7 Nov. 1734, Egmont Papers, 14200, p. 291; McPherson, *Egmont's Journal,* 17 Jan. 1736, pp. 169, 170.

19. Moore, "Voyage to Georgia," pp. 90, 132, 137, 138, 140; Williams, "British-American Officers," pp. 183–87; Forts Committee, Georgia Department of Archives and History, "Fort St. Simons," *Georgia Magazine* 10 (June–July 1966):29. Delegal's Fort is shown on the Spanish map by Antonio de Arredondo, Plano de la Entrada de Goalquini Rio de altura de Polo Septentrional, *CGHS,* 7, pt. 3. Samuel Eveleigh had recommended to Oglethorpe that he secure permission to station the Independent Company of Foot on the Altamaha River. Eveleigh to Oglethorpe, 7 Nov. 1734, Egmont Papers, 14200, p. 291; W. E. May, ed., "His Majesty's Ships on the Carolina Station," *SCHM* 71 (July 1970):163; McPherson, *Egmont's Journal,* 24 Sept. 1735, p. 109.

20. Trevor R. Reese, *Frederica: Colonial Fort and Town* (Saint Simons, 1969),

p. 18; Moore, "Voyage to Georgia," pp. 137, 138; Jones, "Von Reck's Second Report," p. 238; Oglethorpe to the Trustees, 18 May 1736, *CRG,* 21:159, 160.

21. Moore, "Voyage to Georgia," pp. 140–43; Letter from Oglethorpe, June 1736, Egmont Papers, 14201, p. 517; Common Council, 17 Apr. 1737, *CRG,* 2:188.

22. Moore, "Voyage to Georgia," pp. 149–52; TePaske, *Governorship,* pp. 135, 136.

23. Martyn to Oglethorpe, Apr. 1736, CRG, 29:235–37; ibid., 10 June 1736, 265–67.

24. Reese, *Colonial Georgia,* p. 58; Treaty concluded with the Govr. of Fort Augustin, 20 Oct. 1736, Egmont Papers, 14202, p. 197; Herbert E. Bolton, ed., *Arredondo's Historical Proof of Spain's Title to Georgia* (Berkeley, 1925), p. 74.

Chapter V

1. Common Council, 3 Sept. 1735, *CRG,* 2:120; An Act for Maintaining the Peace with the Indians in the Province of Georgia, 3 Apr. 1735, ibid., 1:31–44; Moore, "Voyage to Georgia," p. 102; Duke of Newcastle to Broughton, 11 Oct. 1735, Easterby, *SCCHJ,* 15 Dec. 1736, pp. 128, 129; Martyn, An Account, *CRG,* 3:384; Cooper, *Statutes,* 3:327–34.

2. Moore, "Voyage to Georgia," pp. 102, 103; Oglethorpe to Broughton, 16 Feb. 1736, Easterby, *SCCHJ,* 15 Dec. 1736, p. 126; Oglethorpe's Summons to the Indian Traders, 16 Feb. 1736, ibid., p. 132.

3. Oglethorpe to Broughton, 5 June 1736, ibid., pp. 126, 127; Instructions to Noble Jones, 4 June 1736, Egmont Papers, 14202, p. 1; Instructions for Mr. Lacy, 11 June 1736, ibid., pp. 1, 2; John Gardiner's Journal, 30 Sept. 1736, Easterby, *SCCHJ,* 15 Dec. 1736, p. 135; Thos. John's Journal, 2 Dec. 1736, ibid., p. 138.

4. E. Merton Coulter and Albert B. Saye, eds., *A List of the Early Settlers of Georgia* (Athens, 1949), p. 81; Temple and Coleman, *Georgia Journeys,* pp. 30, 31; Stephens's Journal, 31 July 1738, *CRG,* 4:178; Causton to the Trustees, 26 Aug. 1738, ibid., 22, pt. 1, p. 231.

5. Instructions to Roger Lacy Gent., 11 June 1736, Egmont Papers, 14202, p. 2; Instructions to Samuel Brown (and others), 11 June 1736, ibid., p. 3; Instructions to Noble Jones, 14 June 1736, ibid., p. 4.

6. Trustees' Journal, 23 Sept. 1743, *CRG,* 1:427; John H. Goff, Some Major Indian Trading Paths across the Georgia Piedmont, Manuscript Map, Dr. John H. Goff Collection, Georgia Surveyor General Department, Atlanta; Marion R. Hemperley, informal notes to the author concerning Lacy's probable route, June 1968, Georgia Surveyor General Department; Gardiner's Journal, Easterby, *SCCHJ,* 15 Dec. 1736, p. 135; William Day to Broughton, 5 Aug. 1736, ibid., p. 141; Oglethorpe's Account of Livestock, 19 Oct. 1738, Egmont Papers, 14203, p. 286.

7. Day to Broughton, 5 Aug. 1736, Easterby, *SCCHJ,* 15 Dec. 1736, p. 141.

8. Gardiner's Journal, ibid., p. 135.

9. Ibid., pp. 134–36.

10. Ibid, pp. 136, 137.

11. Ibid., p. 135.

12. Ibid., pp. 135–37.

13. Ibid., p. 137.

14. Mackay to Broughton, 12 July 1735, ibid., p. 123; Johns's Journal, ibid., p. 138; Swanton, *History of the Creek Indians,* plates 1 and 2.

15. Johns's Journal, Easterby, *SCCHJ,* 15 Dec. 1736, p. 140.

16. Ibid., Causton to the Trustees, 14 Dec. 1736, *CRG,* 21:289.

17. Day to Broughton, 5 Aug. 1736, Easterby, *SCCHJ,* 15 Dec. 1736, p. 141.

18. Newcastle to Broughton, 11 Oct. 1735, ibid., pp. 128, 129; Propositions of the Committee to Oglethorpe, 2 Aug. 1736, ibid., pp. 143, 144; P. Spalding, "South Carolina and Georgia," p. 95; Oglethorpe's Answer to the Committee, 5 Aug. 1736, ibid., pp. 145, 146.

19. Ibid., p. 146.

20. Ettinger, *Oglethorpe,* pp. 188–90; Reese, *Colonial Georgia,* pp. 110, 111.

21. Easterby, *SCCHJ,* 18 Jan., 5 Mar. 1737, 179–81, 321.

Chapter VI

1. Easterby, *SCCHJ,* 14 Dec. 1737, pp. 369, 370; Eveleigh to Oglethorpe, 3 Jan. 1737, *CRG,* 21:295–97; Causton to the Trustees, 24 Feb. 1737, ibid, p. 311; Broughton to the Trustees, 7 Feb. 1737, ibid., p. 335.

2. Causton to the Trustees, 24 Feb. 1737, ibid., pp. 311, 315; ibid., 24 Mar. 1737, p. 383; ibid., 25 Apr. 1737, p. 401; John Brownfield to the Trustees, 10 Feb. 1737, ibid., p. 328; ibid., 2 May 1737, p. 417; Noble Jones [Draught of the fort at Savannah], ibid., p. 375.

3. Verelst to Causton, 11 Aug. 1737, *CRG,* 29:419, 420.

4. Francis Moore to Verelst, 20 Sept. 1736, ibid., p. 226; Philip Delegal's Oath, 11 Mar. 1739, ibid., 39:473; Horton to Causton, 7 May 1737, *CRG,* 21:461, 462.

5. Easterby, *SCCHJ,* 14 Dec. 1737, p. 370; Causton to the Trustees, 25 Apr. 1737, *CRG,* 21:401; Ettinger, *Oglethorpe,* p. 196; TePaske, *Governorship,* p. 137.

6. Ettinger, *Oglethorpe,* pp. 196–205; Reese, *Colonial Georgia,* pp. 63, 64; TePaske, *Governorship,* p. 138; McPherson, *Egmont's Journal,* 23 Mar., 19 Oct. 1737, 17 Apr. 1738, pp. 247–51, 314, 315, 347–49.

7. Stephens to the Trustees, 25 July 1738, *CRG,* 22, pt. 1, p. 201.

8. Annual Expenses of the Northern and Southern Divisions, 12 Aug. 1737, *CRG,* 29:430, 431, 433, 435, 436.

9. Ibid., pp. 430, 431; Elbert to the Trustees, 20 Apr. 1742, *CRG,* 23:282–84; Causton to the Trustees, 2 Apr. 1735, CRG, 20:575, 576; Causton to the Trustees, 26 Nov. 1736, *CRG,* 21:274; Common Council, 25 Mar. 1740, ibid., 2:315; Stephens's Journal, 28 Mar. 1738, ibid., 4:113.

10. Easterby, *SCCHJ,* 18 Jan. 1737, p. 180; Verelst to McPherson, 15 May 1735, CRG, 29:117; McPherson to the Trustees, 13 Sept. 1735, ibid., 20:305–7; Stephens's Journal, 24, 28 Mar., 1, 2, 3 Apr., 8 Aug. 1738, *CRG,* 4:110, 113, 115–17, 385. William Stephens had been hired by the trustees in 1737 to serve in Georgia as their secretary. He transmitted voluminous amounts of information, both creditable and rumored, to London in his journals and he seldom had anything good to say about Georgia's military officers. Stephens's Journals are printed in *CRG* 4 and Supplement to 4 (1737–41); E. Merton Coulter, ed., *The Journal of William Stephens, 1741–1743* (Athens, 1958); and E. Merton Coulter, ed., *The Journal of William Stephens, 1743–1745* (Athens, 1959). The journals for the period after 1745 are missing.

11. Annual Expenses of the Northern Division, 12 Aug. 1737, CRG, 29:430; List of Persons to be paid three months Pay, 12 Aug. 1737, ibid., p. 435; Moore, "Voyage to Georgia," p. 108; Stephens's Journal, 20 May 1739, *CRG,* 4:339.

12. List of Persons to be paid three months Pay, 12 Aug. 1737, CRG, 29:435, 436; Oglethorpe's account of expenses, 22 Sept. 1738, Egmont Papers, Supplement, p. 44; Oglethorpe to William Bull, 29 Dec. 1739, Easterby, *SCCHJ,* 1 July 1741, p. 166; Gerard Monger to Francis Nicholson, 24 Sept. 1723, Original Papers, Letters, etc. from the Governors, CO 5/359, microfilm at SC-Ar., fol. 64; Patrick Mackay to the Trustees, 23 Mar. 1735, CRG, 20:538; Mary Musgrove to Oglethorpe, 17 July 1734, Egmont Papers, 14200, pp. 219–21.

13. Annual Expenses of the Northern Division, 12 Aug. 1737, CRG, 29:431; Moore, "Voyage to Georgia," p. 102; Causton's Journal, 12 June 1737, Egmont Papers, 14203, p. 25.

14. Eveleigh to Verelst, 20 July 1736, *CRG,* 21:179, 180; Common Council, 25 Mar. 1740, ibid., 2:318, 319; Annual Expenses of the Northern Division, 12 Aug. 1737, CRG, 29:430; Stephens's Journal, 5 Dec. 1738, *CRG,* 4:241; Instructions for Mr. Lacy, 11 June 1736, Egmont Papers, 14202, pp. 1, 2; To Noble Jones, 14 June 1736, ibid., p. 4; De Brahm, *A Map of South Carolina and a Part of Georgia.*

15. Causton to the Trustees, 14 Dec. 1736, *CRG,* 21:289; ibid., 25 Apr. 1737, p. 401; McPherson, *Egmont's Journal,* 20 July 1736, p. 183; Wesley, Account of Forts, Egmont Papers, 14203, p. 88; Causton's Journal, 7, 18, 23 June, 3, 18 July 1737, ibid., pp. 19, 33, 38, 48, 64; James Wright to the Board of Trade, 15 Nov. 1766, CRG, 28, pt. 2, p. 429. Fort Augusta may have been similar in appearance and construction to the fort built in Savannah during 1737, for Noble Jones, the surveyor, laid out both fortifications. See Jones [Draught of the fort at Savannah], *CRG,* 21:375; To Noble Jones, 14 June 1736, Egmont Papers, 14202, p. 4; Easterby, *SCCHJ,* 26 Mar. 1743, pp. 321, 322; Stephens's Journal, 24 Apr. 1738, *CRG,* 4:133, 134.

16. Ibid., 9, 10 Dec. 1737, 6 Feb., 5, 24, Apr. 1738, pp. 46, 47, 77, 118, 133, 134; Causton's Journal, 23 June 1737, Egmont Papers, 14203, pp. 37, 38; Causton to the Trustees, 26 Aug. 1738, *CRG,* 22, pt. 1, pp. 231–33.

17. Common Council, 10 May 1738, ibid., 2:235; Verelst to Oglethorpe, 17 June 1736, CRG, 29:279. Kent was the only ranger officer to receive a regular army commission in Oglethorpe's regiment after the rangers were disbanded. Notification Book, 1746–55, BPRO, War Office Papers (hereafter cited as WO) 25/135, p. 144; Oglethorpe to Verelst, 19 Oct. 1739, *CRG,* 22, pt. 2, pp. 244, 245.

18. Expense of the Southern Division, 12 Aug. 1737, CRG, 29:433; Common Council, 21 Nov. 1741, *CRG,* 2:374, 379. Although horses were not mentioned for Mackay's rangers after the spring of 1736, Mackay purchased six bridles, twelve double girths, and one pair of stirrup leather on 15 Aug. 1737, CRG, 29:616; Account of Boats, 29 Dec. 1739, ibid., 35:237.

19. Expense of the Southern Division, 12 Aug. 1737, ibid., 29:435; for the location of Amelia Fort, see the map by Emanuel Bowen, *The Provinces of North and South Carolina, Georgia, etc.* (London, 1747); Trustees' Petition to Parliament, 2 Mar. 1737, CRG, 32:502; Stephens's Journal, 1 Feb. 1738, *CRG,* 4:74; Philip Delegal's Oath, 11 Mar. 1739, CRG, 39:473; *The Gentleman's Magazine,* 1740, p. 129.

20. Ettinger, *Oglethorpe,* pp. 144, 186–88.

21. McPherson, *Egmont's Journal*, 6 Feb., 14 Mar., 21 Sept. 1737, pp. 231–33, 243, 303–5; Reese, *Colonial Georgia*, pp. 75, 76; Williams, "British-American Officers," pp. 187, 188. The title of general was actually that of an office rather than a rank. Oglethorpe was not promoted to actual general officer rank until several years later. Ettinger, *Oglethorpe*, pp. 193–99, 249.

22. Estimate of the Forces, 1740, WO 25/3209; McPherson, *Egmont's Journal*, 16 Nov. 1737, p. 316; Proposal relating to the Troops in Georgia, 5 Nov. 1746, CRG, 36:220; A Monthly Return of General Oglethorpes Regiment of Foot, 30 Sept. 1738, ibid., 35:166. The modern British Army regiment that has inherited the Forty-second Regiment's numerical designation is the First Battalion Royal Highlanders, The Black Watch.

23. Manucy, *Fort at Frederica*, pp. 101, 102; Williams, "British-American Officers," pp. 188, 189; Estimate of the Forces, 1740, WO 25/3209; Reese, *Colonial Georgia*, p. 76; McPherson, *Egmont's Journal*, 21 Sept. 1737, pp. 303–5; Ettinger, *Oglethorpe*, p. 205.

24. Williams, "British-American Officers," pp. 188, 189.

25. Ibid., p. 188; McPherson, *Egmont's Journal*, 21 Sept. 1737, p. 303; Ettinger, *Oglethorpe*, p. 206.

26. Cecil C. P. Lawson, *A History of the Uniforms of the British Army*, 5 vols. (London, 1940–67), 2:8, 9, 11, 12, 14, 15, 17, 18, 20, 93; 3:192–94; Manucy, *Fort at Frederica*, pp. 106–8.

27. Lawson, *Uniforms*, 3:194; Peterson, *Arms and Armor*, pp. 161, 165–68.

28. Stephens's Journal, 6, 9–12, 15, 17, 22, 23, 29 May, 7, 16 June, 8 Sept. 1738; 25 Apr. 1739, CRG, 4:141–44, 146, 148, 151, 157, 197, 323; Common Council, 21 Nov. 1741, ibid., 2:374; Expense of the Southern Division, 12 Aug. 1737, CRG, 29:433; "An Impartial Inquiry into the State and Utility of the Province of Georgia," *CGHS*, 1:181, 187.

29. Stephens's Journal, 27 Sept. 1738, 25 Apr. 1739, CRG, 4:206, 323; General Oglethorpe's Account of the Mutiny, 1 Nov. 1738, Egmont Papers, 14203, p. 318; A Monthly Return of General Oglethorpe's Regiment, 30 Sept. 1738, CRG, 35:166; McPherson, *Egmont's Journal*, 19 Mar., 16 Nov. 1737, 30 Mar., 11 May, 6 June 1738, pp. 246, 316, 342, 359, 371.

30. General Oglethorpe's Account of the Mutiny, 1 Nov. 1738, Egmont Papers, 14203, pp. 318, 319; Thomas Jones to Verelst, 12 Nov. 1738, *CSP, AWI*, 1738, p. 240.

31. Ibid.; General Oglethorpe's Account of the Mutiny, 1 Nov. 1738, Egmont Papers, 14203, p. 318.

32. Ibid., p. 319.

33. Ibid.

34. Ibid., p. 319, 320; Jones to Verelst, 12 Nov. 1738, *CSP, AWI*, 1738, p. 240.

35. Ibid.; General Oglethorpe's Account of the Mutiny, 1 Nov. 1738, Egmont Papers, 14203, p. 320; Stephens's Journal, 11 Nov. 1738, CRG, 4:227.

36. Ibid., 3, 4, 10 Mar., 7 Oct. 1739, 293–95, 428; Williams, "British-American Officers," p. 189.

37. Common Council, 10 May 1738, 25 Mar. 1740, CRG, 2:234, 235, 318; McPherson, *Egmont's Journal*, 10 May 1738, pp. 354, 355; Oglethorpe to the Trustees, 7 Oct. 1738, CRG, 22, pt. 1, pp. 279, 280; ibid., 4 July 1739, pt. 2, p. 170;

Thomas Jones to Verelst, 6 Oct. 1740, ibid., p. 427; Egmont's Journal, 4 July 1741, ibid., 5:523, 524; Easterby, *SCCHJ*, 28 Jan. 1740, p. 150; Oglethorpe's account of expenses, 5 July 1739, Egmont Papers, Supplement, pp. 44, 46, 47: The Accompt of James Oglethorpe Esqr . . . for Extraordinary Services . . . from the 22d of September 1738 to the 22d of July 1743, BPRO, Exchequer and Audit Office (hereafter cited as AO) 3/119, 1738, 1739.

38. Stephens's Journal, 21 Mar., 28 Apr. 1739, *CRG*, 4:302, 303, 325, 326; Oglethorpe to the Trustees, 19 Oct. 1738, ibid., 22, pt. 1, pp. 281, 282; ibid., 4 July 1739, pt. 2, p. 169; ibid., 20 Oct. 1739, pp. 252, 253; Oglethorpe's account of expenses, 5 July 1739, Egmont Papers, Supplement, p. 47; The Accompt of James Oglethorpe, AO 3/119, 1738, 1739.

39. Some Transactions in Georgia and Florida in the years 1739 and 1740, Egmont Papers, 14205, p. 229; Oglethorpe to Newcastle, 8 Oct. 1739, CRG, 35:218.

40. Mereness, "Ranger's Report," p. 218; Copy of the Proceedings of the Assembled Estates of all the Lower Creek Nation, 21 Aug. 1739, Egmont Papers, 14204, p. 87; *South Carolina Gazette,* 11 Aug. 1739; Oglethorpe to Verelst, 19 Oct. 1739, *CRG,* 22, pt. 2, p. 245; Samuel Perkins's Oath, 28 Nov. 1741, *CGHS,* 2:106. Thomas Hunt (later a quartermaster in the English Rangers) may have been the author of "A Ranger's Report of Travels with General Oglethorpe, 1739–1742,," Mereness, "Ranger's Report," pp. 218–36.

41. Ibid., pp. 218–21; Memorial & Representation of Mary Bosomworth, 10 Aug. 1747, CRG, 36:260; Copy of the Proceedings of the Assembled Estates of all the Lower Creek Nation, 21 Aug. 1739, Egmont Papers, 14204, pp. 85–87.

42. Mereness, "Ranger's Report," p. 222.

43. Ibid., pp. 222, 223; Roy W. Smith, *South Carolina as a Royal Province, 1719–1776* (New York, 1903), pp. 179–81; Meriwether, *Expansion,* pp. 6, 185; Easterby, *SCCHJ,* 1 July 1741, 83–85; *The Gentleman's Magazine,* 1740, pp. 127, 128.

44. Oglethorpe to the Trustees, 4 July 1739, *CRG,* 22, pt. 2, p. 169; ibid., 5 Oct. 1739, p. 218; ibid., 20 Oct. 1739, p. 252; Oglethorpe to Verelst, 9 Oct. 1739, ibid., pp. 235, 236; The Declaration of the Account of James Oglethorpe, AO 1/162/441, p. 5; Stephens's Journal, 16 Nov. 1739, *CRG,* 4:454.

45. Mereness, "Ranger's Report," p. 222; Easterby, *SCCHJ,* 1 July 1741, p. 83; Copy of the Proceedings of the Assembled Estates of all the Lower Creek Nation, 21 Aug. 1739, Egmont Papers, 14204, p. 87; Oglethorpe to Verelst, 9 Oct. 1739, *CRG,* 22, pt. 2, pp. 235, 236; Stephens's Journal, 13 Feb. 1740, ibid., 4:511; *The Gentleman's Magazine,* 1740, pp. 127, 128; McCord, *Statutes,* 9:112, 113.

46. Oglethorpe to Newcastle, 8 Oct. 1739, CRG, 35:218, 219.

47. Mereness, "Ranger's Report," p. 223; Oglethorpe to Bull, 27 Sept. 1739, Easterby, *SCCHJ,* 1 July 1741, p. 164.

48. Mereness, "Ranger's Report," p. 223; *The Gentleman's Magazine,* 1740, p. 129.

49. Mereness, "Ranger's Report," p. 223.

Chapter VII

1. There is no evidence that the war party included any Spaniards. Some

Transactions in Georgia and Florida in the years 1739 and 1740, Egmont Papers, 14205, p. 230.

2. Ibid.; Egmont's Journal, 4 July 1741, *CRG*, 5:523, 524; The Deposition of Mr. Hugh Mackay, *CGHS*, 1:187; Hugh Mackay, Jr., *A Letter from Lieut. Hugh Mackay of Genl. Oglethorpe's Regiment, to John Mackay, Esq: in the Shire of Sutherland in Scotland* (London, 1742), pp. 13, 14; Oglethorpe to Newcastle, 15 Nov. 1739, CRG, 35:229; Oglethorpe to the Trustees, 16 Nov. 1739, *CRG*, 22, pt. 2, p. 266; Stephens's Journal, 22 Nov. 1739, ibid., 4: 457, 458; *The Gentleman's Magazine*, 1740, p. 129.

3. Mereness, "Ranger's Report," p. 224; Mark Carr to James Campbell, 28 Jan. 1740, Egmont Papers, 14204, p. 326.

4. Mereness, "Ranger's Report," p. 224; An exact Acct . . . of our Forces, and What Loss We Sustain'd during the Siege, Egmont Papers, Supplement, p. 183; Oglethorpe to Newcastle, 22 Jan. 1740, CRG, 35:239.

5. Ibid., pp. 239, 241; The Declaration of the Account of James Oglethorpe, AO 1/162/441, p. 11a.

6. Carr to Campbell, 28 Jan. 1740, Egmont Papers, 14204, pp. 326–28; Oglethorpe to Stephens, 1 Feb. 1740, *CRG*, 22, pt. 2, p. 312; Mereness, "Ranger's Report," pp. 224, 225.

7. Stephens's Journal, 21 Dec. 1739, 2 Jan. 1740, *CRG*, 4:474, 475, 483; Oglethorpe to Newcastle, 22 Jan. 1740, CRG, 35:240, 241; Oglethorpe to Stephens, 1 Feb. 1740, *CRG*, 22, pt. 2, pp. 313, 314; Wright, A Map of Georgia and Florida; TePaske, *Governorship*, p. 134.

8. Ibid., p. 139; Moore, "Voyage to Georgia," p. 128; Moral to Broughton, 13 May 1735, *CRG*, 21:5.

9. Mereness, "Ranger's Report," pp. 225, 226; Oglethorpe to Newcastle 22 Jan. 1740, CRG, 35:241; Oglethorpe to Stephens, 1 Feb. 1740, *CRG*, 22, pt. 2, p. 314; Carr to Campbell, 28 Jan. 1740, Egmont Papers, 14204, p. 329; Mereness, "Ranger's Report," pp. 225, 226.

10. Ibid., p. 226.

11. Ibid.; Oglethorpe to Stephens, 1 Feb. 1740, *CRG*, 22, pt. 2, pp. 314, 315; Carr to Campbell, 28 Jan. 1740, Egmont Papers, 14204, p. 329; Oglethorpe to Newcastle, 22 Jan. 1740, CRG, 35:241, 242.

12. Carr to Campbell, 28 Jan. 1740, Egmont Papers, 14204, pp. 329, 330; Oglethorpe to Stephens, 1 Feb. 1740, *CRG*, 22, pt. 2, p. 315.

13. Ibid.; Mereness, "Ranger's Report," p. 226; Oglethorpe to Newcastle, 22 Jan. 1740, CRG, 35:242.

14. Mereness, "Ranger's Report," pp. 226, 227.

15. Ibid.; Oglethorpe to Stephens, 1 Feb. 1740, *CRG*, 22, pt. 2, p. 315; Carr to Campbell, 28 Jan. 1740, Egmont Papers, 14204, p. 330; Oglethorpe to Newcastle, 22 Jan. 1740, CRG, 35:242; The Declaration of the Account of James Oglethorpe, AO 1/162/441, p. 17.

16. Report of the Committee Appointed to Enquire into the Causes of the Disappointment of Success in the Late Expedition against St. Augustine, Easterby, *SCCHJ*, 1 July 1741, pp. 80, 85, 86; Report of the Committee on the Lieutenant Governor's Message, 12 Dec. 1739, ibid., p. 165.

17. Oglethorpe to Bull, 29 Dec. 1739, ibid., p. 166.

18. Ibid., 24 Jan. 1740, p. 168; The Estimate of Forces . . . Thought Necessary

by General Oglethorpe, 4 Feb. 1740, ibid., pp. 168–70; Report of the Committee, ibid., p. 87.

19. An Estimate of the Expense on General Oglethorpe's Proposal, 5 Feb. 1740, ibid., pp. 171–74; Report of the Committee How far £120,000 Would Go, 9 Feb. 1740, ibid., pp. 174–76.

20. Oglethorpe to Bull, 27 Feb. 1740, ibid., p. 177; Oglethorpe to Newcastle, 19 July 1740, CRG, 35:274, 275.

21. Stephens's Journal, 26 Feb. 1740, *CRG*, 4:520, 521; *The Gentleman's Magazine*, 1740, p. 129.

22. Report of the Committee, Easterby, *SCCHJ*, 1 July 1741, p. 89; Oglethorpe to Bull, 26 Mar. 1740, ibid., p. 178.

23. Report of the Committee, ibid., pp. 89, 90; General Oglethorpe's Plan of Assistance, 29 Mar. 1740, ibid., pp. 178, 179; Oglethorpe to Bull, 29 Mar. 1740, ibid., pp. 179, 180.

24. Report of the Committee, ibid., p. 90; Oglethorpe to Robert Walpole, 23 Jan. 1740, Cholmondeley (Houghton) Manuscripts, Sir Robert Walpole's Archive, University Library, Cambridge, England, letter 2942.

25. Report of the Committee, Easterby, *SCCHJ*, 1 July 1941, pp. 90, 91; Report of the Committee Appointed to Confer with General Oglethorpe, 29 Mar. 1740, ibid., p. 180; The Estimate of the Forces . . . Thought Necessary by General Oglethorpe, ibid., p. 169; Oglethorpe to Walpole, 2 Apr. 1740, Cholmondeley Manuscripts, letter 2948; Cooper, *Statutes,* 3:546–53.

26. Oglethorpe to the Trustees, 29 Dec. 1739, CRG, 35:234; Stephens's Journal 16 Nov. 1739, 20 Sept. 1740, *CRG,* 4:454. 656; The Declaration of the Account of James Oglethorpe, AO 1/162/441, pp. 5, 11a; The Accompt of James Oglethorpe, AO 3/119, 20 Oct. 1739, 8 Apr., 10 Sept. 1740, 29 Sept. 1741; Coulter and Saye, *Early Settlers of Georgia,* p. 2.

27. The Declaration of the Account of James Oglethorpe, AO 1/162/441, pp. 5, 9a, 17; Copy of the Proceedings of the Assembled Estates of all the Lower Creek Nation, 21 Aug. 1739, Egmont Papers, 14204, p. 87.

28. Scroggs officially assumed command of the English Rangers on 28 November 1739. The Declaration of the Account of James Oglethorpe, AO 1/162/441, pp. 5, 9a, 10, 11a, 12; Oglethorpe to the Trustees, 29 Dec. 1739, CRG, 35:234; Stephens's Journal, 29 Nov. 1739, *CRG,* 4:461; James Carwells to the Trustees, 15 Oct. 1741, ibid., 23:115; Edward Kimber, "Itinerant Observations in America," *CGHS,* 4, pt. 2 (1878):14. The Accompt of James Oglethorpe, AO 3/119, 25 June 1740. The British long land musket, a smoothbore flintlock commonly known as the "Brown Bess," was the most common weapon in Georgia. Ordinance Stores delivered to Genl. Oglethorpe in 1737, CRG, 39:140–42; Ordnance & Stores Sent . . . 1739, ibid., p. 155.

29. Stephens's Journal, 4 Dec. 1739, *CRG,* 4:464, 465; Oglethorpe to Bull, 29 Dec. 1739, Easterby, *SCCHJ,* 1 July 1741, p. 166; Carr to Campbell, 28 Jan. 1740, Egmont Papers, 14204, p. 232; An exact Acct . . . of our Forces, and What Loss We Sustain'd during the Seige, ibid., Supplement, p. 183.

30. Oglethorpe to Verelst, 7 Dec. 1741, ibid., 14206, p. 96; Account of Boats, 30 Apr. 1740, CRG, 35:258. The *Speedwell* was Captain Carr's boat. Military Strength of Carolina and Georgia, 7 June 1742, ibid., p. 465; Mackay, *Letter,* p. 30.

31. Stephens's Journal, 18, 22, 24, 28 Apr., 10 May, 11 Aug. 1740, *CRG,* 4:556,

558, 559, 562, 571, 638; Henry A. M. Smith, "Purrysburg," *SCHGM* 10 (Oct., 1909):215.

32. The Declaration of the Account of James Oglethorpe, AO 1/162/441, p. 5; Alexander Mackintosh to William MacKenzie, 27 Sept. 1844, William Mackenzie Papers, Ga. Hist. Soc. Lib., Savannah; Establishment of a Company of Highland Foot, 30 Apr. 1740, CRG, 35:257; John Mackintosh to Alexander Mackintosh, 20 June 1741, ibid., p. 340; Frank Adam, *The Clans, Septs, and Regiments of the Scottish Highlands* (Edinburgh, 1952), pp. 356, 366; Estimate of the charges for a servant for one year, 16 Mar. 1737, Egmont Papers, Supplement, p. 462; Moore, "Voyage to Georgia," Verelst to John Hossack, 23 Apr. 1737, CRG, 29:374; Verelst to Causton, 11 Aug. 1737, ibid., p. 415; Temple and Coleman, *Georgia Journeys,* p. 173; Mackay, *Letter,* pp. 11, 17, 18.

33. Oglethorpe's personal expenses for military items during the period 1738 to 1743 are outlined in The Declaration of the Account of James Oglethorpe, AO 1/162/441; and The Accompt of James Oglethorpe, ibid., 3/119; King's Instructions to Oglethorpe, 9 Oct. 1739, CRG, 35:224–26; Oglethorpe to the Trustees, 16 Nov. 1739, *CRG,* 22 pt. 2, p. 266–68; ibid., 29 Dec. 1739, 287–89; Verelst to Oglethorpe, 29 Mar. 1740, CRG, 30:216, 217.

34. Report of the Committee, Easterby, *SCCHJ,* 1 July 1741, pp. 86, 87, 90, 93, 99, 102; Corkran, *Creek Frontier,* pp. 103, 104, 106; An exact Acct . . . of our Forces, and what loss we Sustain'd during the Seige, Egmont Papers, Supplement, p. 183; Patrick Mackay to Oglethorpe, 29 Mar. 1736, CRG, 20:543; Stephens's Journal, 20 Nov. 1739, *CRG,* 4:456; Carr to Campbell, 28 Jan. 1740, Egmont Papers, 14204, p. 329.

35. An exact Acct . . . of our Forces, and what loss we Sustain'd during the Seige, ibid., Supplement, p. 183; Martyn, An Account, *CRG,* 3:403.

36. Reese, *Colonial Georgia,* pp. 76–78; Report of the Committee, Easterby, *SCCHJ,* 1 July 1741, pp. 84, 91.

37. Ray A. Billington, *Westward Expansion* (New York, 1963), pp. 22–28; TePaske, *Governship,* pp. 134, 135, 140, 141; Wright, A Map of Georgia and Florida; Map of the Coast of Florida from Talbot Island to the mouth of the Musquetta River, 1740; Antonio de Arredondo, Plano del Castillo de Sn Marcos de la Florida, 1737; Arredondo, Plan[o] de la Ciudad De Sn Augustin de la Fla, 1737.

38. Carr to Campbell, 28 Jan. 1740, Egmont Papers, 14204, p. 330; TePaske, *Governorship,* p. 140; Montiano to Güemes, 23 Feb., 24, 25 Mar. 1740, *CGHS,* 7, pt. 1, pp. 43–46, 48.

39. Mackay, *Letter,* pp. 15, 16; Report of the Committee, Easterby, *SCCHJ,* 1 July 1741, pp. 102, 103; Montiano to Güemes, 27 Apr. 1740, *CGHS,* 7, pt. 1, pp. 49–51; An Account of Genl. Oglethorpe's proceedings against Augustine, about 31 Aug. 1740, Cholmondeley Manuscripts, letter 4.

40. Ibid.; Reese, *Colonial Georgia,* pp. 64, 70; King's Instructions to Oglethorpe, 9 Oct. 1739, CRG, 35:224–26.

Chapter VIII

1. Mereness, "Ranger's Report," p. 227; Report of the Committee, Easterby, *SCCHJ,* 1 July 1741, pp. 92, 93; The Deposition of Thomas Wright, 25 May

1741, ibid., p. 184; General Oglethorpe's Journal of his First Proceedings, 14 May 1740, ibid., p. 181.

2. Ibid.; Wright's Deposition, ibid, p. 184.

3. Report of the Committee, ibid., p. 94.

4. General Oglethorpe's Journal, ibid., pp. 181, 182.

5. Ibid., 182; Williams, "British-American Officers," p. 189; Mereness, "Ranger's Report," pp. 227, 229.

6. General Oglethorpe's Journal, Easterby, *SCCHJ,* 1 July 1741, pp. 182, 183; The Accompt of James Oglethorpe, AO 3/119, 8 Apr. 1740, 8 May 1742.

7. Report of the Committee, Easterby, *SCCHJ,* 1 July 1741, p. 95; An Account of Genl. Oglethorpe's Proceedings, Cholmondeley Manuscripts, letter 4; Oglethorpe to Newcastle, 19 July 1740, CRG, 35:274; Mackay, *Letter,* pp. 19, 20.

8. General Oglethorpe's Journal, Easterby, *SCCHJ,* 1 July 1741, p. 183.

9. Vanderdussen to Bull, 27 May 1740, ibid., p. 188; Deposition of Colonel Alexander Vanderdussen, 25 June 1741, ibid., p. 186.

10. Report of the Committee, ibid., pp. 98, 99.

11. Ibid., pp. 99–102; Vanderdussen to Bull, 28 June 1740, ibid., p. 202; An Account of Genl. Oglethorpe's Proceedings, Cholmondeley Manuscripts, letter 4; Mackay, *Letter,* p. 20.

12. Report of the Committee, Easterby, *SCCHJ,* 1 July 1741, p. 92: Wright's Deposition, ibid., pp. 184, 185; Deposition of Lieutenant Bryan, 25 Mar. 1741, ibid., pp. 189–91; Deposition of Captain William Palmer, 19 Feb. 1741, ibid., pp. 196, 198.

13. Report of the Committee, ibid., pp. 101, 102; Resolution of a Council of War, 5 June 1740, ibid., p. 206; An Account of Genl. Oglethorpe's Proceedings, Cholmondeley Manuscripts, letter 4; Oglethorpe to Newcastle, 19 July 1740, CRG, 35:275; Mackay, *Letter,* pp. 21, 22, 25, 26.

14. Vanderdussen apparently was never privy to Oglethorpe's exact battle plans. Vanderdussen's Deposition, Easterby, *SCCHJ,* 1 July 1741, p. 186. The best explanation of the battle plan and its various changes is Oglethorpe's in An Account of Genl. Oglethorpe's Proceedings, Cholmondeley Manuscripts, letter 4.

15. Ibid.; Mackay, *Letter,* pp. 22, 23, 25, 26; Oglethorpe to Newcastle, 19 July 1740, CRG, 35:275; Report of the Committee, Easterby, *SCCHJ,* 1 July 1741, pp. 102, 109–11.

16. Ibid., pp. 111, 112, 114, 115.

Chapter IX

1. This chapter was originally published as Larry E. Ivers, "The Battle of Fort Mosa," *GHQ* 51 (June 1967), 135–53; Mackay, *Letter,* pp. 16, 17; The Declaration of the Account of James Oglethorpe, AO 1/162/441, p. 17; Manuscript Map of Indian Trails, Dr. John H. Goff Collection, Georgia Surveyor General Department; Report of the Committee, Easterby, *SCCHJ,* 1 July 1741, 104. Captain James McPherson had been commissioned commander of the defunct ranger troop upon Oglethorpe's recommendation. Oglethorpe to Bull, 29 Dec. 1739, ibid., p. 166; *South Carolina Gazette,* 11 Apr. 1740. One of Mary Mathews's servants guided the Georgia Rangers to Florida. Mary (Musgrove, Mathews) Bosomworth to Henry Ellis, 23 July 1759, CRG, 27, pt. 1-A, p. 400.

2. Report of the Committee, Easterby, *SCCHJ*, 1 July 1741, pp. 103, 104; Vanderdussen to Pearse, 8 June 1740, ibid., p. 208; Mackay, *Letter*, pp. 22, 23.

3. A company of the South Carolina Regiment was originally supposed to accompany the "flying party," but Oglethorpe assigned it elsewhere. Deposition of Captain Stephen Bull, 23 May 1741, Easterby, *SCCHJ*, 1 July 1741, pp. 210, 211. Mackay's accounts of the flying party's strength are utilized. Being commander of the men he was undoubtedly interested in accurate unit returns. Arrival of some Creek Indians on 14 June probably brought the flying party's total numbers to about 140. Mackay, *Letter*, pp. 23–26, 37: Deposition of Thomas Jones, 9 Apr. 1741, Easterby, *SCCHJ*, 1 July 1741, p. 192; The Accompt of James Oglethorpe, AO 3/119, 29 Sept. 1740; Deposition of Edward Lyng, 8 Sept. 1743, SCCJ, 25 Oct. 1743, SC-Ar, p. 331.

4. Ibid., pp. 331, 332; Mackay, *Letter*, pp. 24, 25, 27; *Boston News Letter*, 13 June 1715, 25 Apr. 1728; Samuel Eveleigh to Boon and Berresford, 7 Oct. 1715, *CSP, AWI*, 1714–15, pp. 296, 297; Historical Commission of South Carolina, *SCCJ*, 1 June 1721; Deposition of Capt John Mackintosh, Quartermaster James McQueen, and Private Ronald Mackdonald, 1743, CRG, 35:431; Jones's Deposition, Easterby, *SCCHJ*, 1 July 1741, pp. 192, 193; Palmer's Desposition, ibid., p. 196; Deposition of William Steads, 13 Mar. 1741, ibid., p. 199; Deposition of Capt Ephrim Mikell, 28 Feb. 1741, ibid., p. 201; Deposition of Col. Barnwell, ibid., p. 210. The South Carolina Assembly report incorrectly stated that Colonel John Palmer's first name was William.

5. Mackay, *Letter*, pp. 26, 27.

6. Report of the Committee, Easterby, *SCCHJ*, 1 July 1741, p. 100.

7. Vanderdussen's Deposition, ibid., p. 187.

8. Mackay, *Letter*, pp. 6, 24–28, 32; Report of the Committee, Easterby, *SCCHJ*, 1 July 1741, pp. 160, 161; Jones's Deposition, ibid., p. 193; Palmer's Deposition, ibid., p. 196; Steads's Deposition, ibid., p. 199; Barnwell's Deposition, ibid., p. 210; Oglethorpe to the Magistrates and Bailiffs of Frederica, ibid., p. 227; Deposition of Mackintosh, McQueen, and Mackdonald, CRG, 35:430, 431.

9. Mackay, *Letter*, pp. 6, 25; see also note 8, this chapter.

10. Mackay, *Letter*, p. 28; Deposition of Mackintosh, McQueen, and Mackdonald, CRG, 35:431; Report of the Committee, Easterby, *SCCHJ*, 1 July 1741, pp. 160, 161; Jones's Deposition, ibid., p. 193; Palmer's Deposition, ibid., p. 196.

11. Deposition of Mackintosh, McQueen, and Mackdonald, CRG, 35:431, 432; Mackay, *Letter*, p. 28.

12. Ibid., pp. 27, 28; Deposition of Mackintosh, McQueen, and Mackdonald, CRG, 35:431.

13. Palmer's Deposition, Easterby, *SCCHJ*, 1 July 1741, p. 196; Jones's Deposition, ibid., p. 193.

14. Mr. Gordon's Journal, 10 June 1740, ibid., pp. 211, 212.

15. Mackay, *Letter*, p. 28.

16. Palmer's Deposition, Easterby, *SCCHJ*, 1 July 1741, p. 196.

17. Ibid., p. 197; Jones's Deposition, ibid., p. 193; Steads's Deposition, ibid., p. 199.

18. Palmer's Deposition, ibid., pp. 195, 196.

19. Ibid., p. 197; Mackay, *Letter*, p. 29.

20. Jones's Deposition, Easterby, *SCCHJ*, 1 July 1741, p. 193; Palmer's Deposition, ibid., p. 197; Steads's Deposition, ibid., p. 199.

21. Mackay to Vanderdussen, 13 June 1740, ibid., p. 213; Palmer's Deposition, ibid., p. 197; Vanderdussen to Mackay, 13 June 1740, ibid., p. 214.

22. Steads's Deposition, ibid., p. 199.

23. Ibid., p. 200; The Indians arrived after the battle. Mackay, *Letter,* pp. 30, 37.

24. Montiano to Güemes, 24 June 1740, *CGHS,* 7, pt. 1, p. 56.

25. Ibid., TePaske, *Governorship,* pp. 142, 143. The modern calendar date would be 25 June.

26. TePaske, *Governorship,* p. 143; Montiano to Güemes, 6 July 1740, *CGHS,* 7, pt. 1, p. 56.

27. Palmer's Deposition, Easterby, *SCCHJ,* 1 July 1741, p. 197; Jones's Deposition, ibid., p. 193.

28. Mackay, *Letter,* p. 31. Jones said they attacked in four parties. Jones's Deposition, Easterby, *SCCHJ,* 1 July 1741, p. 193; Steads's Deposition, ibid., p. 200. The sentry may also have fired a shot.

29. Palmer's Deposition, Easterby, *SCCHJ,* 1 July 1741, p. 197; Jones's Deposition, ibid., p. 193; Steads's Deposition, ibid., p. 200.

30. Jones's Deposition, ibid., p. 193; Mackay, *Letter,* p. 30.

31. Ibid., p. 31; Jones's Deposition, Easterby, *SCCHJ,* 1 July 1741, p. 193.

32. Palmer's Deposition, ibid., p. 197; Steads's Deposition, ibid., p. 200.

33. Jones's Deposition, ibid., p. 193; Mackay, *Letter,* p. 32.

34. Ibid.; Lyng's Deposition, SCCJ, 25 Oct. 1743, SC-Ar, p. 333.

35. Steads's Deposition, Easterby, *SCCHJ,* 1 July 1741, p. 200. Steads's account of the battle is overly dramatic.

36. Mackay, *Letter,* pp. 34, 35; Lyng's Depostion, SCCJ, 25 Oct. 1743, SC-Ar, p. 333.

37. Ibid., p. 332; Mackay, *Letter,* p. 33.

38. Palmer's Deposition, Easterby, *SCCHJ,* 1 July 1741, p. 197.

39. Ibid., pp. 197, 198; Mackay, *Letter,* p. 33.

40. Palmer's Deposition, Easterby, *SCCHJ,* 1 July 1741, p. 198; Mackay, *Letter,* pp. 30, 34.

41. Mackintosh to Mackintosh, 20 June 1741, CRG, 35:341; Deposition of Kenneth Baillie, 11 Mar. 1742, *CRG,* 5:605; Lyng's Deposition, SCCJ, 25 Oct. 1743, SC-Ar, p. 333; Jones's Deposition, Easterby, *SCCHJ,* 1 July 1741, p. 194; Steads's Deposition, ibid., p. 201; Oglethorpe to the Magistrates and Bailliffs of Frederica, ibid., pp. 227, 228; Mackay, *Letter,* pp. 34, 35; An exact Acct . . . of our Forces, and what loss we Sustain'd during the Seige, Egmont Papers, Supplement, p. 183; Montiano to Güemes, 6 July 1740, *CGHS,* 7, pt. 1, p. 57.

Chapter X

1. Montiano to Güemes, 6 July 1740, *CGHS,* 7, pt. 1, p. 56; Gordon's Journal, 20, 21 June 1740, Easterby, *SCCHJ,* 1 July 1741, pp. 219, 221; Report of the Committee, ibid., pp. 116–18; Deposition of Capt. Richard Wright, 28 Mar. 1741, ibid., pp. 204, 205.

2. Deposition of Gabriel Manigault, 25 June 1741, ibid., pp. 246, 247.

3. Declaration of Lt. Patrick Sutherland, 9 Aug. 1744, CRG, 36:202.

4. An Account of Genl. Oglethorpe's Proceedings, Cholmondeley Manuscripts, letter 4; Report of the Committee, Easterby, *SCCHJ,* 1 July 1741, pp. 103, 110;

Vanderdussen to Oglethorpe, 14 June 1740, ibid., p. 214; The Opinion of the Officers of Col. Vanderdussen's Regiment, 17 June 1740, ibid., p. 217; Albert C. Manucy, *Artillery through the Ages* (Washington, 1949), p. 79.

5. Gordon's Journal, 16 June 1740, Easterby, *SCCHJ,* 1 July 1741, p. 216; Oglethorpe to Vanderdussen, 16 June 1740, ibid., p. 216; An Account of Genl. Oglethorpe's Proceedings, Cholmondeley Manuscripts, letter 4.

6. Gordon's Journal, 16, 17 June 1740, Easterby, *SCCHJ,* 1 July 1741, pp. 216–18.

7. Ibid., 25, 26 June 1740, pp. 222, 224; Vanderdussen to Pearse, 25 June 1740, ibid., p. 223; Pearse to Vanderdussen, 25 June 1740, ibid., p. 223; ibid., 26 June 1740, p. 224; Report of the Committee, ibid., p. 125.

8. Ibid., p. 130, 159; Vanderdussen to Bull, 28 June 1740, ibid., p. 225; ibid., 3 July 1740, p. 231.

9. Report of the Committee, ibid., pp. 125, 127; Jones's Deposition, ibid., p. 194.

10. Report of the Committee, ibid., pp. 122, 131; Vanderdussen to Pearse, 27 June 1740, ibid., p. 226; Resolution of a Council of War, 27 June 1740, ibid., p. 226; Gordon's Journal, 2 July 1740, ibid., pp. 228, 229; Pearse to Oglethorpe, 2 July 1740, ibid., p. 229.

11. Vanderdussen to Oglethorpe, 2 July 1740, ibid., pp. 229, 230; Oglethorpe to Pearse, 2 July 1740, ibid., p. 230; Pearse to Oglethorpe, 3 July 1740, ibid., pp. 231, 232.

12. Vanderdussen to Oglethorpe, 4 July 1740, ibid., p. 233.

13. Oglethorpe to Vanderdussen, 4 July 1740, ibid., p. 234; Oglethorpe to Bull, 19 July 1740, ibid. pp. 242, 243; An Account of Genl. Oglethorpe's Proceedings, Cholmondeley Manuscripts, letter 4.

14. Report of the Committee, Easterby, SCCHJ, 1 July 1741, pp. 136, 137, 139–42; Gordon's Journal, 9, 10, 11, 15 July, ibid., pp. 236, 237, 239; Vanderdussen to Oglethorpe, 11 July 1740, ibid., pp. 237, 238; Oglethorpe to Vanderdussen, 13 July 1740, ibid., p. 238.

15. Oglethorpe to Bull, 16 June 1740, ibid., pp. 215, 216; Report of the Committee, ibid., pp. 143–46; Bull to Oglethorpe, 7 July 1740, ibid., p. 241.

16. Gordon's Journal, 15, 21, 22 July 1740, ibid., pp. 239, 244: Vanderdussen to Bull, 20 July 1740, ibid., p. 244; Vanderdussen to Bull, 28 July 1740, ibid., p. 245; Report of the Committee, ibid., p. 101.

17. Ibid., pp. 128, 137–39.

18. Ibid., 148–50; An exact Acct . . . of our Forces and what loss we Sustain'd during the Seige, Egmont Papers, Supplement, p. 183; Mackay, *Letter,* p. 35.

Chapter XI

1. Stephens's Journal, 1 Sept. 1740, *CRG,* 4:653; Ettinger, *Oglethorpe,* p. 237.

2. Ibid., pp. 235–37; Reese, *Colonial Georgia,* pp. 80–82; Cooper, *Statutes,* 3:577–79; Easterby, *SCCHJ,* 1 July 1741, pp. 78–247.

3. Kimber, *A Relation or Journal,* pp. 8, 9; Stephens's Journal, 2 Sept. 1740, *CRG,* 4:654; Martyn, An Account, ibid., 3:403; De Brahm, *A Map of South Carolina and a Part of Georgia;* McKinnon, [Map of Cumberland Island]. The site of Fort Prince William has been washed away.

4. A Monthly Return of Oglethorpe's Regiment, 31 May 1742, CRG, 35:452, 453; Stephens's Journal, 20 May 1741, *CRG,* Supplement to 4, p. 149.

5. Ibid. 2 Sept. 1740, 4:653, 654; Manucy, *Fort at Frederica,* pp. 10, 15, 16; Oglethorpe to Verelst, 29 Mar. 1742, CRG, 35:438; Journal of Mr. Francis Moore of the Spaniards Proceedings, 9 July 1742, ibid., p. 493; Montiano to King Philip, 3 Aug. 1742, *CGHS,* 7, pt. 3, p. 90; Journal kept by the Marquess of Casinas, 17 July 1942, ibid., p. 71, 72; Plan Du Port De Gouadaquini, ibid., shows the fortified complex at the southern tip of Saint Simons Island. See also the Spanish map entitled Descripcion de la Gloriosa y Ecoica entrada quetas tropas de S. dt. Chatolica hisieron al puerto de Gauquinin et dia 16 de Julio de 1742. The site of Fort Saint Simons and Delegal's Fort have been washed away.

6. The Forty-second Regiment had experienced officer promotions and transfers in almost every company. Williams, "British-American Officers," pp. 189–92; A Monthly Return of His Excellency Genll. Oglethorpe's Regiment, 31 May 1742, CRG, 35:452, 453.

7. Oglethorpe to the Trustees, 29 Dec. 1739, *CRG,* 22, pt. 2, p. 287; Reese, *Colonial Georgia,* p. 78; Lawson, *Uniforms,* 2:14–16; Williams, "British-American Officers," p. 190; Moore to Verelst, 3 July 1742, CRG, 35:513.

8. Cook to Vanderdussen, 8 June 1740, Easterby, *SCCHJ,* 1 July 1741, p. 209; Ettinger, *Oglethorpe,* pp. 239, 250; Historical Manuscripts Commission, *The Diary of Lord John Percival, First Earl of Egmont, 1730–1747,* 3 vols., (London, 1920–23), 17, 22, Apr. 1741, 3:213, 216.

9. Stephens's Journal, 1 Jan., 12 June 1740, *CRG,* 4:483, 484, 593; ibid., 23 Jan. 1741, Supplement to 4, p. 77; Williams, "British-American Officers," p. 192.

10. Stephens's Journal, 12 June 1740, *CRG,* 4:593.

11. Ibid., 17 May 1741, Supplement to 4, p. 147; Williams, "British-American Officers," p. 191; Ettinger, *Oglethorpe,* p. 83.

12. Mereness, "Ranger's Report," p. 232; Kimber, "Itinerant Observations," p. 6; B. W. Frobell, Map of Glynn County, 1869, Georgia Surveyor General Department. For an example of a Georgia redoubt see William De Brahm, The Profile of the whole Citadelle of Frederica, ca. 1755, *CGHS,* 7, pt. 3; A Return of the Vessells and Boats, 29 May 1749, *CRG,* 25:468.

13. The Accompt of James Oglethorpe, AO 3/119, 29 Sept. 1741, 15 June 1742; Stephens's Journal, 12 Oct., 11 Nov. 1740, 3 Mar. 1741, *CRG,* Supplement to 4, pp. 12, 27, 28, 93; ibid., 21, 22, 25, 29, 30 Sept., 3 Oct. 1740, 4:656–61.

14. Kimber, "Itinerant Observations," p. 10; The Declaration of the Account of James Oglethorpe, AO 1/162/441, pp. 19, 27a; Samuel Perkins Oath, 28 Nov. 1741, *CGHS,* 2:106.

15. Mackay, *Letter,* p. 35; Egmont's Journal, 11 Mar. 1742, *CRG,* 5:605–7.

16. See the dateline, Mackay to Mackay, 10 Aug. 1740, Mackay, *Letter,* p. 5; Thomas Jones to the Trustees, 23 Feb. 1742, *CRG,* 23:497; The Declaration of the Account of James Oglethorpe, AO 1/162/441, pp. 11, 11a, 18; Casinas's Journal, 26 July 1742, *CGHS,* 7, pt. 3, p. 81.

17. Williams, "British-American Officers," pp. 189, 190, 192.

18. Return of the Men at the Darien, 6 May 1741, Egmont Papers, Supplement, p. 506; A List of the Military Strength of Carolina & Georgia, 7 June 1742, CRG, 35:465.

19. Return of the Men at the Darien, 6 May 1741, Egmont Papers, Supplement,

p. 506; List of the Darien Widows, 6 May 1741, ibid., p. 510; Mackay, *Letter,* pp. 34, 35; Copy of the Certificate of Lieut. Charles Mackay, 7 Dec. 1741, CRG, 35:403; A List of the Military Strength of Carolina & Georgia, 7 June 1742, ibid., p. 465; Invoice of Parcells shipped, 17 Sept. 1741, ibid., 30:382.

20. Stephens's Journal, 30 June 1740, *CRG,* 4:608; ibid., 17 Apr., 11 June, 9 July 1741, Supplement to 4, pp. 126, 164, 187, 271, 272; VerSteeg, *Colony of Georgia,* p. 153; Trustees' Journal, 28 Nov. 1741, *CRG,* 1:388; Proceeding of the President and Assistants, 3 Mar. 1750, ibid., 6:309; The Accompt of James Oglethorpe, AO 3/119, 25 Sept. 1741, 26 Mar. 1742. For the organization of a British troop of dragoons see Estimate of the Forces, 1742, WO 25/3209; A List of the Military Strength of Georgia, 31 Dec. 1742, CRG, 35:556.

21. Stephens's Journal, 9 Sept. 1741, *CRG,* Supplement to 4, pp. 236, 237.

22. Ibid., 13 Feb. 1740, 4:511; Copy of the Proceedings of the Assembled Estates of the Lower Creek Nation, 21 Aug. 1739, Egmont Papers, 14204, p. 87; Coulter, *Journal of William Stephens, 1741–1743,* 27 June 1742, p. 100; McCord, *Statutes,* 9:112, 113.

23. The Declaration of the Account of James Oglethorpe, AO 1/162/441, p. 24; Stephens's Journal, 7 Feb. 1741, *CRG,* Supplement to 4, p. 12; Coulter, *Journal of William Stephens, 1741–1743,* 4 Nov. 1741, 5 July 1742, pp. 5, 105; William Stephens, A State of the Province of Georgia, 10 Nov. 1740, *CRG,* 4:86; De Brahm, *A Map of South Carolina and a Part of Georgia.*

24. Coulter, *Journal of William Stephens, 1741–1743,* 27 June, 5 July 1742, 7 Mar. 1743, pp. 100, 105, 179.

25. Samuel Eveleigh, a prominent Charles Town merchant, had recommended in 1734 that Oglethorpe place a fort on the upper Altamaha River. Eveleigh to Oglethorpe, 5 Aug. 1734, Egmont Papers, 14200, p. 231; Moore to Verelst, 20 Sept. 1736, *CRG,* 21:226. The late Dr. John Goff located the site of Mount Venture after extensive research. See his notes in the Goff Collection, Georgia Surveyor General Department; see also Henry Yonge and De Brahm, A Map of the Sea Coast of Georgia, 1763; and Joseph Purcell, A Map of the Southern Indian District of North America, 1775.

26. Memorial & Represenation of Mary (Musgrove, Mathews) Bosomworth, 10 Aug. 1747, CRG, 36:256, 259, 260; for Mary's career see Merton E. Coulter, "Mary Musgrove, Queen of the Creeks," *GHQ* 11 (Mar. 1927):1–30.

27. Mary Bosomworth to Henry Ellis, 23 July 1759, CRG, 28, pt. 1-A, pp. 397, 398; In 1746 Mary settled another trading fort further up the river at the "Forks," the junction of the Oconee, Okmulgee, and Altamaha Rivers. ibid, p. 402; Oglethorpe to Mathews, 3 Oct. 1740, ibid, 36:274; Thomas Jones to Verelst, 6 Oct. 1740, *CRG,* 22, pt. 2, pp. 427, 428.

28. Oglethorpe to Mathews, 3 Oct. 1740, CRG, 36: 274; Stephens's Journal, 23 Apr., 13 Aug. 1741, *CRG,* Supplement to 4, pp. 130, 217–219.

29. Ibid., 18, 22, 29 Apr. 1741, pp. 127–29, 133; Coulter and Saye, *Early Settlers of Georgia,* p. 74.

30. Stephens's Journal, 3, 4, 12, 13 Aug. 1741, *CRG,* Supplement to 4, pp. 210, 216–19.

31. Coulter, *Journal of Williams Stephens, 1741–1743,* 18 Dec. 1741, 24 Feb., 18 May 1742, pp. 20, 45, 46, 81.

32. Verelst to Oglethorpe, 14 Dec. 1741, Egmont Papers, 14212, p. 117; Coulter,

Journal of William Stephens, 1741–1743, 5, 6 June, 25 Nov. 1742, pp. 89, 90, 142, 143.

33. Oglethorpe to Verelst, 29 Mar. 1742, CRG, 35:435; A List of the Military Strength of Georgia, 31 Dec. 1742, ibid., p. 555; The Declaration of the Account of James Oglethorpe, AO 1/162/441, p. 6a; A Computation of One Year's Expenses . . . proposed by General Oglethorpe in July 1741 . . ., BPRO, Treasury Office Papers (hereafter cited as T) 1/310.

34. Stephens's Journal, 30 Mar. 1741, *CRG*, Supplement to 4, p. 117; Oglethorpe to Newcastle, 28 Apr. 1741, CRG, 35:327.

35. Stephens's Journal, 1 June 1741, *CRG*, Supplement to 4, p. 156; Oglethorpe to Verelst, 29 Mar. 1742, CRG, 35:435; The Declaration of the Account of James Oglethorpe, AO 1/162/441, p. 6a; Lawson, *Uniforms*, 2:22–25, 89.

36. Meeting of the President and Assistants, 12 May 1752, *CRG*, 6:370; Kimber, *A Relation or Journal*, p. 8; A List of the Military Strength of Carolina & Georgia, 7 June 1742, CRG, 35:465; Stephens's Journal, 10 June 1741, *CRG*, Supplement to 4, p. 162; Egmont's Journal, 11 Mar. 1742, ibid., 5:605–7; The Declaration of the Account of James Oglethorpe, AO 1/162/441, p. 28a.

37. Oglethorpe to Verelst, 29 Mar. 1742, CRG, 35:437; A List of the Military Strength of Carolina & Georgia, 7 June 1742, ibid., pp. 465, 466.

38. The Declaration of the Account of James Oglethorpe, AO 1/162/441, p. 28; Coulter, *Journal of William Stephens, 1741–1743*, 14 May, 22 Aug. 1742, pp. 78, 122, 123. For an account of Jones's career see Temple and Coleman, *Georgia Journeys*, pp. 268–91; Williams, "British-American Officers," p. 194; Stephens's Journal, 11 Aug. 1740, *CRG*, 4:638; De Brahm, *A Map of South Carolina and a Part of Georgia*; Kimber, "Itinerant Observations," p. 15; VerSteeg, *Colony of Georgia*, p. 149.

39. A List of the Military Strength of Carolina & Georgia, 7 June 1742, CRG, 35:465, 466; Stephens's Journal, 11 Feb. 1741, *CRG*, Supplement to 4, p. 88; A Return of the Vessells and Boats, 29 May 1749, ibid., 25:468.

40. Oglethorpe to Verelst, about Dec. 1741, CRG, 35:404–9; A List of the Military Strength of Georgia, 31 Dec. 1742, ibid., p. 556; An Account shewing the Annual Charges, ibid., 36:187; South Carolina Council Journals, 8 Feb. 1749, ibid., p. 424. For examples of eighteenth-century armed sloops and schooners see Bjorn Landstrom, *The Ship* (New York, 1961), pp. 174, 175.

41. Mereness, "Ranger's Report," pp. 229–32; TePaske, *Governorship*, pp. 145, 146.

42. Corkran, *Creek Frontier*, pp. 106–9.

43. The Declaration of the Account of James Oglethorpe, AO 1/162/441, pp. 25a, 34a; The Accompt of James Oglethorpe, ibid., 3/119, 29 Sept., 8 Oct., 22 Nov. 1740, 15 Dec. 1741; Olgethorpe, to Newcastle, 12 Nov. 1741, CRG, 35:379; William Horton to Mary Bosomworth, 21 Sept. 1744, *CRG*, 26:10.

44. Milledge's commission is reproduced in Victor Davidson, ed., *Correspondence of John Milledge, Governor of Georgia* (Columbia, 1949); Temple and Coleman, *Georgia Journeys*, pp. 245–57. Milledge did not take command of Fort Argyle until late April 1742. Coulter, *Journal of William Stephens, 1741–1743*, 27 Apr. 1742, p. 70; The Accompt of James Oglethorpe, AO 3/119, 15 June 1742.

45. The Declaration of the Account of James Oglethorpe, ibid., 1/162/441, pp. 12, 23a, 32, 33; VerSteeg, *Colony of Georgia*, p. 149; "An Impartial Inquiry,"

p. 180; Coulter, *Journal of William Stephens, 1741–1743,* 27 Apr. 1742, p. 70.

46. The Declaration of the Account of James Oglethorpe, AO 1/162/441, p. 27a; The Accompt of James Oglethorpe, ibid., 3/119, 18 Aug. 1742. This troop has been erroneously attributed to the command of Noble Jones.

47. Stephens's Journal, 12 Oct. 1740, *CRG,* 4:11, 12; ibid., 24 Mar., 9, 13 May, 4 June 1741, Supplement to 4, pp. 112, 142, 145, 158. It appears that the Ebenezer Rangers were part-time soldiers. Their organization was similar to that of a small militia unit. The Accompt of James Oglethorpe, AO 3/119, 29 Sept. 1741, 15 June, 29 Sept. 1742. Bichler held only the rank of tythingman, a police official, and a noncommissioned officer of militia. Bozius to Martyn, 22 Sept. 1744, *CRG,* 24:314; *South Carolina Gazette,* 13 Dec. 1742.

48. The Declaration of the Account of James Oglethorpe, AO 1/162/441, p. 27a; The Accompt of James Oglethorpe, ibid., 3/119, 28 May, 18 Aug. 1742.

49. Mereness, "Ranger's Report," p. 232; An Account of the Late Invasion of Georgia drawn out by Lieutenant Patrick Sutherland, Dec. 1742, CRG, 35:529, 530; Moore to Verelst, 3 July 1742, ibid., p. 513.

50. Sutherland's Account, ibid., p. 530.

Chapter XII

1. John T. Lanning, "American Participation in the War of Jenkins' Ear," *GHQ* 11 (Sept. 1927):191–204.

2. The new style dates are cited for Spanish letters and journals, but in the text all dates have been converted to old style in order to conform with English dates. José de Campillo (the king's minister) to Juan Francisco de Güemes, 31 Oct. 1741, *CGHS,* 7, pt. 3, p. 22.

3. Ibid., pp. 21–24.

4. Güemes to Montiano, 2 June 1742, ibid., pp. 33, 34; TePaske, *Governorship,* pp. 146, 147.

5. Güemes to Montiano, 14 May 1742, *CGHS,* 7, pt. 3, pp. 27–30; ibid., 2 June 1742, pp. 32—35.

6. Journal Kept by Antonio de Arredondo, 15 June 1742, ibid., pp. 56, 57; Montiano to King Philip V, 3 Aug. 1742, ibid., p. 89; Sutherland's Account, CRG, 35:530.

7. Arredondo's Journal, 5–18 June 1742, *CGHS,* 7, pt. 3, pp. 52–60.

8. Spanish units participating in the invasion are listed on the Spanish map Descripcion de la Gloriosa . . . 16 de Julio de 1742; the British characteristically estimated the Spanish army to be four times its actual size. Sutherland's Account, CRG, 35:529.

9. Arredondo's Journal, 21–23 June 1742, *CGHS,* 7, pt. 3, pp. 61–64; Journal Kept by the Marquess of Casinas, 15, 17, 19, 20 June 1742, ibid., p. 65.

10. Ibid., 20 July 1742, pp. 66, 75, 76; Oglethorpe to Newcastle, 30 July 1742, CRG, 36:32; Journal from Mr. Francis Moore, 9 July 1942, ibid., 35:493.

11. Ibid., pp. 493, 494.

12. Ettinger, *Olgethorpe,* p. 247; Reese, *Colonial Georgia,* p. 82.

13. Oglethorpe to Newcastle, 30 July 1742, CRG, 36:32, 33; Sutherland's Account, Ibid., 35:530; Mereness, "Ranger's Report," pp. 232, 233.

14. See note 13, this chapter. Casinas's Journal, 26 July 1742, *CGHS*, 7, pt. 3, p. 81.

15. Sutherland's Account, CRG, 35:531; Moore's Journal, ibid., p. 495; Easterby, *SCCHJ*, 6 July 1742, p. 566.

16. Sutherland's Account, CRG, 35:530, 531.

17. Casinas's Journal, 29 June 1742, *CGHS*, 7, pt. 3, pp. 66, 67.

18. Ibid., 30 June, 1, 4 July 1742, pp. 67, 68.

19. Sutherland's Account, CRG, 35:531,540; Oglethorpe's Account of the Spaniards Proceedings, 9 July 1742, ibid., p. 491. For the Forty-second Regiment's strength see A Monthly Return of Oglethorpe's Regiment, 31 May 1742, ibid., pp. 452, 453; The Declaration of the Account of James Oglethorpe, AO 1 / 162 / 441, p. 34a; Montiano to the King, 3 Aug. 1742, *CGHS*, 7, pt. 3, p. 90; Coulter, *Journal of William Stephens, 1741–1743*, 18 June, 23 Aug. 1742, pp. 96, 123. See Chapter XI for the probable strengths of the provinical units. *The Gentleman's Magazine*, 1742, p. 496.

20. Ibid.; Casinas's Journal, 16 July 1742, *CGHS*, 7, pt. 3, p. 68.

21. See the Spanish map Descricion de la Gloriosa, for the disposition of the opposing ships, boats, batteries, etc., when the Spaniards sailed into the sound. Oglethorpe to Newcastle, 30 July 1742, CRG, 36:34; Sutherland's Account, Ibid., 35:532; A Return of the Vessells and Boats, 29 May 1749, *CRG*, 25:468; Casinas's Journal, 17 July 1742, *CGHS*, 7, pt. 3, pp. 69, 71; Montiano to the King, 3 Aug. 1742, ibid., p. 90; *The Gentleman's Magazine*, 1742, pp. 496, 661.

22. Ibid., p. 494; Montiano to the King, 3 Aug. 1742, *CGHS*, 7, pt. 3, p. 90; Casinas's Journal, 16 July 1742, ibid., p 69; Mereness, "Ranger's Report," p. 233; Sutherland's Account, CRG, 35:533, 534. The landing site is noted on Plan Du Port De Gouadaquini, and on Descripcion de la Gloriosa.

23. Mereness, "Ranger's Report," p. 233; Casinas's Journal, 16 July 1742, *CGHS*, 7, pt. 3, pp. 69, 70.

24. Ibid.; Montiano to the King, 3 Aug. 1742, ibid, p. 89; Sutherland's Account, CRG, 35:534.

25. Ibid., p. 533; Oglethorpe to Newcastle, 30 July 1742, ibid., 36:34, 35; Mereness, "Ranger's Report," p. 234; *The Gentleman's Magazine*, 1742, p. 496.

26. Ibid.; Proceedings of the President and Assistants, 10, 14, 20 July, 29 Sept. 1742, *CRG*, 6:38–41, 46; Francis Moore's Oath, 14 Feb. 1743, CRG, 36:78–80; Cooper, *Statutes*, 3:595–97.

Chapter XIII

1. Montiano to the King, 3 Aug. 1742, *CGHS*, 7, pt. 3, pp. 90, 91; Casinas's Journal, 16, 17 July 1742, ibid., pp. 70–72.

2. Ibid., 17, 18 July 1742, pp. 71–73.

3. Ibid., 18 July 1742, pp. 72, 73; Montiano to the King, 3 Aug. 1742, ibid., p. 91.

4. Ibid. The trail between Frederica and Fort Saint Simons, sometimes called the military road, is shown in Manucy, *Fort at Frederica*, p. 12. A portion of the trail has been cleared and marked as part of the Fort Frederica National Monument; Sutherland's Account, CRG, 35:534.

5. Ibid.; Mereness, "Ranger's Report," p. 234. Apparently two men by the name

of William Small served in the Georgia rangers; perhaps they were father and son.

6. Oglethorpe to Newcastle, 30 July 1742, CRG, 36:35, 36; Oglethorpe's Account, ibid., 35:489, 490; Sutherland's Account, ibid., p. 534.

7. Ibid., pp. 534, 535; Oglethorpe's Account, ibid., p. 490; A further Account from General Oglethorpe, ibid., p. 527; Mereness, "Ranger's Report," pp. 234, 235.

8. Oglethorpe's Account, CRG, 35:490; Sutherland's Account, ibid., p. 535; Oglethorpe to Newcastle, 30 July 1742, ibid., 36:36; Mereness, "Ranger's Report," p. 234. A small monument marks the traditional site that is apparently incorrect, probably having been based on the traditional account of the battle of Bloody Marsh. See note 16, this chapter; Casinas's Journal, 18 July 1742, CGHS, 7, pt. 3, p. 73.

9. Ibid.; Montiano to the King, 3 Aug. 1742, ibid., p. 91.

10. Ibid., Casinas's Journal, 18 July 1742, ibid., p. 73. Casinas's journal fails to distinguish between the two battles. The journal entry has apparently been incorrectly copied or incorrectly translated. It is apparent, however, that his account is a detailed description of the second battle. Sutherland's Account, CRG, 35:535; Mereness, "Ranger's Report," pp. 234, 235.

11. Oglethorpe to Newcastle, 30 July 1742, CRG, 36:35, 36; Sutherland's Account, ibid., 35:535, 536.

12. Ibid., pp. 536, 537. For Sutherland's commission in Demere's company see Williams, "British-American Officers," pp. 189, 191. Also see A Monthly Return of General Oglethorpe's Regiment, 31 May 1742, CRG, 35:166; Casinas's Journal, 18 July 1742, CGHS, 7, pt. 3, p. 73.

13. Ibid.; Montiano to the King, 3 Aug. 1742, ibid., p. 91; Sutherland's Account, CRG, 35:536.

14. Ibid., pp. 536, 537; Oglethorpe's Account, ibid., pp. 491, 492.

15. Montiano to the King, 3 Aug. 1742, CGHS, 7, pt. 3, p. 92; Casinas's Journal, 18, 19, 20 July 1742, ibid., pp. 73–76.

16. For a different account of the second battle see Margaret D. Cate, "Fort Frederica—Battle of Bloody Marsh," GHQ 27 (June 1943):148–50. Cate relied heavily upon the legendary account given in Thomas Spalding, "A Sketch of the Life of General James Oglethorpe," CGHS 1 (1840):281–84. Spalding repeated the stories that he had learned during his youth on Saint Simons Island from his grandfather and another old man, both of whom were veterans of the battle. Briefly, their account of the battle was as follows: When the Spanish grenadier companies collided with the British force that was blocking the trail, most of the British soldiers became frightened and began retreating up the trail. As they fled past present Bloody Marsh, the rear guard, composed of Lieutenant Sutherland's platoon of regulars and Lieutenant Mackay's Highland Company, halted and prepared an ambush in the dense woods that bordered the west side of the trail. When the pursuing Spaniards reached that site, they halted, stacked their muskets, sat down in the marsh to the east of the trail, and began eating a meal. The British ambush was initiated by a special signal—raising a Highland bonnet on a stick. The Spaniards were slain in great numbers.

An examination of the period documents shows that this legendary account is incorrect. In his letter to Newcastle, Oglethorpe clearly stated that only "Some

Platoons" retreated, while the remainder of the British force remained in their blocking position, as evidenced by the fact that he "heard the firing continue" and "arrived just as the fire was done." Casinas's and Montiano's accounts clearly show that the Spaniards did not conduct a pursuit; in fact, they were not even aware that some of the British soldiers had fled, and they continued to exchange musket fire with those British soldiers who remained. However, Spalding should not be criticized for faulty historical reporting. He first carefully quoted period British accounts before admittedly offering the legendary account for its drama and romance, not for its accuracy. He was obviously aware that one should always parallel the war stories of ancient veterans with period documentary accounts.

17. Mereness, "Rangers' Report," p. 235; Casinas's Journal, 18–22 July 1742, *CGHS,* 7, pt. 3, pp. 74–78.

18. Ibid, 19, 20 July 1742, pp. 74, 75; Montiano to the King, 3 Aug. 1742, ibid., pp. 91, 92.

19. Ibid., pp. 92, 93; Casinas's Journal, 20, 21 July 1742, ibid., pp. 75, 77. Oglethorpe stated that the Spanish reconnaissance was conducted on July 11. Oglethorpe to Newcastle, 30 July 1742, CRG, 36:38, 39.

20. Ibid.; *The Gentleman's Magazine,* 1742, p. 661; Sutherland's Account, CRG, 35:537, 538.

21. Ibid., p. 538; Oglethorpe to Newcastle, 30 July 1742, ibid., 36:39; Casinas's Journal, 24 July 1742, *CGHS,* 7, pt. 3, p. 78.

22. Ibid., p. 79; Oglethorpe to Newcastle, 30 July 1742, CRG, 36:39, 40.

23. At that moment Oglethorpe was planning a coordinated land-sea attack. Oglethorpe to the Commander of His Majesty's Ships at Sea, 14 July 1742, ibid., pp. 44, 45; Montiano to the King, 3 Aug. 1742, *CGHS,* 7, pt. 3, p. 94; Casinas's Journal, 24 July 1742, ibid., pp. 79, 80.

24. Ibid., 25–29 July 1742, pp. 80–83; Montiano to the King, 3 Aug. 1742, ibid., p. 94.

25. Sutherland's Account, CRG, 35:539, 540; Williams, "British-American Officers," p. 191.

26. Montiano to the King, 3 Aug. 1742, *CGHS,* 7, pt. 3, pp. 94, 95; Casinas's Journal, 29 July 1742, ibid., p. 83; Sutherland's Account, CRG, 35:539, 540. The eight rangers received a reward of six pounds each for their brave action. The Accompt of James Oglethorpe, AO 3/119, 18 Aug. 1742.

27. Oglethorpe to Newcastle, 30 July 1742, CRG, 36:42 Sutherland's Account, ibid., 35:540; Coulter, *Journal of William Stephens, 1741–1743,* 16 July, 23 Aug. 1742, pp. 109, 123; Mereness, "Ranger's Report," pp. 235, 236.

28. W. E. May, "Capt. Charles Hardy on the Carolina Station, 1742–1744," *SCHM* 70 (Jan. 1969):5–8; R. Smith, *South Carolina as a Royal Province,* pp. 189, 190; Mereness "Ranger's Report," p. 236; Sutherland's Account, CRG, 35:540; Oglethorpe to Newcastle, 30 July 1742, ibid., 36:42; Lieut. Maxwell's Affidavit, 1 Feb. 1743, ibid., pp. 57, 58; Francis Moore's Narrative, 14 Feb. 1743, ibid., pp. 73–83.

29. TePaske, *Governorship,* pp. 152, 153; May, "Capt. Charles Hardy," p. 8; Mereness, "Ranger's Report," p. 236.

30. Ibid.; TePaske, *Governorship,* p. 153; May, "Capt. Charles Hardy," p. 8.

31. Mereness, "Ranger's Report," p. 236; Oglethorpe to Mary Mathews, 30 July 1742, CRG, 27:4.

Chapter XIV

1. Oglethorpe to Newcastle, 12 Mar. 1743, *CGHS,* 3, pt. 2, p. 150.

2. The Declaration of the Account of James Oglethorpe, AO 1/162/441, p. 26a, 27; The Accompt of James Oglethorpe, ibid., 3/119, 29 Mar., 23 Oct., 29 Dec. 1742; Coulter, *Journal of William Stephens, 1741–1743,* 25 Nov. 1742, pp. 142, 143.

3. *South Carolina Gazette,* 13 Dec. 1742; The Declaration of Nottoway, 22 Nov. 1742, CRG, 36:54.

4. See note 3, this chapter.

5. See note 3, this chapter. A List of the Military Strength of Georgia, 31 Dec. 1742, CRG, 35:555, 556; Coulter, *Journal of William Stephens, 1741–1743,* 19 Feb. 1743, p. 173; The Declaration of the Account of James Oglethorpe, AO 1/162/441, pp. 35a, 36.

6. Coulter, *Journal of William Stephens, 1741–1743,* 5 Feb. 1743, pp. 167, 168.

7. Oglethorpe to Newcastle, 12 Mar. 1743, *CGHS,* 3, pt. 2, pp. 149, 150; Corkran, *Creek Frontier,* pp. 110, 111.

8. Williams, "British-American Officers," p. 191. Dunbar was in England; Kimber, *A Relation or Journal,* pp. 6–8.

9. Ibid., p. 9.

10. Ibid., pp. 9–12.

11. Ibid., pp. 10, 15, 16.

12. Ibid., pp. 15, 23.

13. Oglethorpe to Newcastle, 12 Mar. 1743, *CGHS* 3, pt. 2, 150; Kimber, *A Relation or Journal,* pp. 18–20.

14. Ibid., pp. 20, 21.

15. Ibid., pp. 4, 6, 12, 13, 15, 22, 24, 25, 27–29, 31.

16. Ibid., pp. 21–24, 28.

17. Ibid., pp. 25–27.

18. Ibid., pp. 27, 28.

19. Ibid., pp. 28, 29, 30, 34.

20. Ibid., pp. 29, 30; Lieutenant Noble Jones and his marine company were in Florida from about 15 March to 20 March. Coulter, *Journal of William Stephens 1741–1743,* 7, 27 Mar. 1743, pp. 179, 186.

21. Kimber, *A Relation or Journal,* p. 31: An Account of Extraordinary Services in Georgia, WO 25/3209.

22. Kimber, *A Relation or Journal,* pp. 31–34.

23. TePaske, *Governor,* pp. 153, 154; A letter from one of Oglethorpe's Officers to a friend, 25 Mar. 1743, CRG, 36:155; Oglethorpe to Newcastle, 21 Mar. 1743, ibid., p. 104.

24. Ettinger, *Oglethorpe,* p. 250; Reese, *Colonial Georgia,* pp. 78, 80–83; An Account of Extraordinary Services in Georgia, WO 25/3209.

25. Hist. MSS Comm., *Diary of the Lord John Percival,* 3:266; Williams, "British-American Officers," p. 193; Ettinger, *Oglethorpe,* p. 250.

26. Ibid., p. 251.

Chapter XV

1. Ettinger, *Oglethorpe,* pp. 251, 252; Hist. MSS Comm., *Diary of Lord John Percival,* 12 June 1744, 3:300; William A. Shaw, ed., *A Calander of Treasury Books and Papers, 1729–1745,* 5 vols. (London, 1903), 5:559.

2. Williams, "British-American Officers," p. 193; Ettinger, *Oglethorpe,* pp. 252, 253.

3. Williams, "British-American Officers," p. 193; Meeting of the President and Assistants, 1 Dec. 1745, *CRG,* 6:146.

4. Chitwood, *Colonial America,* p. 315; Temple and Coleman, *Georgia Journeys,* p. 286.

5. Williams, "British-American Officers," p. 193.

6. Horton to Oglethorpe, 26 May 1744, CRG, 36:199; Ettinger, *Oglethorpe,* p. 253; The Royal Warrant for the establishment of the Georgia Rangers, Highland Company, Boatmen, etc., WO 24/222. Bills of exchange were legal tender in Georgia because of the lack of specie. *Collections of the South Carolina Historical Society,* 5 vols. (Charleston, 1857–97), 2:318; The royal warrant was renewed on 25 December 1745, WO 24/251. The establishment of the provincial units was basically the same as Oglethorpe had previously proposed. A Computation of One Year's Expenses . . . proposed by General Oglethorpe in July 1741 . . ., T 1/310. Georgia's provincial officers are not to be found in the following sources that identify British regular officers: Commission Books, WO 25/20–22, pp. 89, 90; The Army Lists, 1738 corrected to 1743, and 1743 corrected to 1753; Notification Books, WO 25/134–36; or the Half Pay Lists, WO 24/696, PMG 4/8. Also see Secretary at War to James Wright, 12 June 1767, Out Letters of the Secretary at War, 1767, WO 4/82.

7. The Royal Warrant for the [Georgia] establishment, WO 24/222. The marine establishment was also ignored. It appears that Oglethorpe may have instructed Major Horton not to disrupt the provincials' existing organization.

8. Henry Laurens to James Crockatt, 3 June 1747, *SCHGM* 28 (July 1927):145; The Accompt of James Oglethorpe, AO 3/119, 12, 15, 16 July 1743; Kimber, *A Relation or Journal,* p. 9; Mary Bosomworth to Henry Ellis, 23 July 1759, CRG, 28, pt. 1-A, p. 402. Mary's settlement at the Forks is designated "Bosomworths Old Trading place," on Yonge and De Brahm, A Map of the Sea Coast of Georgia. The records do not mention the reoccupation of Mount Venture after November 1742. Horton to Thomas Bosomworth, 19 May 1747, CRG, 36:293, 294; The Declaration of the Account of James Oglethorpe, AO 1/162/441, p. 27a, Disbursements from 25 June 1747 to 24 Feb. 1748, CRG, 36:445; Kimber, "Itinerant Observations," pp. 8–11; James Pemberton, Visit to Carolina, 1745, photostat in the Margaret Davis Cate Library, Fort Frederica National Monument, Georgia; Laurens to Crockatt, 3 June 1747, *SCHGM,* 28 (July 1927):145; Coulter, *Journal of William Stephens, 1743–1745,* 4 Nov. 1744, 21, 22 Jan., 19 Dec. 1745, pp. 164, 166, 189, 190, 263.

9. The Declaration of the Account of James Oglethorpe, AO 1/162/441, p. 27. The Accompt of James Oglethorpe, ibid., 3/119, 12 Oct. 1742; Shaw, *Calendar,* p. 310; Coulter, *Journal of William Stephens, 1743–1745,* 22 Sept. 1743, 22 Jan.

1745, pp. 20, 190; Kimber, *A Relation or Journal*, p. 8. The location of Charles Mackay's detachment of the Highland troop can only be conjectured. On 10 Mar. 1747 he witnessed a document for a Highland Ranger at Darien. Georgia Colonial Conveyances, Ga-Ar, Cl, 1750–61, p. 13; Return of the two Troops of Rangers, Highland Company & ca. at Georgia, compared with the Muster Rolls, 18 May 1747, CRG, 36:232, 233. McQueen was originally a quartermaster in the English troop during September 1739. He evidently transferred to the Highland troop after their activation in November 1739. Kimber, "Itinerant Observations," p. 14.

10. Ibid., pp. 13, 14. Gentlemen in the Scottish Highlands wore tartan trews when riding horseback. Trews were expensive, however, and the Highland Rangers probably wore the standard buckskin breeches. Adam, *The Clans*, p. 357, plate V. A bonnet, a tartan jacket, and perhaps a shoulder plaid (during cold weather) were probably the only Highland items they wore. See lists of clothing for Highland indentured servants in Estimate of charges for a servant for one year, 16 Mar. 1737, Egmont Papers, Supplement, pp. 462, 465; Verelst to John Hossack & Co., 23 Apr. 1737, CRG, 29:374; Verelst to Causton, 11 Aug. 1737, ibid., p. 415. Also see the advertisement for a runaway Scot servant from Georgia in the *South Carolina Gazette*, 29 June 1734; Inventory of the Trustees' magazine at Savannah, 29 Sept. 1738, Egmont Papers, 14203, pp. 254–56; for Highland weapons see Lawson, *Uniforms*, 2:66–68. Most of the provincial soldiers probably carried Brown Bess muskets, which were very plentiful in Georgia. Verelst to John Pye, 17 Sept. 1744, CRG, 30:382, 383; Ordinance Stores delivered to Genl. Oglethorpe in 1737, ibid. 39:141, 142; An Account of Ordinance & Stores sent . . . 1739, ibid., p. 155. There are many other accounts evidencing the delivery of Brown Bess muskets to Georgia. Rangers probably sawed off parts of the barrels on their muskets for easier handling on horseback among the thick woods.

11. Memorandum from Gen. Oglethorpe, 28 Mar. 1746, CRG, 36:217; Return of the two Troops of Rangers, Highland Company & ca., 18 May 1747, ibid., pp. 232, 233; Robert Wright, *A Memoir of General James Oglethorpe* (London, 1867), pp. 355, 356. There is other evidence suggesting that a blue coat with red facings was intended as the rangers' uniform. Georgia rangers on duty during the French and Indian War wore a uniform, but its appearance is unknown. *The Georgia Gazette*, 19 Jan. 1764. However, when rangers were ordered raised again in 1773, six years after their disbandment, the prescribed uniform was a blue coat faced with red. Gov. James Wright's instruction to Edward Barnard, 1773, Loyalist Claims, Bundle 38, microfilm at Ga-Ar.

12. Notification Book, 1746–55, WO 25/135, p. 144; Coulter, *Journal of William Stephens, 1741–1743*, 30 Aug. 1742, p. 125; Easterby, *SCCHJ*, 26 Mar. 1743, p. 321; The Accompt of James Oglethorpe, AO 3/119, 26 Mar. 1742; Return of the two Troops of Rangers, Highland Company & Ca., 18 May 1747, CRG, 36:232, 233; The Declaration of the Account of James Oglethorpe, AO 1/162/441, p. 28; Proceedings of the President and Assistants, 14 June 1742, *CRG*, 6:36; Wilbur R. Jacobs, ed., *The Appalachian Indian Frontier: The Edmond Atkin Report and Plan of 1755* (Lincoln, 1957), p. 64.

13. Meriwether, *Expansion*, pp. 70, 71, 191, 193–96.

14. Finlay to Horton, 14 Jan. 1747, CRG, 36:221; Horton to Oglethorpe, 21

Feb. 1747, ibid., p. 222; Stephens to Verelst, 4 Feb. 1742, *CRG,* 23:206; Jacobs, *Indians,* pp. 23, 24.

15. The Declaration of the Account of James Oglethorpe, AO 1/162/441, p. 27a; Laurens to Crockatt, 3 June 1747, *SCHGM* 28 (July 1927):145; Kimber, *A Relation or Journal,* pp. 7, 9; Coulter, *Journal of William Stephens, 1743–1745,* 5 June 1744, pp. 109, 110; Horton to Mary Bosomworth, 21 Sept. 1744, CRG, 36:283.

16. Laurens to Crockatt, 3 June 1747, *SCHGM* 28 (July 1927):144, 145; Coulter, *Journal of William Stephens, 1743–1745,* 17, 19 Nov. 1743, 13 Aug., 18 Oct. 1744, 22 Nov. 1745, pp. 41, 134, 158, 253, 254; Meeting of the President and Assistants, 24 Nov. 1743, 10 Dec. 1747, *CRG,* 6:87, 198, 199; Bolzius to Van Munch, 6 May 1747, ibid., 25:171; Martyn to President and Assistants, 16 Mar. 1746, CRG, 31:117, 118.

17. The Accompt of James Oglethorpe, AO 3/119, 26 Feb. 1743; Horton to Oglethorpe, 21 Feb. 1747, CRG, 36:222; Coulter, *Journal of William Stephens, 1743–1745,* 22 Jan. 1745, p. 190; Georgia Colonial Conveyances, Ga-Ar, Cl, p. 34.

18. Bichler's commission as quartermaster may not have been granted until just prior to the rangers' disbandment. Bolzius to Verelst, 27 Apr. 1747, *CRG,* 25:157, 158; Bolzius to the Trustees, 1 May 1747, ibid., 159; Meeting of the President and Assistants, 30 Mar. 1744, ibid., 6:100; Bolizius to Martyn, 22 Sept. 1744, ibid., 24:314.

19. Mark Carr to James Campbell, 28 June 1740, CRG, 36:67, 68.

20. Ibid.

21. Return of the two Troops of Rangers, Highland Company & Ca., 18 May 1747, ibid, pp. 232, 233; Lawson, *Uniforms,* 1:43–45; Easterby, *SCCHJ,* 12 Feb. 1737, p. 234; A Monthly Return of Oglethorpe's Regiment, 31 May 1742, CRG, 35:452, 453. The British secretary at war was convinced that large-scale frauds were being perpetrated because muster rolls were never submitted. Henry Fox to Newcastle, 18 May 1747, ibid., 36:227, 228.

22. Shaw, *Calendar,* p. 310; The Royal Warrant for the [Georgia] establishment, WO 24/222; Adam, *The Clans,* pp. 445, 446. It is possible that the mutineers were assigned to the Forty-second Regiment; however, the strength of the Highland Company and the Highland Rangers in 1746 suggests a large influx subsequent to 1741. Return of the two Troops of Rangers, Highland Company & Ca., 18 May 1747, CRG, 36:232, 233.

23. Lawson, *Uniforms,* 2:56–58, 65, 66.

24. Oglethorpe to Verelst, about 7 Dec. 1741, CRG, 35:403; Establishment of a Company of Highland Foot, 30 Apr. 1740, ibid., p. 257; Lawson, *Uniforms,* 2:54–64, 66–68, 73; Adam, *The Clans,* pp. 356, 360, 361; Kimber, "Itinerant Observations," p. 13, 14.

25. Kimber, *A Relation or Journal,* p. 8; Horton to Mary Mathews, 20 Mar. 1744, CRG, 27:8.

26. Return of the two Troops of Rangers, Highland Company & ca., 18 May 1747, ibid., 36:232, 233; "William Logan's Journal of a Journey to Georgia, 1745," *Pennsylvania Magazine of History and Biography* 36 (1912), 15, 18 Nov. 1745, p. 173.

27. Coulter, *Journal of William Stephens, 1741–1743,* 27 Mar. 1743, p. 186; Notification Book, 1746–55, WO 25/135, 6 Feb. 1748; The Declaration of the Account of James Oglethorpe, AO 1/162/441, p. 28; Kimber, "Itinerant Observations, " pp. 15, 19; Return of the two Troops of Rangers, Highland Company & Ca., 18 May 1747, CRG, 36:232, 233.

28. Ibid.

29. A List of the Military Strength of Georgia, 31 Dec. 1742, ibid., 35:557.

30. The Declaration of the Account of James Oglethorpe, AO 1/162/441, p. 30.

31. Return of the two Troops of Rangers, Highland Company & Ca., 18 May 1747, CRG, 36:232, 233; An Account shewing the Occasion of General Oglethorpe's drawing Bills for His Majesty's Service which yet remain unsatisfied, ibid., pp. 186, 187. For examples of eighteenth-century frigates, schooners, and sloops see Landstrom, *The Ship,* pp. 174, 175, 178, 179; Temple and Coleman, *Georgia Journeys,* p. 260; Letter from a Gentleman in Charles Town, 18 May 1745, CRG, 36:207; Horton to Oglethorpe, 19 May 1746, ibid., pp. 213, 214.

32. Stephens to Verelst, 22 Jan. 1744, *CRG,* 24:207.

33. Stephens's Journal, 24 Mar. 1738, *CRG,* 4:110; Coulter, *Journal of William Stephens, 1741–1743,* 5 Feb. 1743, pp. 167, 168; ibid., *1743–1745,* 22 Sept. 1743, p. 20; Easterby, *SCCHJ,* 18 Jan. 1737, p. 180.

34. Instructions for Mr. Patrick Mackay Agent to the Creeks, 27 Apr. 1734, Miscellaneous Records, EE, 1741–43, SC-Ar, p. 56; Manucy, *Fort at Frederica,* pp. 115–18; "William Logan's Journal," 15 Nov. 1745, p. 173; Easterby, *SCCHJ,* 26 Mar. 1743, p. 321; Verelst to John Pye, 17 Sept. 1741, CRG, 30:382, 383; Coulter, *Journal of Peter Gordon,* p. 43; Kimber, *A Relation or Journal,* p. 6; Stephens's Journal, 31 Mar. 1741, *CRG,* Supplement to 4, p. 118.

35. Meeting of the President and Assistants, 10 Dec. 1747, 17 Nov. 1748, 12 May 1752, *CRG,* 6:198, 199, 229, 370; Stephens to Verelst, 31 Mar. 1746, ibid., 25:41; Temple and Coleman, *Georgia Journeys,* pp. 260, 278; "William Logan's Journal," 4, 10, 14–20 Nov. 1745, pp. 169, 171–73.

36. Ibid., 25 Nov. 1745, pp. 174, 175; Stephens's Journal, 24, 28 Mar. 1738, *CRG,* 4:110, 113; Stephens to Verelst, 22 Jan. 1744, ibid., 24:207; Temple and Coleman, *Georgia Journeys,* pp. 22, 23, 26, 27, 55, 63, 183, 292–94; Miller, *First Frontier,* pp. 140, 141, 237–41; Jones, *Detailed Reports,* 1:111.

37. The author lived with South Vietnamese provincial soldiers in similar forts, on similar terrain, and under similar circumstances during 1966–67. Kimber, "Itinerant Observations," pp. 12, 13; Jones, *Detailed Reports,* 1:60; Mackintosh to Oglethorpe, 15 Nov. 1737, *CRG,* 22, pt. 1, p. 12; Verelst to Hossack & Co., 23 Apr. 1737, CRG, 29:373; Miller, *First Frontier,* p. 184; Chitwood, *Colonial America,* p. 481.

38. SCCHJ, 9 Mar. 1734, SC-Ar, Commons House Journals No. 8, 1734–35, p. 58; Temple and Coleman, *Georgia Journeys,* pp. 15, 168–71; Miller, *First Frontier,* pp. 182, 183; Chitwood, *Colonial America,* p. 487.

39. Stephens's Journal, 4 Dec. 1740, 17 May, 12 Aug. 1741, *CRG,* Supplement to 4, pp. 43, 44, 147, 216, 217; "William Logan's Journal," 27 Oct. 1745, p. 166. Few soldiers could read or write, as evidenced by "marks" in lieu of signatures on wills, conveyances, etc. It is the author's observation that vulgar speech and manners become the norm among soldiers who spend long periods in primitive

isolated circumstances, regardless of educational or social backgrounds.

40. Atlanta Town Committee, *Abstracts of Colonial Wills in the State of Georgia*, (Atlanta, 1962), p. 67.

41. Stephens's Journal, 22 Apr. 1741, *CRG*, Supplement to 4, pp. 128, 129; Mereness, "Ranger's Report," p. 221; Meriwether, *Expansion*, pp. 191, 192, 232; Crane, *Southern Frontier*, p. 125. Adultery with a married Indian woman, however, was a serious incident. Jones, *Detailed Reports*, 1:67, 199, 200.

42. Cooper, *Statutes*, 2:397; Temple and Coleman, *Georgia Journeys*, pp. 161, 162, 167; Chitwood, *Colonial America*, pp. 490–92; Coulter, *Journal of William Stephens, 1741–1743*, 18 Dec. 1741, 27 June 1742, pp. 20, 100; ibid., *1743–1745*, 22 Jan. 1745, p. 190; Georgia Colonial Conveyances, Ga-Ar, Cl, p. 34.

43. Ettinger, *Oglethorpe*, pp. 255, 256, 259–61.

44. Ibid., pp. 263–65, 269.

45. Ibid., pp. 264, 265, 268, 269.

46. Ibid., pp. 266–69.

47. Ibid., pp. 269, 270.

48. Reese, *Colonial Georgia*, pp. 83, 84; Fox to Oglethorpe, 20 Oct. 1746, Out Letters of the Secretary at War, WO 4/42; ibid., 18 Nov. 1746; Fox to Oglethorpe, 26 Dec. 1746, Ibid., 4/43; Proposal relating to the Troops in Georgia, 5 Nov. 1746, CRG, 36:219, 220; Extract of Mr. Fox's Memorial to the Lords of the Treasury, 2 Dec. 1746, ibid., pp. 229–31; Fox to Newcastle, 18 May 1747, ibid., pp. 227, 228.

49. Horton to Thomas Bosomworth, 6 July 1747, ibid., p. 296; Expense of the Frontier of Georgia during Lt. Col. Heron's late Command, 8 Mar. 1750, ibid., pp. 464, 479; A Pay Bill of the Boatmen, 25 Feb. 1747, 24 Sept. 1748, ibid., pp. 372–78; Reese, *Colonial Georgia*, pp. 6, 30, 31, 40–50; Stephens to Verelst, 22 Jan. 1744, *CRG*, 24:207; President and Assistants to Martyn, 2 Oct. 1747, ibid., 25:233, 234.

Chapter XVI

1. Petition of Granville County settlers to the Duke of Newcastle, 3 Feb. 1748, *Collections of the South Carolina Historical Society*, 2:298; Trustees' Journal, 4 Apr. 1748, *CRG*, 1:514.

2. Proceedings of the President and Assistants, 31 Dec. 1745, 3 Mar. 1750, ibid., 6:146, 309; John Terry to the Trustees, 13 Feb. 1743, and 27 Aug. 1744, ibid., 24:248–52; John Pye to the Trustees, 10 Mar. 1745, ibid., 25:20–23; Terry to the Trustees, 25 Mar. 1746, ibid., pp. 31–33; ibid., Dec. 1747, p. 248; Horton to the Trustees, 20 Sept. 1746, ibid., pp. 120, 121.

3. Expense of the Frontier, 8 Mar. 1750, CRG, 36:464; Certification of John Pye, 29 Oct. 1748, ibid., p. 363; Copy of Orders from Genl. Oglethorpe, 18 May 1748, ibid., p. 402; Kimber, "Itinerant Observations," pp. 8, 9, 19, 20.

4. Copy of Orders from Genl. Oglethorpe, 18 May 1748, CRG, 36:402; Proceedings of the President and Assistants, 4 Jan. 1749, *CRG*, 6:235; Disbursements from 25 Feb. 1748 to 29 May 1749, CRG, 36:455.

5. Williams, "British-American Officers," pp. 191–95; Copy of Orders from Genl. Oglethorpe, 18 May 1748, CRG, 36:402; Depositions by various persons, 4 Mar. 1749, ibid., p. 435.

6. Heron to the Duke of Bedford, 29 Aug. 1748, ibid., p. 398; ibid., 20 Mar. 1749, p. 418; Certification of John Pye, 29 Oct. 1748, ibid., p. 363; An Account Current of the Magazine at Frederica, 25 Feb. 1748 to 29 May 1749, ibid., p. 459; *South Carolina Gazette,* 23 Feb. 1747.

7. Heron to the Duke of Bedford, 10 Feb. 1749, CRG, 36:527, 528; Depositions of various persons, 4 Mar. 1749, ibid., p. 426; Proceedings of the President and Assistants, 19 Apr. 1749, *CRG,* 6:241, 242.

8. "William Logan's Journal," 27 Oct., 25 Nov. 1745, pp. 166, 174, 175; John Calwell to the Trustees, 1 Aug. 1744, *CRG,* 24:285; Terry to the Trustees, 13 Feb. 1743 and 27 Aug. 1744, ibid, 252–55; ibid., 11 July 1745, 406, 407, 410, 411.

9. Ibid., 13 Feb. 1743 and 27 Aug. 1744, pp. 259, 260; ibid., Dec. 1747, 25:246–48.

10. Ettinger, *Oglethorpe,* p. 250; Manucy, *Fort at Frederica,* pp. 109, 111, 114, 115; Terry to the Trustees, 3 May 1745, *CRG,* 24:387–89; Proceedings of the President and Assistants, 22 Sept., 12 Oct., 27 Dec. 1748, 4, 19 June 1749, ibid., 6:222–24, 233, 235–37; Pye to Verelst, 12 Dec. 1746, ibid., 25:97; William Logan's Journal, 30 Oct., 1, 4, 9, 10, 14 Nov. 1745, pp. 168–72.

11. Heron to the Duke of Bedford, 20 Mar. 1749, CRG, 36:417.

12. Ibid., pp. 417, 418; South Carolina Council Journals, 8 Feb. 1749, ibid., pp. 420–25.

13. Ibid., pp. 424, 425. Muster rolls of boatmen are in A Pay Bill of the Boatmen, 25 Feb. 1747 to 24 Feb. 1748, 25 Feb. to 24 July 1748, and 25 July to 24 Sept. 1748, ibid., pp. 372–78; A Return of the Vessells and Boats, 29 May 1749, *CRG,* 25:468.

14. Easterby, *SCCHJ,* 2, 10 Mar. 1743, pp. 259, 289, 3 July 1744, p. 224, 23 Mar. 1745, p. 419, 18 Jan., 19 Mar. 1746, pp. 52, 53, 154, 155, 17 Feb., 11 June 1747, pp. 191, 192, 362, 363; Miscellaneous Records, 1743–46, FF, SC-Ar, 4:92, 93; R. Smith, *South Carolina as a Royal Province,* pp. 183, 184, 188–92.

15. Ibid., pp. 193–95; Williams, "British-American Officers," pp. 290–92; Lawson, *Uniforms,* 2:14.

16. R. Smith, *South Carolina as a Royal Province,* pp. 194, 195; Easterby, *SCCHJ,* 29 Nov. 1746, 5 June 1747, pp. 72, 325, 7 Apr., 4, 20 May 1748, pp. 171, 210, 281; Meriwether, *Expansion,* pp. 64, 199.

17. Arrell M. Gibson, *The Chickasaws* (Norman, 1971), pp. 42–56; Jacobs, *Indians,* pp. 42, 45, 66–71.

18. Horton to Mary Bosomworth, 15 Sept. 1744, CRG, 36:282; Letter from Charles Town, 30 May 1745, ibid., p. 208; Letter from Frederica, 27 Apr. 1745, ibid., p. 205. For a period description of the Creek nations see Jacobs, *Indians,* pp. 43, 54–65.

19. Corkran, *The Creek Frontier,* pp. 118–23.

20. John Dobell to the Trustees, May 1746, *CRG,* 25:48.

21. Corkran, *The Creek Frontier,* pp. 123–25; Heron to the Duke of Bedford, 29 Aug. 1748, CRG, 36:398, 399.

22. Perhaps the last battle of King George's War in southeastern North America was the raid on Brunswick, North Carolina, by a small flotilla of Spanish privateers during 3–8 September 1748. Lawrence Lee, *The Lower Cape Fear in Colonial Days* (Chapel Hill, 1965), pp. 232–34; Williams, "British-American Officers," pp. 292,

293; Ettinger, *Oglethorpe,* p. 254; Fox to Oglethorpe, 27 Dec. 1748, WO 4/45, p. 348.

23. Proceedings of the President and Assistants, 22 Apr., 5, 23 May, 10 June 1749, *CRG,* 6:244, 247–49.

24. President and Assistants to Martyn, 26 Oct. 1749, ibid., 25:431.

25. Verelst to Heron, 1 Aug. 1749, CRG, 36:436.

26. Ettinger, *Oglethorpe,* pp. 254, 271–90.

27. Henry Bruce, *Life of General Oglethorpe* (New York, 1890), p. 250, sketch of Oglethorpe in old age.

Bibliography

I. Manuscript Sources

A. British Public Record Office, London

Exchequer and Audit Office
> AO 3/119, The Accompt of James Oglethorpe . . . for Extradordinary Services Incurr'd . . . from the 22d of September 1738 to the 22d of July 1743.
> AO 1/162/441, The Declaration of the Account of James Oglethorpe . . . Between the 22d of September 1738 and Michaelmas 1743.

Treasury Office
> T 1/310, A Computation of One Year's Expenses . . . proposed by General Oglethorpe in July 1741. . . .

War Office
> WO 4/40–45, 82, Out Letters of the Secretary at War.
> WO 24/222, 251, The Royal Warrant for the Establishment of the Georgia Rangers, Highland Company, Boatmen, etc.
> WO 24/696, PMG 4/8, Half Pay Lists.
> WO 25/20–22, 89, 90, Commission Books.
> WO 25/134–36, Notification Books.
> WO 25/3209, Estimate of the Forces.

B. University Library, Cambridge, England

Cholmondeley (Houghton) Manuscripts, Sir Robert Walpole's Archive.

C. Georgia Department of Archives and History, Atlanta

Chandler, Allen D., and Lucian L. Knight, eds. The Colonial Records of the State of Georgia. Vols. 20, 27–39.

Georgia Colonial Conveyances, 1750–76. 9 vols.

Records in the British Public Record office Relating to Loyalist Claims, microfilm.

D. University of Georgia Libraries, Athens

Egmont Papers, Phillipps Collection. 20 vols. Special Collections Library.

E. South Carolina Department of Archives and History, Columbia

Loose Plats.
Miscellaneous Records, 1732–76. 10 vols.
Plat Books, 1731–75. 23 vols.
Proprietary Grant Books, 1732–75. 46 vols.
Public Treasurer Ledgers, 1725–73. 4 vols.
Records in the British Public Record Office Relating to South Carolina, microfilm.
South Carolina Commons House Journals (see Charles E. Lee, and Ruth S. Green, "A Guide to the Commons House Journals of the South Carolina General Assembly, 1692–1721," *South Carolina Historical Magazine* 68 [Apr. 1967]:85–96, and ibid., 1721–75, 68 [July 1967]:165–83).
South Carolina Council Journals (see Lee and Green, "A Guide to South Carolina Council Journals, 1671–1775," *South Carolina Historical Magazine* 68 [Jan. 1967]:1–13).
South Carolina Upper House Journals (see Lee and Green, "A Guide to the Upper House Journals of the South Carolina General Assembly, 1721–1775," *South Carolina Historical Magazine* 67 [Oct. 1966]:187–202).

F. Other Manuscript Sources

Mackenzie, William, Papers. Georgia Historical Society Library, Savannah.
Pemberton, James. Visit to Carolina, 1745. Photostat in Margaret Davis Cate Library, Frederica, original in Library of Congress, Washington.

II. Printed Sources

A. Diaries and Journals

Barnwell, Joseph W., ed. "Fort King George—Journal of Col. John Barnwell." *South Carolina Historical and Genealogical Magazine* 27 (Oct. 1926):189–203.
Coulter, E. Merton, ed. *The Journal of Peter Gordon, 1732–1735.* Athens, 1963.
————. *The Journal of William Stephens, 1741–1743,* Athens, 1958.
————. *The Journal of William Stephens, 1743–1745.* Athens, 1959.
Dampier, William. *A New Voyage Round the World.* 3 vols. London, 1717.
Historical Manuscripts Commission. *The Diary of Lord John Percival, First Earl of Egmont, 1730–1747.* 3 vols. London, 1920–23.
Jones, George F., ed. *Detailed Reports on the Salzburger Emigrants Who Settled in America . . . Edited by Samual Urlsperger.* 3 vols. Athens, 1968–72.
————. "Von Reck's Second Report from Georgia." *The William and Mary Quarterly* 22 (Apr. 1965):319–33.
Jones, Katharine M., ed. *Port Royal Under Six Flags.* New York, 1960.

A Journal of a Voyage from Gibraltar to Georgia. London, 1738.
Kimber, Edward. "Itinerant Observations in America." *Collections of the Georgia Historical Society* 4, pt. 2 (1878):1–64.
———. *A Relation or Journal of a Late Expedition to the Gates of St. Augustine in Florida.* London, 1744.
Lefler, Hugh T., ed. *A New Voyage to Carolina by John Lawson.* Chapel Hill, 1967.
McPherson, Robert, ed. *Journal of the Earl of Egmont, 1732–1738.* Athens, 1962.
Mereness, Newton D., ed. "A Ranger's Report of Travels with General Oglethorpe, 1739–1742." *Travels in the American Colonies.* New York, 1916:218–36.
Moore, Francis. "A Voyage to Georgia Begun in the Year 1735." *Collections of the Georgia Historical Society* 1 (1840):80–152.
"A New Voyage to Georgia." *Collections of the Georgia Historical Society* 2 (1842):39–60.
"The Spanish Official Account of the Attack on the Colony of Georgia." *Collections of the Georgia Historical Society* 8, pt. 3 (1913):1–110.
"William Logan's Journal of a Journey to Georgia, 1745." *Pennsylvania Magazine of History and Biography* 36 (1912):1–16, 162–86.

B. Documents

Atlanta Town Committee. *Abstracts of Colonial Wills of the State of Georgia.* Atlanta, 1962.
Candler, Allen D., and Lucian L. Knight, eds. *The Colonial Records of the State of Georgia.* Vols. 1–19, 21–26. Atlanta, 1904–16.
Collections of the South Carolina Historical Society. 5 vols. Charleston, 1857–97.
Cooper, Thomas, and David J. McCord, eds. *The Statutes at Large of South Carolina.* 10 vols. Columbia, 1836–41.
Coulter, E. Merton, and Albert B. Saye, eds. *A List of the Early Settlers of Georgia.* Athens, 1949.
Headlam, Cecil, and others, eds. *Calendar of State Papers, Colonial Series, America and the West Indies.* 35 vols., in progress. London, 1860–.
May, W. E., ed. "His Majesty's Ships on the Carolina Station." *South Carolina Historical Magazine* 71 (July 1970):162–69.
McCord, David J. *Statutes.* See Cooper, Thomas.
McDowell, W. L. ed. *Documents Relating to Indian Affairs, 1750–1754.* Columbia, 1958.
———. *Journals of the Commissioners of the Indian Trade, 1710–1718.* Columbia, 1955.
Salley, A. S., and Mable L. Webber, eds. *Death Notices in the South Carolina Gazette, 1732–1775.* Columbia, 1954.
Shaw, William A., ed. *A Calendar of Treasury Books and Papers, 1729–1745.* 5 vols. London, 1897–1903.
Williams, W. R., ed. "British-American Officers, 1720–1763." *South Carolina Historical and Genealogical Magazine* 33 (July 1932):183–96; (Sept. 1932):290–96.

C. *Correspondence*

Barnwell, Joseph W., ed. "Correspondence of Henry Laurens." *South Carolina Historical and Genealogical Magazine* 28 (July 1927):141–68.
Davidson, Victor, ed. *Correspondence of John Milledge, Governor of Georgia, 1802–1806.* Columbia, 1949.
"Letters from General Oglethorpe." *Collections of the Georgia Historical Society* 3, pt. 2 (1873):1–156.
"Letters of Montiano; Siege of St. Augustine." *Collections of the Georgia Historical Society* 7, pt. 1 (1909):1–70.

D. *Other Contemporary Works*

Bolton, Herbert E., ed. *Arredondo's Historical Proof of Spain's Title to Georgia,* Berkeley, 1925.
Cadogan, George. *The Spanish Hireling Detected.* London, 1743.
Cumming, William P., ed. *The Southeast in Early Maps.* Chapel Hill, 1958.
A Full Reply to Lieut. Cadogan's Spanish Hireling, &c. and Lieut. Mackay's Letter Concerning the Action at Moosa. London, 1742.
An Impartial Account of the Late Expedition Against St. Augustine. London, 1742.
"An Impartial Enquiry into the State and Utility of the Province of Georgia." *Collections of the Georgia Historical Society* 1 (1840):153–202.
Jacobs, Wilbur R., ed. *Indians of the Southern Colonial Frontier.* Columbia, 1954.
Mackay, Hugh. *A Letter from Lieut. Hugh Mackay of Genl. Oglethorpe's Regiment, to John Mackay, Esq; in the Shire of Sutherland in Scotland.* London, 1742.
Milling, Chapman, Jr., ed. *Colonial South Carolina: Two Contemporary Descriptions by Governor James Glen and Doctor George Milligen–Johnson.* Columbia, 1951.
Muller, John. *A Treatise Concerning the Elementary Part of Fortification.* London, 1746.
VerSteeg, Clarence L., ed. *A True and Historical Narrative of the Colony of Georgia by Patrick Tailfer and Others with Comments by the Earl of Egmont.* Athens, 1960.

E. *Newspapers and Periodicals*

Boston News Letter.
The Gentleman's Magazine.
The Georgia Gazette.
The London Magazine.
The South Carolina Gazette.

III. Maps

A. *Contemporary Manuscript Maps*

Arredondo, Antonio de. Descriptio Geographica, de la part que los

Españoles possen Actualmente en el Continente de la Florida, 1742. Original in the Archives of the Indies, Sevilla. Reproduced in Verne E. Chatelain, *The Defenses of Spanish Florida, 1565 to 1763.* Washington, 1941.

———. Plan[o] de la Ciudad De Sn Augstin de la Fla, 1737. Original in the Arch. of the Indies, Seville. Reproduced in Chatelain, *Defenses of Spanish Florida.*

———. Plano de la Entrada de Gualquini Rio de St. Simon Situada en 31 orados de altura de Polo Septentrional, 1737. Original in the Arch. of the Indies, Sevilla. Reproduced in *Collections of the Georgia Historical Society (CGHS)* 7, pt. 3.

———. Plano del Castillo de Sn Marcos de la Florida, 1737. Original in the Arch. of the Indies, Seville. Reproduced in Chatelain, *Defenses of Spanish Florida.*

Barnwell, John. A Plan of King George's Fort, 1722. Original in the British Public Record Office (BPRO), London. Photostat in the Georgia Surveyor General Department, Atlanta.

———. [Southeastern North America], ca. 1722. Original in the BPRO, London. Tracing in the South Carolina Department of Archives and History, Columbia.

Bonar, William. A Draught of the Creek Nation, 1757. Original in the BPRO, London. Photostat in the Ga. Surv. Gen. Dept., Atlanta.

Bull, William. [Southeastern North America], 1738. Original in the BPRO, London. Photostat in the Ga. Surv. Gen. Dept., Atlanta.

Castello, Pablo. Plano del Presido de Sn. Augustin, 1764. Original in the Ministry of Marine, Madrid. Reproduced in Chatelain, *Defenses of Spanish Florida.*

Crenay, Baron de. Carte De partie de la Louisianne, 1733. Original in the Ministry of the Colonies, Paris. Reproduced in John R. Swanton, *Early History of the Creek Indians and Their Neighbors.* Washington, 1922.

De Brahm, William. A Map of Savannah River . . . also the Four Sounds Savannah, Hossabaw and St. Katharines . . . Likewise Newport or Serpent River . . ., ca. 1750. Photostat in the Ga. Surv. Gen. Dept., Atlanta.

———. The Profile of the whole Citadelle of Frederica, ca. 1755. Original in the BPRO, London. Reproduced in *CGHS* 7, pt. 3.

Descripcion de la Gloriosa y Ecoica entrada quetas tropas de S. dt. Cha tolica hisieron al puerto de Gauquinin et dia 16 de Julio de 1742. Original in the National Library, Madrid. Photostat in the Ga. Surv. Gen. Dept., Atlanta.

The Fort at Frederica in Georgia as layd down by a Swiss Engineer facing the princiapl Street of the Town, 1736. Original in the John Carter Brown Library, Providence. Photostat in the Margaret Davis Cate Library, Frederica.

Frobell, B. W. Map of Glynn County, 1869. Original in the Ga. Surv. Gen Dept., Atlanta.

Jones, Noble. [Draught of the Fort at Savannah], 1737. Original in the

BPRO, London. Reproduced in Allen D. Candler and Lucian L. Knight, eds. *The Colonial Records of the State of Georgia,* Vol. 21.

McKinnon, John. [Map of Cumberland Island], 1802. Photostat in the Ga. Surv. Gen. Dept., Atlanta.

Map of the Coast of Florida from Talbot Island to the mouth of the Musquetta River, ca. 1740. Original in the British Museum, London. Photostat in the St. Augustine Historical Society Library, St. Augustine.

Mapp of Beaufort in South Carolina, 1721. Original in the BPRO, London.

Moncrief, James. Plan of Fort Picalata on St. John's River, 1765. Original in the Library of Congress, Washington. Reproduced in Chatelain, *Defenses of Spanish Florida.*

Plan dun petit Fort pour L'Isle de St. Andre, ca. 1765. Original in the British Museum, London. Reproduced in *CGHS* 7, pt. 3.

A Plan of Frederica a Town in the Plantation of Georgia in the Province of Carolina as layd out by Mr. Oglethorpe, 1736. Original in the John Carter Brown Library, Providence. Photostat in the Margaret Davis Cate Library, Frederica.

Purcell, Joseph. A Map of the Southern Indian District of North America, 1775. Original in the Newberry Library, Chicago.

Roworth, Sam. A Plan of the Land Between Fort Mossy And St. Augustine, ca. 1765. Copy in the Lib. of Cong., Washington. Reproduced in Chatelain, *Defenses of Spanish Florida.*

[Sketch Map of the Rivers Santee, Wateree, Saludee, &c., with the road to the Cuttauboes], ca. 1736. Original in the BPRO, London. Reproduced in Douglas S. Brown, *The Catawba Indians: The People of the River.* Columbia, 1966.

Yonge, Henry, and William De Brahm. A Map of the Sea Coast of Georgia 1763. Original in the British Museum, London. Photostat in Ga. Surv. Gen. Dept., Atlanta.

Wright, Thomas. A Map of Georgia and Florida, 1763. Original in the BPRO, London. Photostat in the Ga. Surv. Gen. Dept., Atlanta.

B. Contemporary Printed Maps

Bowen, Emanuel. *The Provinces of North and South Carolina, Georgia, etc.* London, 1747. Copy in the University of Georgia Special Collections Library, Athens.

Campbell, Archibald. *Sketch of the Northern Frontiers of Georgia.* London, 1780. Photostat in the Ga. Surv. Gen. Dept., Atlanta.

De Brahm, William. *A Map of South Carolina and a Part of Georgia.* London, 1757. Photostat in the Ga. Surv. Gen. Dept., Atlanta.

Delisle, Guillaume. *Carte de la Louisiane.* Paris, 1718. Reproduced in William P. Cumming, ed. *The Southeast in Early Maps.* Chapel Hill, 1958.

Gordon, Peter. *A View of Savanah as it stood the 29th of March 1734.* London, 1734. Copy in the Univ. of Ga. Spec. Coll. Libr., Athens.

Hughes, Andrew. *A Draught of South Carolina and Georgia from Sewee to St. Estaca.* London, ca. 1740. Reproduced in *CGHS* 7, pt. 1.

Jefferys T., and William Faden, eds. *A Plan of Port Royal in South Carolina.*

London, ca. 1776. Copy in the University of South Carolina Caroliniana Library, Columbia.

———. *A Plan of the River and Sound of D'Awfoskee, in South Carolina.* London, ca. 1776. Copy in the Lib. of Cong., Washington.

Lotter, T. F. *A Map of the County of Savannah.* London?, 1740. Copy in the Univ. of Ga. Spec. Coll. Library, Athens.

Mitchell, John. *A Map of the British and French Dominions in North America.* London, 1755. Photostat in the Ga. Surv. Gen. Dept., Atlanta.

Moseley, Edward. *A New and Correct Map of the Province of North Carolina.* London, 1733. Reproduced in Cumming, *Southeast in Early Maps.*

Nairn, Thomas. *A Map of South Carolina.* London, 1711. Reproduced in Cumming, *Southeast in Early Maps.*

A New and Accurate Map of the Province of Georgia in North America. London, 1780. Copy in the Univ. of Ga. Spec. Coll. Lib., Athens.

A Plan of the Town, Castle, and Harbour of St. Augustine (and the adjacent Coast of Florida) with the Disposition of the Forces in the Expedition under General Oglethorpe, in the Year 1740. Reproduced in *CGHS* 7, pt. 1.

Plan Du Port De Gouadaquini now called Jekil Sound in the Province of Georgia in North America. London?, ca. 1741. Reproduced in *CGHS* 7, pt. 3.

Seale, R. W. *Georgia [and] Part of Carolina.* London, 1741. Copy in the Univ. of Ga. Spec. Coll. Lib., Athens.

Silver, Thomas. *A View of the Town and Castle of St. Augustine, and the English Camp before it June 20, 1740.* Reproduced in William B. Stevens, *A History of Georgia,* Vol. 1.

Stuart, John. *A Map of South Carolina and a Part of Georgia.* London, 1780. Photostat in the Ga. Surv. Gen. Dept., Atlanta.

Toms, W. H. *The Ichnography of Charles-Town at High Water.* London, 1739. Reproduced in the *Charleston Year Book.* Charleston, 1884.

A View of the Town of Savannah, in the Colony of Georgia, in South Carolina. London, 1741. Copy in the Univ. of Ga. Spec. Coll. Lib., Athens.

IV. Secondary Works

Adam, Frank (revised by Thomas Learney). *The Clans, Septs, and Regiments of the Scottish Highlands.* Edinburgh, 1952.

Arnade, Charles W. *The Siege of St. Augustine in 1702.* Gainesville, 1959.

Billington, Ray A. *Westward Expansion.* New York, 1963.

Bruce, Henry. *Life of General Oglethorpe.* New York, 1890.

Chatelain, Verne E. *The Defenses of Spanish Florida, 1565–1763.* Washington, 1941.

Chitwood, Oliver P. *A History of Colonial America.* New York, 1961.

Crane, Verner W. *The Southern Frontier, 1670–1732.* Ann Arbor, 1959.

Corkran, David H. *The Cherokee Frontier, Conflict and Survival, 1740–1762.* Norman, 1962.

———. *The Creek Frontier, 1540–1783.* Norman, 1967.

Ettinger, Amos A. *James Edward Oglethorpe, Imperial Idealist.* Oxford, 1936.

Gibson, Arrell M. *The Chickasaws.* Norman, 1971.

Ivers, Larry E. *Colonial Forts of South Carolina, 1670–1775.* Columbia, 1970.

Jones, Charles C. *The History of Georgia.* 2 vols. Boston, 1883.

Klingberg, Frank J. *An Appraisal of the Negro in Colonial South Carolina.* Washington, 1941.

Landstrom, Bjorn, *The Ship.* New York, 1961.

Lawson, Cecil C. P. *A History of the Uniforms of the British Army.* 5 vols. London, 1940–67.

Lee, Lawrence. *The Lower Cape Fear in Colonial Days.* Chapel Hill, 1965.

Manucy, Albert C. *Artillery through the Ages.* Washington, 1949.

_____. *The Fort at Frederica.* Tallahassee, 1962.

Meriwether, Robert L., *The Expansion of South Carolina, 1729–1765.* Kingsport, 1940.

Miller, John C., *The First Frontier: Life in Colonial America.* New York, 1966.

Milling, Chapman J. *Red Carolinians.* Columbia, 1969.

Peterson, Harold L. *Arms and Armor in Colonial America, 1526–1783.* New York, 1956.

Reese, Trevor R. *Colonial Georgia: A Study in British Imperial Policy in the Eighteenth Century.* Athens, 1963.

_____. *Frederica: Colonial Fort and Town.* Saint Simons, 1969.

Sirmans, Eugene M. *Colonial South Carolina: A Political History, 1663–1763.* Chapel Hill, 1966.

Smith, Roy W. *South Carolina as a Royal Province, 1719–1776.* New York, 1903.

Stephens, William B. *A History of Georgia from Its First Discovery by Europeans to the Adoption of the Present Constitution in 1798.* 2 vols. New York, 1847–59.

Swanton, John R. *Early History of the Creek Indians and Their Neighbors.* Washington, 1922.

_____. *The Indians of the Southeastern United States.* Washington, 1946.

_____. *Indian Tribes of the Lower Mississippi Valley and Adjacent Coast of the Gulf of Mexico.* Washington, 1911.

Temple, Sarah B. G., and Kenneth Coleman. *Georgia Journeys.* Athens, 1961.

TePaske, John J. *The Governorship of Spanish Florida, 1700–1763.* Durham, 1964.

Tunis, Edwin. *Colonial Living.* Cleveland, 1957.

Wright, Robert. *A Memoir of General James Oglethorpe.* London, 1867.

V. Articles

Cate, Margaret D. "Fort Frederica-Battle of Bloody Marsh." *The Georgia Historical Quarterly* 27 (June 1943):111–74.

Coulter, E. Merton. "Mary Musgrove, Queen of the Creeks." *The Georgia Historical Quarterly* 11 (Mar. 1927):1–30.

De Vorsey, Louis, Jr. "The Colonial Southeast on an Accurate General Map." *The Southeastern Geographer* 6 (1966):20–32.

Forts Committee, Georgia Department of Archives and History. "Fort St. Andrews, Fort Prince William." *Georgia Magazine* 11 (Aug.–Sept. 1967):22–24.

————. "Fort St. Simons." *Georgia Magazine* 10 (June–July 1966):29–31.

Goff, John H. "The Path to Okfuskee Upper Trading Route in Georgia to the Creek Indians." *The Georgia Historical Quarterly* 39 (Mar. 1955):1–36; (June, 1955):152–71.

————. "Short Studies of Georgia Place Names, No. 110, Sterling Creek." *Georgia Mineral Newsletter* 17 (1964–65):67.

Harden, William. "James Mackay of Strothy Hall, Comrade in Arms of George Washington." *The Georgia Historical Quarterly* 1 (June, 1917):77–98.

Ivers, Larry E., "The Battle of Fort Mosa." *The Georgia Historical Quarterly* 51 (June 1967):135–53.

————. "Scouting the Inland Passage, 1685–1737." *The South Carolina Historical Magazine* 73 (July 1972):117–29.

Lanning, John T. "American Participation in the War of Jenkins' Ear." *The Georgia Historical Quarterly* 11 (Sept. 1927):191–215.

May, W. E. "Capt. Charles Hardy on the Carolina Station, 1742–1744." *The South Carolina Historical Magazine* 70 (Jan. 1969):1–19.

Peeples, Robert E. "A Miles Genealogy." *The South Carolina Historical Magazine* 66 (Oct. 1965), 229–40.

Smith, Henry, "Purrysburg." *The South Carolina Historical and Genealogical Magazine* 10 (Oct. 1909):187–219.

Spalding, Phinizy. "James Edward Oglethorpe. A Biographical Survey." *The Georgia Historical Quarterly* 61 (Fall 1972):332–48.

————. "South Carolina and Georgia: The Early Days." *The South Carolina Historical Magazine* 69 (Apr. 1968):83–96.

Spalding, Thomas. "A Sketch of the Life of General James Oglethorpe." *Collections of the Georgia Historical Society* 1 (1840):239–95.

Index

A

Abercorn, Georgia, 24, 29, 161
Agencourt, the, 101
Alabama Fort, 45. *See also* Fort Toulouse
Altamaha River, 9, 10, 12, 21, 29, 42, 50, 51, 56, 60, 61, 64, 72, 73, 97, 113, 135, 139, 174, 175, 186, 187
Amelia, the, 77, 85, 90, 97, 101
Amelia Fort, Georgia, 56, 78, 85, 91, 93, 133, 135, 145
Amelia Island, Georgia, 3, 56, 78, 85, 90, 100, 176, 189
Anastasia Island, Flordia, 109–13, 116, 126, 127, 172, 182
Apalachee, Florida, 3, 12, 41, 92, 95
Apalachee Indians, 6, 87
Apalachicola Indians, 6, 23
Artillery, 92, 96, 98, 154, 163, 168
Assembly, South Carolina, 11, 28, 32, 33, 45, 48, 70, 96–99, 133, 141, 150, 210
Augusta, the, 76
Augusta, Georgia, 75–77, 87, 102, 125, 140, 157, 164, 189, 206, 214
Augusta Rangers, 85, 140, 157, 185, 187, 188, 202, 206

B

Bachelor's Redoubt, Georgia, 135, 137, 149, 150, 186, 187
Bachelor's Redoubt, the, 137
Bagpipes, 194
Baillie, Lieutenant Kenneth, 119, 120–24, 138, 145, 146, 195
Barba, Captain Antonio, 165, 166
Barnard, Captain John, 141, 192
Barnwell, Colonel John, 7
Barracks, 77, 134, 149, 196, 197, 206, 211
Barrimacke, Georgia, 80, 83
Barton, John, 39, 41, 48
Bathesda, the, 195, 209
Batteries, 57, 60, 94, 109–11, 113, 126–29, 134, 156, 160, 206

Battle of Bloody Marsh, 166, 167, 244–45 (n. 16). *See also* Grenadier Fight
Battle of Fort Mosa, 115, 120–24, 130
Baugh, Gabriel, 106, 107
Bayonets, 80, 121, 122, 194, 195, 208
Beaufort, South Carolina, 7, 8, 12, 23–25, 38, 48, 53, 72, 82, 114, 134, 151, 152, 172, 210, 211
Beaufort Fort, South Carolina, 7–9
Beaufort Galley, the, 209, 210
Bellinger, Captain William, 23, 25
Bichler, Quartermaster Thomas, 149, 192, 193, 242 (n. 47), 249 (n. 18)
Bienville, Governor Jean, 212
Bigwall, George, 175
Black Watch tartan. *See* Government tartan
Blockade, 99, 103, 129, 132
Blockhouse, 45, 94, 95, 134, 137, 145, 146
Board of Trade, 9, 10, 50
Boatmen, 202, 203, 209, 214
Boats, 50, 58, 60, 61, 85, 91, 96, 97, 103, 107, 111, 112, 122, 127–29, 137, 145, 150, 153, 155, 156, 159, 161, 168–71, 178, 196, 208, 209
Bolzius, Rev. John, 192
Bonnets, 51, 100, 188, 194
Bosomworth, Mary, 186, 189, 192, 212, 213. *See also* Mathews, Mary; Musgrove, Mary
Bosomworth's Trading Fort, Georgia, 186, 187, 247 (n. 8)
Bray, Dr. Thomas, 10
Britain, 44, 71, 73, 172, 194, 200, 213
British, the, 31, 63, 64, 85, 92, 95, 102, 120, 126, 151, 153, 165–67, 172, 173, 176, 196, 197, 200, 211
British flag, 37, 50, 161
British government, 7, 10, 28, 29, 61, 63, 66, 69, 98, 104, 136, 154, 183, 185, 189, 202, 208, 213
British navy. *See* Royal Navy
British soldiers. *See* Regulars
Broadsword, 51, 83, 194
Brooks, Francis, 77, 90, 97

Broughton, Lieutenant Governor Thomas, 47–49, 69–71
Brown Bess, 80, 194. *See also* Long land musket, Muskets
Brown, Samual, 85
Bull, Colonel William, 10, 13, 29, 33, 71, 88, 96, 98, 103, 130, 131
Burnside, James, 38
Burntpot Island, Georgia, 146

C

Cadogan, Captain Lieutenant George, 206
Caesar, a chief of the Over Hills Cherokee, 68
Calwell, John 205
Campbell, Mrs., 207
Camps, 39, 53, 60, 83, 93, 105–8, 110, 113, 116–18, 120, 128–31, 137, 162, 168, 177–79, 181, 182
Cannons, 20, 28, 51, 62, 76, 78, 94, 95, 104, 107, 108, 111, 126, 130, 131, 134, 153–55, 159–61, 171, 172, 177
Canoes, 40, 53, 55, 58, 90, 91, 119, 145, 194, 209, 210
Canoochee Creek, 18, 19, 135, 187
Carbines, 14, 40
Carolina, the, 15, 28, 29, 53, 54, 58, 71, 77, 101
Carolina Rangers, Troop of, 114, 116–21
Carr, Captain Mark, 144–46, 159, 166, 167, 169, 176, 182, 194, 195
Carr's Fort, Georgia, 135, 145, 187, 194. *See also* Hermitage
Carteret's Point, Georgia. *See* Bachelor's Redoubt
Cartridge box, 14, 26, 36, 80
Castillo de San Marcos, Florida, 93, 103, 110, 112, 131, 179. *See also* Fort San Marcos
Catawba Indians, 5, 6, 12, 210
"Cathole" toilets, 21
Cattle, 11, 12, 74, 85, 91, 139, 162, 182, 197
Causton, Thomas, 38, 42, 74
Cellars, 21, 58, 145
Charles Town Galley, the, 182, 209, 210. *See also* Galleys, South Carolina
Charles Town, South Carolina, 4–9, 11, 12, 22, 25, 28, 32, 33, 35–37, 40, 45–48, 71, 72, 80, 84, 87, 88, 96, 98, 139, 147, 150, 152, 161, 171, 204, 209–11
Chattahoochee River, 12, 31, 39, 40, 43, 47, 189, 210
Chattooga River, 67
Cherokee Indians, 5, 6, 8, 12, 37, 66, 68, 75, 76, 85–87, 102, 105, 106, 181, 210, 213. *See also* Lower Cherokee Indians, Middle Cherokee Indians, Over Hills Cherokee Indians, Valley Cherokee Indians
Chickasaw Indians, 5, 7, 12, 32, 43, 44, 66, 76, 92, 102, 125, 140, 157, 164, 210, 211; war with French, 7, 44, 211; best ally of British, 211
Chigelley, principal mico of the Lower Creek, 40, 86, 87, 102, 142, 147, 176
Children, 42, 51, 72, 82, 90, 140, 145, 161, 199
Choctaw Indians, 5, 7, 12, 32, 44, 75, 147, 204, 210, 211
Clark, William, 39
Cloake, Seaman Samuel, 168, 169
Clothing, 100, 101, 125, 180, 188, 194, 198
Cockran, Lieutenant Colonel James, 79, 80, 84, 134, 136
Colony Piragua, the, 61, 97, 101
Combahee River, 6, 11, 14, 15, 24
Commons House of Assembly, South Carolina, 33, 96, 98, 99
Congaree Fort (1718–22), South Carolina, 6–8
Congaree Fort (1748–54), South Carolina, 210, 211
Conservators of the Peace, 140, 205
Constables, 29, 34, 65, 67, 68, 192, 193, 205
Cook, Lieutenant Colonel William, 79, 82, 136, 137, 183, 184
Cooke, Lawrence, 16
Coosa River, 7, 31, 32, 43
Corn, 12, 22, 25, 28, 41, 58, 140, 148, 197, 198
Corporal-guards, 117, 124, 144
Council, South Carolina, 33, 96, 99, 171, 209
Court-martial, 84, 183, 184, 201, 207
Coweta, the principal town of the Lower Creek, 38, 40–44, 47, 86, 87, 142
Cowpen, 12, 143, 144
Creek Indians, 5–7, 27, 31–34, 36–38, 41, 43, 46–48, 61, 63, 65, 66, 69, 75, 85–87, 92, 114, 141, 143, 144, 147, 164, 178, 204, 211; culture and customs, 31, 42–44; political policy of neutrality, 31, 45, 176, 213; raids on Florida, 147, 148, 212. *See also* Lower Creek, Indians, Upper Creek Indians
Cuban half-galleys, 97, 104, 108, 109, 111–13, 116, 126, 127, 129, 152–56, 159, 160, 168, 170–72
Cumberland Island, Georgia, 56, 58, 62, 77, 80, 85, 102, 134, 139, 148–50, 154, 155, 170, 171, 176, 188, 205

Cussita, a principal Lower Creek town, 44. *See also* Kasihta
Cuthbert, Captain John, 51, 52, 74, 75, 85, 86, 88
Cutlass, 26, 36
Cutter, the, 101, 146, 154, 182

D

Danner, Quartermaster, 100
Darien, Georgia, 9, 51, 52, 55, 56, 58, 63, 72–74, 91, 100, 101, 113, 135, 142, 149, 154, 157, 161, 187, 188, 206, 210
Darien, the, 101, 139, 146, 181
Darien Fort, 72, 73
Davis, Captain Celeb, 182, 207
Delegal, Lieutenant Philip, Sr., 61
Delegal's Fort, Georgia, 56, 61, 80, 82, 134, 158
Demere, Captain Raymond, 134, 136, 163–67, 206
Demetre, Sergeant Daniel, 146, 209, 212
Dempsey, Charles, 60, 62, 63
Desbrisay, Captain Lieutenant Albert, 79, 83, 84, 134, 136, 137
Diego River, 107, 110, 116, 118, 119, 122, 123, 177
Disabled veterans, 193
Disease, 21, 119, 129, 131, 136, 197, 198. *See also* Health
Doctors, 25, 26, 138
Don, Lieutenant Archibald, 206
Dragoons, 13, 140, 181, 193; Spanish, 95, 120, 148, 152, 153, 176, 212
Drums: Indian, 87; British, 118, 120, 194, 214, 215
Duels, 137
Duke of Newcastle, British Secretary of State, 60
Dunbar, Captain George, 86, 92, 94, 97, 106, 131, 134, 136, 156, 176

E

Ebenezer, Georgia, 24, 29, 51, 86, 100, 101, 135, 141, 149, 187, 192, 206, 210
Ebenezer Rangers, 149, 202, 242 (n. 47)
Edgecomb, Lieutenant Arthur Ogle, 74
Edisto River, 6–10, 14, 26
Edwards, William, 46, 47
Eels, Private, 181
Elbert, Lieutenant William, 22, 23, 29, 74
Ellick, a mico of Kasihta, 69
England, 3, 4, 7, 10, 13, 32, 35, 47, 50, 61, 79, 82, 84, 86, 130, 133, 136, 137, 138, 145, 150, 183, 184, 189, 193, 195, 200, 201, 205, 208
English Rangers, Troop of, 99, 100, 106, 113, 114, 116, 117, 120, 138, 143, 174, 176, 185, 202; in Battle of Fort Mosa, 120–24; encounter with Yemassee, 149, 150; encounter with Spaniards, 164
Equipment, 35–37, 129, 131, 155, 161, 162, 164, 189
Establishments: Southern Rangers, 14, 74; Palachacola Garrison, 23, 25, 26; Palachacola Rangers, 28; Independent Company of Rangers, 35; Ranger parties, 52; Southern Scouts, 53; Forty-second Regiment, 79; English and Highland Rangers, 100; Highland Company, 101, 193; South Carolina Regiment, 125; Augusta Rangers, 140, 187; Marine Company, 144, 195; Georgia, 185
Evans, Captain Rowland, 25, 27
Eveleigh, Samuel: advises Oglethorpe, 225 (n. 2), 226 (n. 18), 240 (n. 25)
Eyles, Doctor, 137

F

Faulcon, the, 157, 159
Ferguson, Captain William, 53, 54, 58, 71, 77
Finley, William, 16
Finlay, Quartermaster William Atcheson, 189
First Fort, Georgia, 23, 24, 27; initially called Fort Argyle, 18. *See also* Old Fort
Fisher, Nicholas, 35
Fitchet, William, 16
Flamborough, the, 152, 168
Fletcher, Margaret, 207
Florida, 3, 4, 9, 12, 14, 17, 47, 48, 50, 60–63, 70, 87–89, 92, 93, 96, 97, 100, 102, 113, 129, 133, 136, 137, 145, 147, 151, 169, 170–72, 176, 179, 180, 182, 183, 189, 194, 204, 206, 210, 211, 213
Flying party, 114–24, 236 (n. 3)
Food, 39, 41, 97, 100, 108, 113, 119, 133, 161, 162, 182, 183, 212
Fort Argyle, Georgia, 18, 24, 27–29, 38, 74, 85, 99, 135, 137–39, 143, 148, 149, 161, 174, 186, 187, 192, 206, 210; construction of, 19–21; depiction of, 22; reconstruction of, 148
Fort Argyle, the 149
Fort Augusta, Georgia, 52, 75–77, 85, 87, 139, 206, 209, 214, 229 (n. 15)
Fort Diego, Florida, 93, 103, 105–8, 115, 116, 120, 130, 180
Fort Frederica, Georgia, 51, 55, 57, 102, 134, 138, 158, 168, 187; depiction of, 59

Fort Frederick, South Carolina, 11, 12, 24, 72, 85, 134, 211

Fort Johnson, South Carolina, 7, 8, 12, 209, 210

Fort King George, South Carolina (modern Georgia), 9, 12, 50, 51, 73

Fort Matanzas, Florida, 172, 179, 182, 210

Fort Moore, South Carolina, 6, 8, 12, 23, 27, 40, 47, 66, 67, 69, 75, 76, 87, 88, 209–12

Fort Mosa, Florida, 93, 103, 108, 111–13, 115, 117–19, 125, 126, 131, 138, 160, 167, 169, 172, 177; Battle of, 120–24

Fort Mount Pleasant, Georgia, 26, 135, 141, 187

Fort Picolata, Florida, 92–94, 103

Fort Prince George, South Carolina, 8, 12, 15, 24–28, 35, 37, 38, 52, 75, 88, 140, 141. *See also* Palachacola Fort

Fort Prince William, Georgia, 93, 102, 134, 135, 139, 145, 149, 153, 155–57, 167, 170, 176, 179, 187, 205, 208, 210; Spaniards attack, 150, 153, 171; rebuilt, 177, 206

Fort Pupo. *See* Fort San Francisco de Pupo

Fort Saint Andrews, Georgia, 56, 58, 60, 62, 77, 80, 82–84, 91, 135, 139, 153, 155, 158, 167, 170, 188, 205

Fort Saint George, Florida, 56, 62–64, 78, 92, 93, 105, 106, 131

Fort Saint Simons, Georgia, 82, 134, 135, 138, 152, 153, 155–62, 165–99, 205

Fort San Francisco de Pupo, Florida, 42, 47, 48, 92–96, 103, 120

Fort San Marcos, Saint Augustine, Florida, 12, 97, 99, 109, 117, 119, 120, 126, 177, 210. *See also* Castillo de San Marcos

Fort San Marcos de Apalachee, Florida, 12, 92, 103, 210

Fort Toulouse, Louisiana (modern Alabama), 7, 12, 43, 44, 189, 210

Forty-second Regiment of Foot, 78, 80–82, 84, 86, 90–92, 96, 97, 109, 111, 113, 116, 126, 129, 133, 134, 136–39, 142, 147, 152–54, 163, 175, 177, 178, 181, 184, 202, 204, 206, 208, 211, 213; establishment, 79, 136; mutiny in, 83; invades Florida, 102, 105, 106, 114, 122, 123, 130, 131; during Spanish invasion, 157, 161, 163, 166, 167, 169

France, 28, 32, 44, 65, 87, 189, 200, 208

Francis, Lieutenant William, 143, 144, 174, 186

Francis, Mrs. William, 174, 175

Frederica, Georgia, 51, 52, 55–58, 61, 63, 66, 74, 83, 86, 89, 90, 95, 99, 101, 105, 131, 133, 135, 137, 143, 147–49, 152, 153, 155, 157, 161, 162, 165–68, 171–74, 176, 178, 186, 189, 199, 204–10, 212, 214

Frederica, the, 101, 146, 209

Frederica River, 54, 158, 159, 168, 169

G

Galleys, 152, 153, 159–61, 168, 172

Gardiner, John, 68

Garrisons of Rangers. *See* Augusta Rangers, Ebenezer Rangers, Mount Pleasant Rangers, Mount Venture Rangers, Okfuskee Rangers

Gascoigne, James, 61, 62

Gascoigne Bluff, 62, 158, 163

Georgia, 3, 7, 10, 11, 13, 16, 20, 21, 23, 25–31, 33–37, 44, 46, 51, 63–65, 70–72, 77–79, 82, 85, 91, 97, 100, 101, 105, 133, 136, 139, 140, 141, 145, 146, 149, 152, 153, 164, 170, 171, 174–76, 182, 183, 185, 192–95, 200–206, 210, 211, 213, 215; defenses, 7, 16, 28–30, 63, 84, 85; divided into military divisions, 74

Georgia, the, 58, 62, 77, 101, 122, 123, 145

Georgia's navy, 147, 159, 182, 195, 202

Georgia Trustees, 13, 16, 21, 23, 28, 31–33, 44, 46, 48–52, 57, 63, 65, 66, 70–72, 74, 80, 85, 90, 100, 102, 141, 205, 206, 214, 215

Germain, Sergeant William, 145

Glen, Governor James, 209

Glover, Colonel Alexander, 27

Government tartan, 194

Grant, Peter, 206

Grant, Cadet Peter, 137

Gray, John, 38, 39

Gray, Captain William, 164

Great Tellico, a town in the Over Hills Cherokee, 68

Greenfield, Sarah, 23

Grenadier Fight, 165–67, 244–45 (n. 16). *See also* Battle of Bloody Marsh

Grenadiers, 125, 136, 150, 154, 160, 161, 165–67, 176, 183; depiction of, 81

Grove, the, 93, 115, 179–81

Guale, Florida, 3, 10, 12, 50

Guards, 39, 51, 117, 121, 162, 196, 197, 208

Güemes, Governor Juan Francisco de, 151, 152

Gunners, 42, 94, 126, 152, 159, 160, 172, 177

H

Half-galleys. *See* Cuban half-galleys
Halfway, an Upper Creek town, 43, 44
Hand grenades, 136, 155
Hanover, the, 209
Harbor, of Saint Augustine, 97, 104, 107, 108, 109, 111, 112, 126, 129, 153, 172
Hardy, Captain Charles, 171, 182
Harry, chief of Kiawah Indians, 14
Harvey, William, 199
Hatchets, 14, 26, 100, 148, 161
Hawk, the, 61, 62, 63
Headmen, Indian, 41, 45, 47, 48, 68, 87
Health, 25, 26, 41, 49, 108, 165
Hearn, John, 7
Hearn's Fort, 8
Hermitage, a plantation, 144, 145, 194, 195. *See also* Carr's Fort
Hermsdorf, Captain Christian, 62
Hernández, Captain Nicholas, 162–64, 168
Heron, Lieutenant Colonel Alexander, 79, 82, 136, 154, 155, 170, 172, 175, 184, 202, 205–8, 213
Hewit, James, 113
Highland dress, 51, 100, 101, 118, 188, 194; depiction of, 191
Highlanders, 52, 55, 58, 83, 90, 91, 106, 107, 111, 120–24, 139, 146, 164–66, 193, 194, 196, 202, 204, 205
Highland Independent Company of Foot, 101, 106, 107, 114, 116–18, 123, 133, 155, 157, 163, 176, 186, 202, 206; Battles of, 120–24, 163–66
Highland militia, 62, 72
Highland Rangers, Troop of, 91, 94, 95, 100, 113, 114, 118–24, 138, 139, 145, 146, 150, 157, 185, 202; in Battle of Fort Mosa, 120–24; depicted, 190
Hirsh, Doctor, 35, 37, 39, 41, 46
Hobohatchey, mico of Abihkutci in the Upper Creek, 69
Hodgson, Captain Robert, 211
Horse Quarter, 16, 24
Horses, 11, 13, 36–40, 42, 57, 67, 100, 107, 108, 123, 139, 145, 148, 153, 155, 157, 161, 163, 164, 166, 167, 170, 176, 180, 181, 196, 198, 199, 208, 212
Horton, Major William, 52, 60, 62, 63, 79, 82, 136, 150, 154, 157, 158, 167, 176, 185, 189, 202, 204, 206, 208
House of Commons, Britain, 183, 184
Houses, 20, 38, 58, 77, 78, 83, 90, 105, 106, 115, 119, 133, 134, 139, 141, 143, 145, 149, 150, 174, 206, 207, 208
Howarth, Lieutenant Probart, 207

Hunt, Quartermaster Thomas, 86, 138, 157, 186, 231 (n. 40)
Huts, 21, 38, 41, 51, 80, 83, 91, 118, 134, 138, 141, 171, 206

I

Independent Companies of Foot, 9, 61, 79, 211, 213, 214
Independent Company of Rangers, 33–35, 37–41, 44, 48, 52, 61, 67
Indians, 5, 6, 23, 31, 32, 60, 65, 90, 102, 107, 111, 112, 114, 116, 117, 120–24, 129, 147, 148, 153, 154, 157, 160, 162, 164, 167–69, 176, 180, 182, 202. *See also* Apalachee Indians, Apalachacola Indians, Catawba Indians, Cherokee Indians, Chickasaw Indians, Choctaw Indians, Creek Indians, Yemassee Indians
Indian trade. *See* Trade
Indian traders. *See* Traders
Inland Passage, 7, 9, 29, 53, 58, 62, 77, 78, 80, 97, 145, 154, 170, 171, 176, 195, 209
Intracoastal Waterway. *See* Inland Passage

J

Jekyll Island, Georgia, 56, 154, 158, 170, 189
Jekyll Sound, 52, 55, 150. *See also* Saint Simons Sound
Johns, Thomas, 69
Johnson, Governor Robert, 9, 10, 13 34–36, 44, 47, 49, 71
Jones, Captain Lieutenant Noble, 66, 101, 146, 171, 195. *See also* Northern Company of Marines
Jones, Captain Thomas, 75, 85, 102, 114, 120–24, 147, 149, 157, 164, 171, 189, 192
Jones's Fort, Georgia, 135, 146, 187. *See also* Jones, Captain Lieutenant Noble
Jones's Rangers, 149, 157, 163, 164, 171, 185, 189. *See also* Jones, Captain Thomas
Josephs Town, Georgia, 24, 33, 37, 39, 48, 49, 75, 85
July, a Negro scout leader, 131

K

Kasihta, a principal Lower Creek town, 43, 69, 87. *See also* Cussita
Kent Captain Richard, 76, 77, 85, 87, 139, 140, 157, 188, 192, 206, 229 (n. 17). *See also* Augusta Rangers

King George II, 46, 70, 78, 88, 89, 96, 101, 102, 104, 185, 192, 195, 200, 202, 204
King George's War, 184, 202, 204, 213, 214
King Philip V, 73, 151
Knott, Jeremiah, 69

L

Lacanela, Florida, 93, 105
Lacy, Mary, 66, 77
Lacy, Captain Roger, 52, 53, 66–69, 75–77
Laffite, Captain Peter, 101
Latrines, 21, 220 (n. 24)
Latter, John, 77, 85
Launch, 97, 156, 210
Leman, Ensign John, 137
Letters of marque, 103, 147
"Lewd house," 207
Licko, a Creek mico, 41, 42, 47, 48
Lieutenant, a Creek Indian, 47
Little Kilt, 101, 194; depicted, 191
Livestock, 140, 141, 162
London, England, 21, 48, 51, 82, 183, 184, 201, 205, 210, 215
Long land musket, 80, 100, 233 (n. 28), 248 (n. 10). *See also* Brown Bess, Muskets
Louisiana, 7, 10, 12, 44, 102, 184, 204, 210, 211, 212
Lower Cherokee Indians, 12, 67, 210
Lower Creek Indians, 12, 31, 32, 38, 40–42, 44, 47, 48, 68, 69, 86, 87, 102, 142, 144, 147, 157, 176–78, 181, 213
Lower Trading Path, 40, 43, 87, 189
Loyer, Lieutenant Adrain, 38, 44, 47
Lyng, Private Edward 123

M

Mace, Ensign Sanford, 95, 129
Mackay, Charles, 33
Mackay, Captain Charles, 121, 139, 157, 164–67, 176, 181. *See also* Highland Independent Company of Foot, Highland Rangers
Mackay, Hugh, 33
Mackay, Captain Hugh, Jr., 35, 39, 46, 51, 52, 57, 58, 62, 79, 80, 83, 85, 86, 90, 91, 95, 100, 103, 113, 114, 116–18, 121–24, 138, 139, 146, 150, 157, 186. *See also* Highland Rangers
Mackay, Captain Hugh, Sr., 33, 51, 58, 62, 79, 80, 82, 134, 153, 184, 185; mutiny in his company, 83, 84
Mackay, James, 33
Mackay, Captain James, 206
Mackay, John, 90

Mackay, Captain Patrick, 33–37, 39–52, 65, 67, 69, 86
Mackay River, 158
Mackintosh, Captain Aneas, 27–29, 37, 52 85, 86, 88, 140. *See also* Palachacola Rangers
Mackintosh, Captain John, 140, 141. *See also* Palachacola Rangers
Mackintosh, Captain John Mohr, 72, 101, 114, 117, 122, 123, 139, 186, 188, 193, 194, 206. *See also* Highland Independent Company of Foot
Mackintosh, Lachlan, 99, 100, 137, 138
Mackintosh, William, 122
Macleod, Angus, 90
McNeal, Mark, 175
McPherson, Captain James, 11–23, 27–29, 35, 52, 71, 74, 85, 88
McPherson, Rachel Miles, 12
McPherson, Lieutenant Robert, 100, 113, 138
McPherson, Sergeant William, 14, 15
McQueen, Quartermaster James, 123, 138, 188
Malatchi, principal mico of Lower Creek, 213
Marine Boat, the, 61
Marine Company of Boatmen, 144–46, 166, 169, 176, 194, 195, 202
Marines, 53, 144, 146, 154, 156, 159, 167, 182, 194–96, 202–5; depicted, 191. *See also* Marine Company of Boatmen, Northern Company of Marines
Maryland, 3, 144, 145, 175
Matanzas River, 110, 111, 127–29, 179
Mathews, Captain Jacob, 142–44, 174, 186
Mathews, Mary, 142, 157, 175, 176. *See also* Bosomworth, Mary; Musgrove, Mary
Maxwell, Lieutenant Edmond, 23, 25
Men-of-war: Spanish, 55, 103, 153, 159; British, 102, 112, 126–29, 147, 149, 152, 154, 161, 171, 172, 210
Merchants, Charles Town, 35, 36, 47, 49, 65, 70, 71, 189, 196
Middle Cherokee Indians, 12, 67, 210
Midnight, the, 52, 55
Militia: South Carolina, 4, 6, 7, 9, 29, 30, 88, 116, 161; Georgia, 21, 28, 29, 48, 51, 61, 62, 72, 73, 77–79, 82, 91, 101, 148; Spanish, 120, 151, 153
Milledge, Quartermaster John, 148, 186
Mission provinces. *See* Apalachee, Guale, Timucua
Mississippi River, 12, 210–12
Mistresses, 25, 82, 140
Mobile, Louisiana (modern Alabama),

12, 204, 210

Montiano, Governor Manuel de, 91, 103, 108, 123, 125, 130, 133, 147, 162, 163, 165, 167, 177, 178, 181–83; invades Georgia, 151–71

Moral, Governor Francisco del Sánchez, 60, 61, 63, 64, 78

Morrison, Sergeant Ambrose, 188

Morrison, Cornet Hugh, 139, 157, 188

Muklasa, an Upper Creek town, 43, 147

Mortars, 111, 168

Mount Pleasant, Georgia, 26, 135, 141, 187

Mount Pleasant Rangers, 141, 192

Mount Venture, Georgia, 135, 142–44, 149, 154, 174–76, 186, 192

Mount Venture Rangers, 143, 144, 149, 174

Musgrove, Captain John, 13, 143, 186

Musgrove, Mary, 13. *See also* Mathews, Mary; Bosomworth, Mary

Muskets, 35, 40, 51, 54, 77, 80, 83, 84, 90, 107, 112, 121, 122, 130, 148, 159, 163, 165, 166, 169, 174, 177, 178, 194, 195, 197, 208, 209, 212, 214, 233 (n. 28), 248 (n. 10). *See also* Brown Bess, Long land musket

Mutiny, 82–84, 194, 249 (n. 22)

N

Negroes, 85, 108, 151, 153

Negro slaves. *See* Slaves

Nelson, Captain Pascall, 211

Norbury, Captain Richard, 79, 82, 85, 136, 137

North Carolina, 4, 6, 12, 175, 192, 210

Northern Company of Marines, 146, 171, 195, 202

Northern military division, 74

Northern Rangers, Company of, 7

Nottoway, an Indian slave, 175

O

Ogeechee River, 8, 17–19, 24, 29, 40, 53, 63, 74, 135, 138, 149, 187, 192

Oglethorpe, General James Edward, 10, 11, 13, 18, 21, 22, 26–29, 31–33, 35, 36, 38, 44, 46, 49–53, 55, 58, 60, 61, 66, 69, 70, 75, 77, 78, 83–86, 88–90, 92, 99–109, 111, 114–16, 119, 123–34, 136, 138, 141–49, 152–55, 157, 159, 161, 164–66, 169–72, 174, 175, 178–84, 192, 193, 195, 200–202, 204–6, 214, 215; personality and background, 16, 17; schemes to give control of the Indian trade to Georgia, 33–35, 46, 49, 65, 66; occupies Anglo-Spanish border, 50–64; recruits a regiment under his command, 78–80, 230 (n. 21); quells mutiny, 83, 84; peace expedition to Creek, 86–88; leads raids on Flordia, 91–95, 178–82; receives military aid from South Carolina, 88, 89, 96–99; unsuccessfully attacks Saint Augustine, 105–31; successfully defends Georgia against Spanish invasion, 153–71; marries, 200; in Jacobite Rebellion, 200; court-martialed and acquitted, 201; withdraws from public life, 201, 202; Georgia command terminated, 214

Okfuskee, a principal Upper Creek town, 43, 45–48, 52, 75, 188

Okfuskee Fort, Upper Creek, 32, 34, 37, 45–47, 66, 85, 141, 188

Okfuskee Rangers, 47, 48, 52, 66, 69, 85

Old Fort, 18. *See also* First Fort

Old Scout Boat, the, 145

One Eyed King, a Creek mico, 213

One Handed King, the Okfuskee mico, 47

Over Hills Cherokee Indians, 12, 67, 68, 210

P

Packhorsemen, 35, 37–40, 52, 140

Palachacola, South Carolina, 8, 17, 23, 25, 26, 35, 37, 88, 135, 141

Palachacola Fort, 7, 24, 26, 88

Palachacola Garrison, 23, 25–28

Palachacola Rangers, 28, 37, 52, 75, 85, 141

Palachacola Town, 23

Palmer, Colonel John, 9, 114–24; in Battle of Fort Mosa, 120–22

Palmer, Captain William, 114, 118, 121, 122

Parker, Lieutenant Robert, Jr., 35, 37, 38

Parliament, British, 16, 50, 63, 77, 78, 101, 102, 104, 202

Parmenter, Lieutenant Phileman, 25–28

Parties of rangers, 52, 74, 75, 77, 85, 86, 88

Paths, 39, 40, 90, 92, 94, 206

Pearse, Commodore Vincent, 99, 102, 107–9, 111, 127, 128, 132

Pepper, Captain Daniel, 87, 189

Percival, Sir John, 10

Peters, Captain William, 14, 15

Pickets, companies of, 152

Pioneers, 96, 97, 177

Piraguas, 13, 37, 55–58, 101, 146, 153, 156, 170, 176, 177

Pistols, 14, 26, 100, 122, 126, 141, 164, 178, 194

Plaid, belted, 51, 55, 100, 101, 194

Point Quartell, Florida, 107, 108, 110–13, 119, 122, 123, 126, 129

Pon Pon, South Carolina, 8, 14, 37, 75

Port Royal, South Carolina, 6, 9, 11, 24, 27, 28, 53, 208, 209

Presents, Indian, 31, 37, 38, 44, 47, 87, 97, 101, 209

Prince Charles, 200, 201

Prince George, the, 209

Prisoners of war, 109, 123, 131, 138, 148, 169, 174, 175, 194, 195

Privateers, 92, 103, 146, 147, 207

Privates, Forty-second Regiment, depicted, 81

Privy Council, British, 46

Prostitutes, 199, 207

Punishment, 130, 131, 169, 180

Purrysburg, South Carolina, 8, 10, 12, 13, 24, 60, 75, 88, 96, 101, 135, 187, 210

Q

Queen Anne's War, 4, 7, 53

R

Raids, 42, 77, 91, 94, 97, 98, 133, 147, 168, 169, 176, 180, 182, 196, 197, 204, 206, 212

Rangers, 26, 38, 48, 92, 100, 106, 111, 121, 160, 161, 163, 166, 168, 188, 202, 204, 205, 248 (n. 10); South Carolina, 7, 9, 12–15, 23, 28, 118, 161, 209; Georgia, 35, 37, 39, 46, 49, 51, 57, 58, 63, 66, 67, 74, 75, 77, 85, 86, 88, 91, 100, 105, 106, 109, 111, 165, 170, 171, 181, 193, 196; depicted, 15, 190, 191. *See also* Garrisons of Rangers, Parties of rangers, Troops of Rangers

Rangers Fort. *See* Saltcatchers Fort

Rape, 207

Rawlings, James, 7

Ray, John, 58, 77, 85

Reconnoitering party, Spanish, 164, 165, 168

Recreation, 199

Religion, 25, 31, 199

Regulars, British, 78, 79, 82, 83, 85, 91, 94, 95, 97–99, 102, 105, 106, 108, 112, 118, 130, 131, 133, 134, 142, 147, 154, 155, 159, 164, 165, 167, 172, 176–78, 204, 208, 211; in Battle of Fort Mosa, 122, 123; flee from Grenadier Fight, 166; character of, 207. *See also* Forty-second Regiment of Foot, Indepen-

dent Companies of Foot

Regulars, Spanish, 151, 152, 156, 163, 164, 168

Richards, Major James, 60–63

Roads, 57, 108, 130, 163, 180

Ross, Private, 83

Royal Navy, 96, 99, 109, 127, 128, 129, 132, 150, 168, 171

Royal warrant, 185–87

Rum, 21, 22, 25, 36, 45, 74, 82, 87, 143, 199, 200, 214

Rye, the, 171, 181, 182

S

Saddles, 11, 14, 39, 40, 100, 153, 157, 196

Saint Andrews, the, 77, 101, 139, 146

Saint Andrews Sound, 154

Saint Augustine, Florida, 3, 4, 9, 12, 17, 47, 60, 84, 86, 88–93, 95, 97, 99, 102–4, 106–13, 115–18, 111, 119, 123, 127–31, 148, 150, 152, 153, 155, 168, 170, 171, 174–82, 195, 209, 210, 212; defenses of, 103

Saint Johns River, 42, 60, 61, 64, 77, 91, 92, 94, 95, 103, 105–7, 113, 116, 131, 137, 171, 177, 179–82, 195, 206, 212

Saint Phillip, the, 147, 195

Saint Simons Island, Georgia, 51, 52, 54–56, 61, 62, 80, 82, 145, 146, 148, 149, 152–56, 158, 161, 170, 171, 186, 205, 208

Saint Simons Sound, 55, 63, 152, 153, 156-61, 167, 170, 186. *See also* Jekyll Sound

Salgado, Lieutenant Colonel Antonio, 120, 160

Salkehatchie River, 8, 14

Saltcatchers Fort, 8, 11, 12, 15, 16, 24, 27, 28, 219 (n. 8)

Saltchatchers River. *See* Salkehatchie River

Salzburgers, 51, 100, 106, 206

Sambrooke, Elizabeth, 200

Sánchez, Captain Sebastian, 163, 164

Savannah, Georgia, 13, 17, 18, 21, 24, 27, 29, 31, 33, 37, 38, 42, 45, 47, 48, 51–53, 55, 57, 60, 66, 68, 69, 72, 76, 77, 80, 87, 89, 101, 135, 138, 140, 141, 143, 144, 146, 148, 149, 155, 161, 171, 186, 187, 189, 192, 195, 198, 199, 205, 208, 210, 214; fort constructed in, 72; in northern military division, 74

Savannah, the, 101, 146

Savannah River, 6–13, 15, 17, 23, 25–29, 40, 51–3, 61, 63, 67, 72, 73, 76, 80,

87, 88, 102, 135, 141, 187
Savannah Town, 8, 75
Scalps, 42, 178, 181
Schooners, 101, 130, 153, 154, 156, 176, 182, 195
Scout boats, 53, 60, 61, 72, 77, 85, 90, 92, 97, 101, 133, 139, 142, 144–46, 153, 154, 156, 161, 168, 172, 176, 177, 182, 196, 202, 209, 212; depiction of, 15, 54. See also *Agencourt, Amelia, Carolina, Cutter, Darien, Frederica, Georgia, Hanover, Marine Boat, Prince George, Saint Andrews, Savannah, Skidaway, Speedwell*
Scout company, Spanish, 153, 163
Scouts, 71; South Carolina, 9, 15, 55, 58, 60, 114, 131; depicted, 15; Indian, 39, 167, 178; Georgia, 58, 60, 77, 83, 85, 86, 95, 144, 146; Spanish, 153, 163, 164, 182
Scouts' Fort, Georgia, 24, 53
Scroggs, Captain Richard, 88, 99, 100, 114, 122, 137, 149, 150, 157, 174, 176, 186, 233 (n. 28); in battle, 122, 164
Seamen, 107, 109, 111, 125, 126, 128, 129, 147, 152, 153, 162, 168, 169, 190
Second battalion, Forty-second Regiment, 175. See also Virginia recruits
Secretary of State, 60, 66, 70, 86. See also Duke of Newcastle
Secretary at war, 202, 213
Sentries, 73, 112, 117, 120, 180, 181
Servants, 37, 46, 100, 126, 143, 174; indentured, 51, 58, 80, 85, 90, 97, 100, 138, 157, 199, 208
Shad, Solomon, 175
Shannon, Cadet, 137
Shannon, William, 138
Ships, 72, 73, 146, 156, 186, 208; British, 52, 102, 103, 109, 127, 129, 150, 155, 170, 171; Spanish, 103, 133, 139, 147, 150, 156, 159, 169, 170
Skee, a Yamacraw Indian warrior, 21
Skidaway, Georgia, 24, 29
Skidaway, the, 146
Skidaway Island, Georgia, 53
Slaves, 5, 6, 10, 30, 87, 88, 103, 105, 140, 151, 208, 214
Sloops, 52, 61–63, 92, 95, 101, 102, 104, 128, 152, 153, 156, 157, 161, 195
Small, William, 16, 35, 163
Soldiers, 17, 54, 91, 101, 107, 114–25, 128, 134, 142, 167, 172–74, 178, 180–83, 200, 204; Georgia, 35, 36, 74, 77, 98, 115, 117, 131, 136, 177, 178, 196; French, 32, 204; South Carolina, 72, 105, 115, 118, 125, 129, 131, 136; Spanish, 64, 73, 94, 95, 97, 150–52, 160, 162, 177; lifestyle, 196–200. See

also Highlanders; Marines; Rangers; Regulars, British; Regulars, Spanish; Scouts
South Carolina, 4–9, 11, 16, 17, 20, 21–24, 26, 28–30, 32–35, 44, 45, 49, 50, 52, 53, 58, 61, 66, 67, 70, 72, 87, 92, 96–100, 105, 111, 113, 115, 126, 129, 130, 133, 139–42, 145, 149–52, 155, 161, 164, 170, 171, 174, 188, 189, 200, 204, 209–11, 213, 214; systems of defense, 6, 7, 27–30; assistance to Georgia, 10, 11, 49, 171
South Carolina Regiment of Foot, 96–98, 101, 105, 111, 125, 126, 128–31, 146, 211
Southern military division, 74, 77
Southern Rangers, Company of (1716–18), 7, 23
Southern Rangers, Company of (1726–37), 11–23, 27, 29, 52, 71, 74
Southern Scouts, 53
South Point, Georgia, 186, 187
Spaniards, 3, 4, 9–11, 31, 34, 41, 42, 50, 53, 60, 63, 72, 78, 84, 91, 92, 94–96, 98, 103, 105, 112–15, 117, 119, 125, 126, 130, 131, 139, 148, 159–68, 170, 173, 175–79, 181, 184, 200, 204, 208, 209, 211, 212
Spain, 4, 10, 28, 44, 65, 73, 78, 86–88, 103, 138, 146, 151, 184, 192
Spanish, the, 42, 64, 70, 72, 73, 76, 85, 91, 196, 205
Speedwell, the, 101, 145
Spinosa, Diego, 106
Squirrel, the, 104
Squirrel King, a Chickasaw mico, 102, 123, 157, 164
Steads William, 121
Stephens, William, 74, 196, 205, 208, 228 (n. 10)
Sterling, Lieutenant George, 207, 208
Sterling's Fort, Georgia, 24, 29, 192, 221 (n. 40)
Stewart, Lieutenant Alexander, 170, 171
Stewart, Sergeant John, 166
Success, the, 153, 157, 159, 161, 182, 195
Suicides, 141, 208
Sutherland, Captain Patrick, 137, 166, 206
Swamps, 37, 39, 67, 72, 88, 106
Swivel-guns, 53, 54, 61, 139, 145–47, 154
Swords, 14, 80, 83, 84, 95, 100, 162, 173, 195, 208

T

Tallapoosa River, 7, 31, 32, 43, 44, 45

Tallassee, an Upper Creek town, 43, 44
Tanner, Ensign John, Jr., 52, 66, 68, 69, 79
Target, 51, 121, 194
Tarter, the, 104
Tennessee, a town in the Over Hills Cherokee, 68
Tennessee River, 12, 67, 210, 211
Terry, John, 205, 207
Thompson, Captain William, 157, 182
Thunderbolt, Georgia, 24, 29, 53, 66, 77
Timucua, Florida, 3, 12
Tolson, Lieutenant William, 134, 137, 154, 155
Tomochichi, mico of the Yamacraw, 31, 58, 60, 89, 157
Toonahowi, a Yamacraw Indian, 157, 164, 178, 194, 195
Trade, 31, 32, 35, 45, 46, 49, 65, 66, 70, 75, 86, 96, 116, 148, 204
Traders, 5–7, 34, 36, 37, 39, 40, 44, 45–49, 65–69, 75, 114, 140, 147, 189, 199, 213
Trading act; Georgia, 34, 46, 48, 65, 70; South Carolina, 66
Trails, 86, 148, 161–65, 167, 168
Treasury Office, 184
Troops of Rangers, 96, 98–101, 113, 157, 166, 167, 169. *See also* Carolina Rangers, English Rangers, Highland Rangers, Jones's Rangers, Williams's Rangers
Tukabahchee, an Upper Creek town, 43, 69
Tuscarora Indians, 4, 5
Tustegoes, a Lower Creek town, 44
Tybee Roads, 51, 52, 55, 80
Tythingmen, 29, 205
Tythings, 29

U

Uchee, an Indian town, 26, 38, 39, 86, 88, 138, 141
Uchee Fort. *See* Fort Mount Pleasant
Uchee Indians, 8, 24, 26, 38–41, 75, 76, 92, 102, 114, 141, 148
Uniforms; rangers, 48, 100, 188, 248 (n. 10); Forty-second Regiment, 80; marines, 144, 145, 195; Highlanders, 194
Upjber, Joseph, 175
Upper Creek Indians, 7, 12, 31, 32, 38, 43–48, 52, 75, 86, 141, 147, 181, 188, 210, 211, 213
Upton, Thomas, 146

V

Valley Cherokee Indians, 12, 67, 210

Vanderdussen, Colonel Alexander, 107, 111, 113, 118, 119, 122, 126–32, 211
Virginia, 3, 6, 144, 145, 149, 175, 192
Virginia recruits, 176–78, 180

W

Walker, the, 147, 153, 156, 157, 159, 161, 176, 180, 182, 195, 209
Wall, Lieutenant James, 176
Walpole, Sir Robert, 78
War of Jenkins's Ear, 104, 133, 214
War Office, 79, 183, 201, 202
Warren, Captain Peter, 126, 127
Warriors, 31, 44, 60, 69, 87, 89, 90, 96, 102, 119, 147, 148, 174, 176–78, 181, 190, 199, 211, 212
Water Passage Fort, South Carolina, 7, 8
Weapons, 39, 40, 97, 100, 118, 162, 164, 188, 197, 212
Weather, 13, 39, 73, 97, 98, 109, 138, 153, 156, 165, 168, 196, 198
Western Rangers, Company of, 7
White Post. *See* Bachelor's Redoubt
Wiggins, Captain Thomas, 38, 39, 45, 46, 68, 69, 141
Williamsburg, Georgia, 187, 192
Williams, Captain John, 149, 157, 175, 176, 192. *See also* Williams's Rangers
Williams's Rangers, 149, 157, 175, 176, 185, 192
Willy, Lieutenant Anthony, 47, 48, 52, 66, 69, 75, 85, 141
Wolf of Muccolossus, an Upper Creek mico, 147
Women, 42, 44, 45, 51, 72, 82, 90, 101, 126, 138, 145, 148, 161, 199, 207, 211
Wood, Alexander, 46
Woodward, John, 7
Woodward's Fort, 8
Wormsloe, a plantation, 146, 195

Y

Yamacraw Bluff, 13
Yamacraw Indians, 8, 13, 17, 21, 24, 28, 29, 39, 42, 52, 54, 55, 58, 114, 122, 148, 157, 164, 178
Yemassee Indians, 5–7, 12, 14, 66, 92, 94, 106, 107, 114, 115, 118–20, 122, 123, 125, 138, 142, 163, 168, 176, 181, 195, 196; raids into South Carolina, 9, 15, 23, 27; raids into Georgia, 42, 60, 90, 144, 145, 162, 174, 175, 194, 213
Yemassee War, 6, 7, 10, 23, 25, 96
Yeomen farmers, 5, 10, 214
Yuchi Indians. *See* Uchee Indians